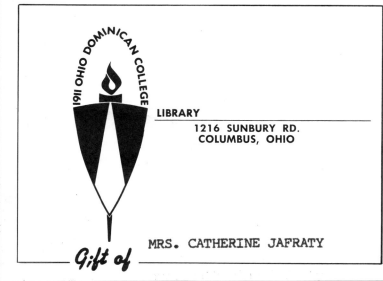

THE WORLD OF RENAISSANCE FLORENCE

Text by:

MAURILIO ADRIANI
of the University of Florence

MARIO APOLLONIO
Director of the School of Advanced Journalism

ANNAMARIA BRIZIO
of the University of Milan

GIORGIO CHIARELLI
Director of the Florence Tourist Office

RAFFAELE CIASCA
Dean of the Faculty of Political Science, Rome

ULRICH MIDDELDORF
Director of the Kunsthistorisches Institut, Florence

IRIS ORIGO
of Harvard University

GUIDO PAMPALONI
of the State Record Office, Florence

GIULIANO PROCACCI
of the University of Rome

VASCO RONCHI
*President of the International Association for the
History of Science*

FERDINANDO ROSSI
Director of the Pietre Dure Works, Florence

NICOLAI RUBINSTEIN
of the University of London

MARIO SALMI
President of the National Institute of Renaissance Studies

PIERO SANPAOLESI
of the University of Florence

ARMANDO SAPORI
Rector of the Bocconi University, Milan

CESARE VASOLI
of Cagliari University

ALBERTO VIVIANI
of the Academy of the Fine Arts, Rome

Organised and directed by:
The publishing office, Bemporad Marzocco

Consultation by: ARMANDO SAPORI

THE WORLD OF

RENAISSANCE FLORENCE

edited by GIUSEPPE MARTINELLI

300 illustrations in colour

G. P. PUTNAM'S SONS ~ NEW YORK

This translation by Walter Darwell

First published in Italy in 1964
as TUTTO SU FIRENZE RINASCIMENTALE
by BEMPORÀD MARZOCCO, Florence
© 1964 BEMPORÀD MARZOCCO, Florence

This translation
© 1968 MACDONALD & Co. (Publishers) Ltd.

Printed in Italy

This volume, continuing the series begun with « The World of Ancient Rome », which has met with the highest praise, has been published to conform to the same high standards and with the same purpose in view. « The World of Renaissance Florence » aims, in fact, to reconstruct, with the greatest scientific accuracy, the daily life and the great intellectual and artistic experiences of a society which has so often been the object of the most widely differing interpretations. We have also been concerned to offer to the public a truly living picture of the civilisation of the Renaissance in the city which was its cradle, captured in all its forms and in all its manifestations, at the various levels of its economic, political and cultural activities, and in the humble, productive labour of its artisans and its working classes. For this reason the story, which is a collaboration of the most eminent authorities, is illustrated by a wealth of documentary material, without, however, following the usual pattern of art books.

Renaissance Florence, reconstructed in the complex of its architecture and town-planning, and in the most characteristic and salient features of its daily life, from the sumptuous feasts in the Medici villas to the burning piety of Girolamo Savonarola and his followers, from the serene wisdom of its humanists to the patient skill of its craftsmen, from the glory of its artists to the shrewd ability of its bankers and merchants, this Florence can still live again after half a millennium, with the same freshness and joy we can find in the lives of those whose time on earth spanned the age from Dante to Galileo.

This book also aims to pay homage to Florence and to its mission of civilisation: to the luminous city of yesteryear, to that of today and that of tomorrow.

CONTENTS

Contributors: Francesco Adorno, Maurilio Adriani (Religious Life), Mario Apollonio, Ferruccia Cappi Bentivegna, Annamaria Brizio (The Workshops), Giorgio Chiarelli, Raffaele Ciasca (Physicians and Apothecaries), Elio Conti, Ulrich Middeldorf (Furnishing), Iris Origo (Slaves in Florence), Guido Pampaloni (Topography), Giuliano Procacci, Vasco Ronchi, Ferdinando Rossi, Nicolai Rubinstein (Political Institutions after the Fall of the Medici), Mario Salmi, Piero Sanpaolesi (Architecture; The House), Armando Sapori (Economic Life), Cesare Vasoli and Alberto Viviani.

CHRONOLOGY

1267 Guelf faction triumphed over Ghibelline rivals in Florence. Corps of Guelf Captains created.

1280 Population of Florence 80,000.

1282 Creation of Signoria (chief magistrature).

1294 Building of Cathedral began.

1301 Dante exiled from Florence. Population of Florence 105,000

1304 Attempt by Ghibellines to seize Florence frustrated.

1313 Florence put itself under the protection of Robert of Anjou, King of Naples.

1314 Building of Palazzo Vecchio finished.

1321 Studium set up in Florence for the teaching of medicine.

1327 Municipal Council's plan for street widening.

1333 Third outer wall finished.

1338 Population of Florence 90,000.

1340 Population of Florence 75,000.

1348 Florence struck by the plague.

1359 Cathedral bell-tower finished.

1362-4 Campaign against Pisa.

1363 Priors allowed unlimited importation of slaves into Florence.

1375-8 Florence at war with Avignon Popes who were trying to extend their dominion over Perugia.

1377 Birth of Brunelleschi, Florentine architect.

1378 Ciompi uprising against Guelf oligarchy.

1380 Population of Florence down to 59,747.

1382 Rule of Albizzi oligarchy began.

1386 Birth of Donatello, Florentine sculptor.

1392-1421 Intermittent war between Florence and Milan.

1403-24 Ghiberti made his first Baptistery door.

1421-44 Brunelleschi built the Ospedale degli Innocenti, one of the first Renaissance buildings.

1425-52 Ghiberti made the second pair of Baptistery doors.

1434 End of Albizzi oligarchy. Cosimo Medici's rule began.

1436 Cathedral consecrated under Pope Eugenius IV.

1439 Ecumenical Council held in Florence.

1443-8 Medici banished.

1445 Birth of Botticelli.

1446 Death of Brunelleschi.

1452 Birth of Leonardo da Vinci.

1456 Cathedral dome finished.

1465 Birth of Michelangelo.

1466 Death of Donatello.

1478 Pazzi conspiracy against the Medici.

1494 Florence became a republic after the second banishment of the Medici and placed herself under the protection of Charles VIII of France.

1498 Execution of Savonarola.

1509 Pisa reconquered.

1510 Death of Botticelli.

1512 Battle of Ravenna ended French domination of Italy. Return of the Medici under Giuliano, son of Lorenzo the Magnificent.

1513 Election of the Medici Pope Leo X.
Machiavelli published « The Prince ».

1519 Death of Leonardo da Vinci.

1527 Guelf Captains abolished. Third banishment of the Medici. Siege of Florence by the combined forces of Pope Clement VII and Charles V of Spain to restore the Medici. Sack of Rome by Imperialist Lutherans supporting Charles V of Spain.

1530 Signoria of Florence lost legislative power to Grand Council. Siege of Florence by Imperialist forces under Philibert of Orange to restore the Medici.

1531 Medici restored under Alessandro.

1537 Alessandro murdered by Lorenzino de' Medici and succeeded by Cosimo.

1564 Death of Michelangelo.

1582 Creation of Crusca (Florentine literary academy).

MAP OF MONUMENTS AND OTHER BUILDINGS MENTIONED IN THIS WORK

1. Santa Maria del Carmine
2. Santo Spirito
3. Roman Gate
4. Palazzo Pitti
5. Forte Belvedere
6. San Niccolò Gate
7. San Frediano Gate
8. Santa Trinità Bridge
   (Francavilla's statue of « Spring »)
9. Ponte Vecchio
10. Uffizi
11. Loggia Orcagna
12. Palazzo Vecchio
13. Bargello

14. Palazzo Strozzi
15. Palazzo Antinori
16. Santa Trinità
17. Palazzo Davanzati
18. Palazzo Albizzi
19. Palazzo Peruzzi
20. Cathedral (Santa Maria del Fiore, formerly Santa Reparata)
21. Belltower (Giotto)
22. Baptistery
23. San Lorenzo
24. San Procolo
25. Palazzo Medici Riccardi
26. San Marco

27. Laurentian Library
28. Loggia del Bigallo
29. All Saints' Church (Ognissanti)
30. Santissima Annunziata
31. Santa Croce
32. Oricellari Gardens
33. Palazzo Frescobaldi
34. Santa Maria Novella
35. Orsanmichele and Palazzo dell'Arte della Lana
36. Palagio di Parte Guelfa
37. Loggia Rucellai
38. Palazzo Rucellai
39. Palazzo Guadagni

BOBOLI GARDENS

FLORENCE AND HUMANISM

In 1518, a great German scholar, Philipp Melanchthon, speaking to his students, paid tribute to the city of Florence as the first to welcome the humanist masters, and thus help to save from extinction the priceless heritage of classical language and literature. In a Europe which still lay under the shadow of the Barbarian, said Melanchthon, where ignorance and a general decline of culture were effacing the already fading memories of the past, Florence had opened her gates to scholars of all lands who had proved their devotion to a learning too often misunderstood and despised elsewhere. These were the beginnings of a great change in European civilisation, which Melanchthon's age was still experiencing. In Florence the Muses again found a home and a refuge. From Florence sprang the first impulse of a movement of reform, never to be reversed, which affected all the institutions of the Western Christian world, civil, educational, political and religious, and brought into being a newly enlightened phase of human history. For this, all civilised men owe to the people of Florence a great debt of gratitude and admiration; thanks to them classical art and letters again shone out to the eyes of a world reborn.

Philipp Melanchthon's words, spoken at a time when Europe was the scene of the fiercest political discord and the bitterest religious dissension, reflect an opinion commonly held by cultured men of the sixteenth century, and it is not difficult to find, amongst the writings of the greatest European humanists, this same moving testimony to the part which Florence had played for more than a century as the ideal, the natural home and the focus of all that was most dynamic in the new culture.

In her schools, her academies, in the great houses of her wealthy citizens, in the Chancellery of the Republic, and in the peaceful atmosphere of her churches and cloisters, Florence had given to humanism the most suitable climate for growth, and a complex of historical, social and political conditions exceptionally suited to the taste and intellectual demands of the humanist scholars.

The new culture may indeed have flowered as quickly and as happily in other centres also, such as the Lombard courts and the Venetian Republic, owing to the personality of men like Vittorino da Feltre and Guarino Veronese, but it was only in Florence that the new vision of man entered so deeply into the lives of all citizens and made such a decisive and lasting imprint on city life.

To those men who in the mid-sixteenth century carried the torch of the « studia humanitatis » throughout Europe, Florence and humanism were one and the same thing, unique and inseparable. The city which had summoned to its Council the most cultured and refined humanist scholars of the time; and which had built up the first great libraries; and which had expressed in its streets and houses, built to the measure of man, the new concept and value of life, was the perfect model of that republic of scholars to which the wisest consciences of Europe aspired as they smarted under barbarism and apparently insuperable divisions. For centuries the myth of a new Athens had been a constantly recurring theme in the humanist movement and, like that ancient Greek city, Florence was to become the chosen home of a civilisation soon to spread throughout the Western world, her archives and monuments were to constitute the very sources of the « rebirth », and she was in herself to offer a complete picture of a whole age of human history.

By her very nature Florence seemed destined to play this rôle. She was a busy, thriving city, rapidly developing both economically and socially, so that already by the 13th century she had reached a standard of living unknown to other great European towns. Rich and opulent, Florence had successfully combined a judicious adventurousness in business matters with a taste for culture and a high regard for intellectual eminence such as that which won universal fame for the works of Dante in the early decades of the fourteenth century. But her destiny as the future centre of humanism was influenced above all by the Florentine origins of the man considered by all humanists as their true spiritual father, Francesco Petrarch, whose family roots lay in the neighbouring countryside and whose father, Ser Petrarch, had been seriously involved in the same political troubles which had caused the exile of Dante. Although he lived for many years between Avignon and Northern Italy, and in other more distant lands, whither his unsatisfied curiosity as a scholar and his duties as a master of rhetoric had taken him, Petrarch always maintained the closest relationships with some of the most important leaders of Florentine cultural life.

His friend and warm admirer was Giovanni Boccaccio who, in the long years of his stay in Florence, where he acquired a solid classical education, was the acknowledged master of a generation of young men who were devoted to Petrarch and passionate students of his writings. It was to Boccaccio and his Florentine friends that Petrarch often turned when he needed classical texts and manuscripts, documents and memoirs of the ancients which he collected so assiduously. But the author of *Africa* and *De viris illustribus* was always regarded by the young humanists of Florence as the supreme example of a mind free of all scholasticism, which considered itself and man's destiny in the light of the eloquent philosophy of Cicero or Seneca and the intimate religious experience of St. Augustine. From the mid-fourteenth century until his death in 1374, Petrarch dominated the spiritual horizon of Florence and inspired not only the masters of the « studia humanitatis », but also the formation of a new class of thinkers who believed as he did that goodness and virtue should permeate every aspect of civic life and unite with the ideal of civic glory. It is not surprising that Florence should welcome the direct heir of Petrarch, Coluccio Salutati, elected Chancellor of the Republic in 1375.

COLUCCIO SALUTATI (1331-1406)

These were among the most dramatic years in the history of the Florentine republic, years of crisis which culminated in the revolt of the Ciompi (a popular uprising against the Guelf oligarchy which secured constitutional rights for the Lesser Guilds, 1378), the differences between Church and State and the increasing threat from Milan. The oligarchy of merchants and bankers which governed the city and its vast outlying territory had to face enormous political problems, which depended for their solution on the survival of the republican State and its capacity to stand up against the ambitions of its powerful neighbour. But Coluccio Salutati, the man of letters, the reader of Cicero, the admirer of Petrarch, succeeded in turning his humanistic discipline into a powerful arm of Florentine politics, and in strengthening his appeal to the precious lessons of the ancients with a call for the defence of « Florentine liberty » and for a clear conception of the civil and political duties of a man of culture.

In the elegant letters he wrote from the City Hall, attempting to form alliances between free cities against all « tyrants » and appealing to the ancient republican dignity of which Florence proclaimed herself the heiress, Ser Coluccio transformed his elegant Latin into a powerful political weapon more capable than any faithless mercenary militia of arresting the ambitions of his Milanese rival Giangaleazzo Visconti.

In his moral tracts which circulated throughout humanist Italy, he outlined the ideal of the scholar who leads a working life in the city and contributes to the common good, refusing to shut himself up in his ivory tower. Citizen and Chancellor of the Republic, Salutati thus rejected the temptation of a self-sufficient culture, setting himself and his friends quite a different task: to be the true spiritual guide of a city republic,

Head of Matteo Palmieri (Rossellino) against a background of Florentine buildings (Domenico di Michelino). A pharmacist's son, Matteo Palmieri was educated by famous humanists and became a politician, writer and student of antiquities.

where liberty still had meaning and value, and to participate in the lives of those merchants and craftsmen who were bringing to Florence her wealth and political strength. For this reason, in his letters, both as Chancellor and as a private individual, he turns again and again to praise Florence and her citizens. But even these apologiae, sometimes perhaps dictated by forces of circumstance, are set in their proper context of a wider, freer view of human destiny, in the call for virtue won in the hard daily struggle and for a nobility founded, not on ancient feudal privileges, but on honest work.

Thus closely linked with that bourgeois oligarchy which had transformed the city into a true regional State, Coluccio Salutati was not, however, only the able politician and the illustrious Chancellor of the Palazzo Vecchio. He was the master who was gradually shaping a new generation of humanists, better trained for political warfare than their old fourteenth century predecessors. In his house, and in their own fine villas and town mansions, these young men conversed with Coluccio and his friends, with famous teachers from the Studium and with men who had come from all over Italy to meet the Chancellor of Florence. They engaged in free discussion without condescension or arrogance, of the most diverse subjects closest to the heart of a band of learned men who combined the practice of politics, the exercise of the liberal professions or teaching, and a close knowledge of the immortal writings of the ancients. But whether they were discussing the origins of Florence, smiling over old legends, arguing over a passage of Cicero or the meaning of a Latin word, or praising the art of rhetoric (which enables man both to express himself and to praise civic virtues), their attention was forever directed towards the daily life of the city in which they lived and to the events which wove the complex web of Florentine society. Thus the men of Salutati's circle were able to interpret present reality through the lessons of the past, without the pedantry and bigotry which were later to dry up the vital springs of humanism.

The constant attention to the lessons of history (which, as Coluccio wrote in a famous letter, teaches us to use the past to illuminate the present and the future), the willingness to recognise in the ancient world the same principles and ideals which inspired their daily lives, led them to turn the study of the classics into a lesson of moral, civil and political conduct. It is not surprising that Coluccio's lead should find such an enthusiastic following among those merchants and bankers who felt, almost by instinct, the connection between the ideas of their Chancellor and their own position as typical representatives of a new leading class, emerging from the decadent world of the feudal aristocracy.

It is for this reason that in Florence more than anywhere else, the study of ancient texts was in itself a great formative influence, reaching out far beyond the narrow circles of the teachers and their scholars to the men and families most representative of the city's ruling class. The wealth acquired in distant lands to the north and east, when not employed in splendid buildings which reflected the humanist's good taste, was often spent on bringing to light some long-forgotten document, some long-buried tradition, once more breathing life into the bones of the ancients. Niccolò Niccoli was a merchant who abandoned his lucrative calling to devote himself wholly to classical research, and even imitated the ancients in his way of life and mode of dress. Palla Strozzi was the son of a family of bankers who was to be for many years the patron of humanism in Florence, and he collected together at his own expense a library even richer than that of Ser Coluccio. Thus a fine aristocratic culture came within the grasp of men who, until that time, had functioned only in the exclusive world of medieval scholasticism. Florence was the first to set the example of a new method of humanistic training and showed her respect for Salutati's teaching by continuing to shelter in her schools and her administration the friends and disciples of her Chancellor, and by freely opening her purse to attract the most famous and learned scholars to her Studium.

Thus one of Coluccio Salutati's greatest desires was realised: the institution in Florence of the first regular course of Ancient Greek which would teach his young friends to know at first hand those pages of Homer, Demosthenes or Plato which neither he nor Petrarch nor Boccaccio had been able to read. The appointment to the Studium of the Byzantine scholar Manuele Crisolora (1397) was a memorable step in the return of Greek studies to the West. In the Studium were trained expert philologists such as Leonardo Bruni and Jacopo Angeli da Scarperia, and future teachers such as Pier Paolo Vergerio. Above all, however, Manuele

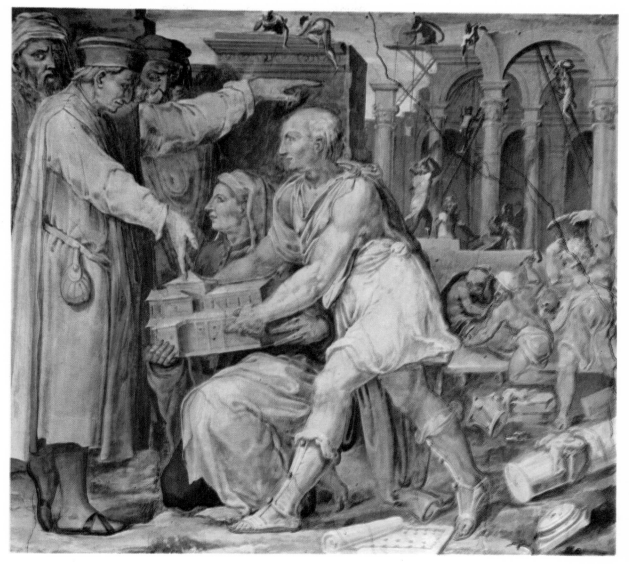

The model of the San Lorenzo Basilica being presented to Cosimo de' Medici by Filippo Brunelleschi (Palazzo Vecchio fresco by Vasari).

Crisolora's teaching was eloquent proof that Florence was willing to undertake by herself the most ambitious programmes of humanistic education, and to continue that patient and impassioned reconquest of the Ancient World to which Petrarch had devoted the whole of his life.

There were, of course, even in Florence those who opposed the spread of humanism on the grounds that liberal study was a threat to Christianity. A high-minded Dominican, the future Cardinal Giovanni Dominici, openly criticised the new methods of education. The Blessed Giovanni Delle Celle and his followers thundered against the pleasure-seeking youths who devoted themselves to the study of « Vanity », and even a sensitive musician, Francesco Landino, wrote verses in defence of the scholastics. These arguments,

however, fell on deaf ears and did not affect the increasing sympathy which the citizens of Florence showed for the new culture, personified for them by Ser Coluccio, who, moreover, had no difficulty in reminding Florentines that the knowledge of sacred texts presupposed grammatical and literary exercises, and that the knowledge of the tongue and the doctrines of the Ancients would help to fortify the truths of Christianity.

THE GENERATION OF LEONARDO BRUNI

The death of Salutati in 1406 did not interrupt the development of the humanistic tradition in Florence, as this was so closely bound to the history and the

Fifteenth-century miniature. Part of a Virgil manuscript showing an episode from the Trojan War, but set in Florence (Biblioteca Riccardiana).

destiny of the city. A new generation of scholars was ready to take his place and to carry on his teaching with renewed vigour. Amongst the young men who had grown up in his school, the most outstanding were Leonardo Bruni and Poggio Bracciolini, whose names were already being mentioned in other parts of Italy where humanism was spreading. Leonardo (1374?- 1444), a disciple of Coluccio, who was to succeed him as Chancellor in 1410, echoed his master's words when he praised the city which had welcomed him as a tender pupil, brought him to his masters and opened to him, through Manuele Crisolora, the wonderful world of Hellas. To Florence, hub of the Italian world, heiress of Roman liberty, guardian of Republican institutions, he dedicated, in his *Laudatio urbis florentinae*, pages of the rarest eloquence, as he described the perfect symmetry of the squares, the superb yet not inhuman dimensions of her great houses and the unrivalled splendour and wealth of a community which had not allowed financial success to distract it from seeking through education all that was refined and spiritual. He was, however, to pay her even greater tribute in his *Historiae populi florentini*, in which he combined an enthusiastic apologia for the new humanistic Athens with the most careful research into history, rejecting the fantastic imaginings of the medieval chroniclers, and seeking out historical truth in documents and archives. His complete devotion to the new humanistic education did not, however, cause Bruni to neglect the traditions of the fourteenth century which had a particular significance for Florence, and he made a comparative study of Petrarch and Dante, setting the solitary ivory tower reputation of the former against Dante the man of action, the Florentine and the soldier who served his city and his fellow citizens so well.

HUMANISM AND CITY LIFE

Humanism was so closely bound up with citizenship in Florence that the new method of education, new cultural tastes, the new outlook on life and the ideal of the new humanist man permeated every aspect of city life, inspired young artists like Brunelleschi, Donatello and Masaccio, penetrated the workshops of the craftsmen and the tiny offices of the copyists and, in full and joyous measure, enlivened the festivals and the sumptuous pomp of religious ceremonies. In a city which saw the creation, one after the other, of the greatest works of art of fifteenth century sculpture and where the new style of the young Masaccio was born, humanism was not only a cultural phenomenon, but a way of life which was spreading to an ever-increasing number of social groups. If the high culture of humanism was at first an élite culture, reserved for a small minority of patricians, their example was followed by men in all walks of life in the second half of the century.

Humanism was the great driving force in the first decades of the fifteenth century, the dominant factor in Florentine culture and civic life. Around Leonardo Bruni were other scholars and masters who, although often divided in the bitter arguments which arose inevitably in the humanist movement, stood solidly behind his work as an educator and a doughty defender of the new culture. Niccolò Niccoli, whom Vespasiano da Bisticci the Florentine biographer (1421-98), describes as an old man at this time, was still hale and active, and his rich merchant's house was one of the centres of the Italian humanist movement. Here were delivered from all parts of Europe ancient manuscripts and codices which Niccolò himself copied in his beautiful hand. Poggio Bracciolini, who was kept away from Florence by his duties in the Roman Curia,

wrote often to Niccolò asking for information and telling him and his Florentine friends of the discovery of long-awaited codices, such as a text of Quintilian which he had found in the dreadful « prison » attic of a Swiss monastery at San Gallo. He describes Quintilian now as a prisoner finally liberated from the anguish of oblivion. Or he could have announced the discovery of Lucretius' *De natura rerum*, or other priceless documents which bore witness to the unequalled glory of the Ancients.

News such as this circulated rapidly amongst humanist friends (and adversaries), reached Palla Strozzi's town house, where he was always looking for new codices for his library, was conveyed to Messer Leonardo at the Chancellery, or filtered through to a peaceful cell in the Monastero degli Angeli where a pious Camaldolese humanist, Ambrogio Traversari, divided his time between translating Diogenes Laertius and studying Hebrew for a better understanding of the language of the Scriptures. But often these and other discoveries, news of which arrived from all over Italy and Europe, were commented upon in the workrooms of the copyists, where a young man was becoming known, a young man destined soon to be the kindly, witty recorder of the humanist world of Florence: Vespasiano da Bisticci. Other letters then left Florence destined for fellow-humanists: letters taking up former discussion and debate; letters of information

Another miniature from the same Virgil manuscript. The Greek and Trojan heroes are shown with their Latin names (Biblioteca Riccardiana).

Lorenzo the Magnificent (Giorgio Vasari).

about new problems of philology; or letters conveying friendly or controversial argument.

Florence was thus connected by a network of correspondence to the other humanist centres in Ferrara, Mantua, Milan, Venice, to Jean de Montreuil and Nicolas de Clamanges in Paris and to the learned prince, Humphrey of Gloucester, at the court of England. These letters, often circulated and copied with loving care, bore the precious result of long and difficult studies, and were the means of spreading ideas and theories dear to a whole generation of scholars now to be found in all the nerve-centres of Italian intellectual life. Many of them bore praises of Florence, the city which humanist princes took as a model for the rebuilding of their own town houses, or the fine villas of their capital cities, and which their secretaries and scholars remembered with nostalgia.

FLORENCE AND THE ECCLESIASTICAL COUNCIL (1439-1443)

These were the proudest and happiest years in fifteenth-century Florence, when the city was host to the Council for Union which seemed to crown the hopes, so dear to humanists, for a general reconciliation of all Christianity. The Tuscan capital was then the meeting-place of some of the most learned men of Western and Eastern Christendom, and the humanists, of whom there were already many in the papal Curia, had again the occasion of renewing discussion with their friends in Florence. Distinguished visitors included a most learned authority on Hellenic culture, the Byzantine Cardinal Bessarione, a scholarly humanist Tommaso Parentuccelli, destined to rise to the papal throne, and the old sage Gemisto who brought to the West the secret wisdom of Platonic meditation. The sceptical Curia secretaries were there too, adding a more light-hearted note to the solemn gathering, and more eager to expound a line of Virgil or Homer than to listen to long disquisitions and controversies in Council about subtle points of theology.

In the long intervals between Council sessions the scholars often met in learned conversation or went into the bookshops in search of some rare manuscript written out in a fine « humanist » hand.

The good Vespasiano, then very young, has left us glowing accounts of these meetings, which often took

Giuliano de' Medici, brother of Lorenzo the Magnificent (Botticelli, Museo Carrara, Bergamo).

place on the popular Piazza della Signoria under the ancient roofs built by Pisan prisoners. Here one might have heard the ironic, elegant scepticism of Carlo Marsuppini, another humanist from Arezzo, destined to rise to the Chancellorship of the Republic in 1444, or the gentle piety of Traversari, always warmly enthusiastic for union with the brothers of the Eastern faith, or the sharp argumentative tongue of Bracciolini, so quick to deride the sloth and hypocrisy of the false priests, or the steadfast faith of Parentuccelli, already busy at work on plans for the new library at the Dominican monastery of San Marco. The dominating figure was that of Messer Leonardo, now old and near to death, but still capable of making his warning voice heard in the great assemblies of the Republic. A young man of another generation who had grown up in the cult of civic liberty in his town, a merchant who at the age of twenty-five had become a student and had mastered both Greek and Hebrew, listened attentively to the words of Ser Coluccio's old disciple. He was Giannozzo Manetti, soon to praise the memory of Leonardo in a moving funeral oration. Meanwhile, in his apothecary's shop in the Canto alle Rondini, Matteo Palmieri was poring over the *Libro della vita civile* which is still today the best expression of the integration of humanism with civic loyalty.

On the free debating-grounds of the squares and loggias of Florence, in the fine patrician houses where sometimes they stayed, these men, free of affectation in speech and dress, talked freely amongst themselves, without disdaining the company of merchants, tradesmen or those « most excellent craftsmen » who were making the old city the worthy capital of humanism. Their speech was not the pedantic lesson or the boring sermon of the schoolman, but the lively conversation of friends working together in the search for a common truth. Men of the Government or the Church, orators serving princes or the republics, masters from the Studium or prelates, all had the feeling of belonging to a unique body, and of holding, for present and future generations, the new concept of man, free, rational and peace-loving. This concept was reflected for them in the monuments of the new art, in the figures carved by the chisel of Donatello, in the solemn majesty of the Carmine frescoes by the young Masaccio, or in the fine mansions which were rising to celebrate the new measure of man's dignity. Over all floated the newly-finished dome of Santa Maria del Fiore, the cathedral which Maestro Filippo had crowned on the shrewd advice of Paolo Toscanelli, a merchant, scientist and friend of the humanists.

THE RULE OF COSIMO DE' MEDICI (1434-1464)

However, in the period which followed, Florence was no longer the free city dreamed of by Coluccio Salutati, or the republican state extolled by the young Bruni. Palla Strozzi's fine library no longer welcomed learned humanist scholars. The munificent patron now lived in exile in far-away Padua after the fall of the Albizzi oligarchy in 1434. The assemblies of the Republic were still held in the Palazzo Vecchio, it is true, and the Chancellor Messer Leonardo was still writing his elegant missives with his accustomed skill and wisdom.

But the real master of Florence was elsewhere, in the Palazzo in the Via Larga, the princely mansion of Cosimo de' Medici, where humanist scholars and masters were being attracted by the generosity of the great banker. A munificent patron, protector of the arts and letters, Cosimo aimed to make his house and his beautiful villas a haven of refuge for men of genius, and to bind the humanist intellectuals to the political fortunes of his family. Because he was a fervent admirer of the new culture, he desired the humanists and the masters of the *studia humanitatis* to educate his sons and adorn his court.

The humanism of Ser Coluccio and the young Bruni was now at an end. Even the old Chancellor had to yield to the power of the rich Signore who in a few years had sent the stern Manetti into exile and driven out of his post Filippo Peruzzi, a learned authority on Church reformation, and an indefatigable collector of ancient and medieval scientific manuscripts.

Then, in 1444, when Messer Leonardo was lowered into the fine tomb prepared for him by Rossellino in Santa Croce, the happiest and most formative period of humanism came to an end. For a further nine years Carlo Marsuppini, the new Secretary of the Republic, continued with his clear and elegant style the literary and philological traditions set by his predecessor in the Palazzo Vecchio. He was succeeded by Poggio Bracciolini, one of the most famous humanists of the first half of the century, but now a tired old man, who held the office of Chancellor for the next five years and saw his duties reduced to the monotonous (but well paid) task of turning the imperious decrees of Cosimo into elegant Latin. This was the end of an epoch in the long history of the city of Florence, and the funeral cortège which followed Poggio Bracciolini to his grave on October 30th, 1459, was also mourning the heroic age of humanism, now enshrined forever in the exemplary writings of Salutati and Bruni.

THE ACADEMIES

The outlook and form of humanism changed around the mid-fifteenth century. Its centre shifted from the Republican Chancellery to the Court of the Medicis, where Cosimo, Piero, and especially Lorenzo, collected together one of the richest libraries in Europe. But also in the Studium, once the undisputed domain of

Niccolò Machiavelli seen against the background of the « Hall of Lilies » in the Palazzo Vecchio. Even in his caustic denunciation of the failure of the Italian States, in some of the harshest pages of Il Principe, *the Secretary of the Second Chancellery of the Republic never abandoned the myth of the classical republics.*

the schoolmen, the humanist masters had for some time predominated with their philosophical methods, their cult of the classics, and their new vision of culture and the value of the *studia humanitatis*. Among the masters who worked in Florence in the latter half of the fifteenth century it will suffice to mention here

Francesco Filelfo, Bartolomeo Platina, Demetrio Calcondilla, and especially the learned Byzantine scholar Giovanni Argiropulos, translator of Aristotle and a notable commentator of his philosophical works. Argiropulos's school produced a philologist-poet of the first order, the man who perhaps saw and expressed more clearly than anyone else the feelings of an age so full of the joy of living, yet so keenly aware of its coming downfall: Agnolo Poliziano. Yet the tradition of Florentine humanism lived on, not so much in the Studium, or in the learned and refined discussions of the scholars in the Medici circle, as in the personalities and the writings of two men who at this time were living far away from the city: Leon Battista Alberti, whose family had long been in exile and who, though born in Genoa, had always felt closely tied to the city of his ancestors, and Giannozzo Manetti, whom Cosimo's displeasure had driven to find refuge, first in the Roman Curia, then in the Aragonese Court at Naples.

Alberti's *Della famiglia* (1437-1440) had already devoted chapters to a most eloquent apologia of that healthy, sane and fearless band of town merchants who gave humanism its natural home, where a moving evocation of the past could combine with a pursuit of a new concept of life, where a firm vindication of liberty opposed the blindness of chance, and where people realised the ideal of virtue in dignified moderation and purposeful work for society, and saw the value of a man capable of forging his own destiny. Similarly Giannozzo Manetti nurtured during his exile the lesson he had learned in his early youth, and in his *De dignitate et excellentia hominis* he praised the admirable proportions of the human frame, the wonderful creative power of the mind, capable of devising all the arts and skills, of changing the face of the world and of shaping the inert forces of nature into a rational design.

The ideas of Alberti and Giannozzo had been dear to a generation now disappearing, as the historical setting in which they had grown up was itself changing also. The intellectuals of the new generation which grew up under the shadow of the great mansion of the Medici in the company of Cosimo's sons and young friends, had different ideas and aspirations.

About the year 1459, a young doctor from Figline, Marsilio di Diotifeci, began to work in Cosimo's library on the Plato manuscripts which the Signore of Firenze had collected. Diotifeci was a profound Christian and a fervent admirer of Plato, who was searching for a way to reconcile his religious faith with the truths expressed by the greatest pagan thinkers. In the fantasies, the myths and the warmth and poetic beauty of Plato's Dialogues, « Ficino », as he came to be called, discovered that secret link between time and

Above: « *The grammar lesson* ». Below: « *Plato and Aristotle* ». (*Luca della Robbia, Belltower of Santa Maria del Fiore*).

One of the famous Florentine craftsmen's workshops (Nanni di Banco, predella of altarpiece of Quattro Santi Coronati, Orsanmichele, formerly a public granary).

eternity, between the world on earth and the perfect world above, between human destiny and its divine origin. In the Medici villa at Careggi he gathered round him a group of friends who strove to drive away their worldly cares with the joys of meditation. One might have listened in vain in their discourse for praises of the Republic of Florence, or of the virtue of work or civic loyalty: rather were they lost in admiration before the harmony and perfection of an ideal world, all light and beauty, in which man is the link between God's infinite wisdom and its revelation in the immutable order of creation. One of these men, Cristoforo Landino, announced in his *Camaldulenses disputationes* the new ideal of the scholar who, though not despising the virtue of action, nevertheless subordinated it to the superior life of contemplation.

From the learned concourse which Ficino's friends and admirers held in his house was to rise the Platonic Academy. Though it aimed to revive the teaching, the institutions and the quasi-religious observances of the school founded by Plato in Athens so many centuries before, the Academy in fact encouraged the group-forming tendencies so characteristic of humanist intellectuals.

It is true that the harsh repressive measures of the Medicis had dissolved the *contubernium*, a group of

scholars which had gathered round Niccolò della Luna, the teacher of Greek. Among this group were the young sons of Palla Strozzi. In 1455, however, four young humanists, Alamanno Rinuccini, Andrea Alamanni, Antonio Rossi and Marco Parenti had begun to meet « to practise literary exercise together ». They were joined by other patrician youths, such as Pietro and Donato Acciaiuoli, and soon this free association of literary men took upon itself the title of *Achademia*, after the school of Plato. But it was particularly after the arrival in Florence of Argiropulos that this small group of young humanists, gathered round the great Byzantine master, began to exert a notable influence on Florentine intellectual life. They formed the *Chorus Achademiae florentinae* (1456), which attracted the most learned and scholarly youths of the time, among them Lorenzo de' Medici. Giovanni Argiropulos gave them private lessons in the house put at his disposal by the Republic, lessons of a novel kind, interspersed with free discussion and argument on every topic of literature and philosophy, and often ending up under the shade of a fine laurel tree in the cloisters of Santa Maria de' Servi. Masters and scholars did not fail to visit the house of Cosimo, who had begun to protect the *Achademia* and even deigned personally to join in their debates, or partake of the banquets and symposia which the *Chorus* held twice yearly in the richly-furnished mansion of Messer Franco Sacchetti. Here the members of the Academy spent two or three days in literary or philosophical discussion, and occasional political debate, in between feasting at the expense of their munificent host. These young men were very close friends, united by the bonds of veneration for their master and the similarity of their intellectual tastes. Some of their letters which have come down to us paint a lively and pleasing picture of these joyful gatherings, the wisdom of their Byzantine master and the ardent enthusiasm for argument displayed by his young disciples.

Marsilio Ficino's *Accademia platonica*, also attended by several members of the *Chorus*, had a more strictly philosophical programme and kept more closely in its teaching to the doctrines of the great Athenian. Around Marsilio who, though having the melancholy temperament, as he said himself, of one born under Saturn, was a gay and witty conversationalist, there gathered men of varied ages, origins and culture, but united in their enthusiasm for the « divine » Plato. Ficino himself took Plato as his model even for his ordinary everyday behaviour, as well as in his mode of speech and writing, and his friends also copied the behaviour of Plato's disciples. Wherever they were, in the Medici villa at Careggi or his town house, or out walking in the Fiesole hills to young Poliziano's villa, their conversation was always about the pages of Plato which Marsilio read and commented on to them, freely inviting them to answer his questions, and never standing on his academic dignity. All the members of the Platonic Academy were conscious of belonging to the « Platonic family », calling Ficino « Prince of Academicians » or « Father of the Platonic family » and themselves « Brothers in Plato »; when they met their prescribed form of address was « greetings in Plato ».

THE « SYMPOSIA »

Naturally, like those of any academy, the Platonists' meetings were devoted to philosophical arguments and narrow discussion on the texts of the master, but their most characteristic feature was the symposium held on the anniversary of Plato's birth and death which tradition held to have occurred on the same date, November 7th. Recalling the markedly religious character, virtually that of a devout fraternity, of the ancient Platonic school, the members of Ficino's Academy endeavoured to respect the ritual associated with the symposium in ancient times. The ancient custom was thus renewed on November 7th, 1474, under the auspices of Lorenzo the Magnificent. The banquet organiser, called *tisarca* or *architriclino* was Francesco Bandini, whose duty was to choose the guests, nine after the number of the ancient Muses: Antonio degli Agi, bishop of Fiesole, doctor Diotifeci da Figline, the poet Cristoforo Landino, the rhetorician Bernardo Nuzi, Tommaso Benci, Giovanni Cavalcanti, Cristoforo and Carlo Marsuppini and Ficino himself. After the meal, sumptuously provided by Lorenzo in his villa at Careggi, Nuzi began a reading of Plato's *Symposium*, and then asked each of the guests to comment on one of the dialogues. Ficino's comment, which he wrote down on the pretence that it related what was discussed on that day, was, of course, of much wider import, and a vehicle for the expression of some of his most cherished ideas. It is very likely, however, that the proceedings were very much as described by Ficino, with a reading together of a text of Plato and a subsequent commentary. The banquet was repeated the following year, this time in Francesco Bandini's house in Florence.

LORENZO DE' MEDICI AND GIROLAMO SAVONAROLA

The Academy thus contained in the second half of the fifteenth century the flower of Florentine culture: poets, jurists, scholars, Churchmen, doctors and musicians rubbed shoulders with well-known figures in the political life of the city, such as Bernardo Vettori, Piero Soderini, Bernardo del Nero, Bartolomeo and Filippo Valori. Lorenzo himself deigned to profess the Platonic faith and to consider himself a friend of the Academy. Around Ficino and within the Medici court, in Lorenzo's library, in the drawing rooms and the gardens, at the Carnival festivities, the jousts, the feasting and merry hunting parties, there were to be seen men of quite distinctive stature, easily distinguished from courtier and politician, men who represented all that was best in humanistic culture. A familiar of the Medici court, although often on bad terms with Lorenzo, was Agnolo Poliziano, the poet, philosopher and learned critic of the *Pandette* and professor of Greek in the Studium. In his *Stanze per la giostra* and *Favola d'Orfeo* he expressed the fleeting enchantment of a world so perfect yet so near to extinction. Another intimate of the villa at Careggi was the very young philosopher, the prodigy of his time, Giovanni Pico, Count of Mirandola, who had come to Florence to find the ideal place in which to exercise his mind, ever open to nobility and truth. In his *De dignitate nominis* he extolled human liberty and man's capacity to meet every need, to overcome every restriction and to win for himself glory and salvation. Here at Careggi he conceived his great plan for gathering together, at his own expense, all the intellectual leaders of the world in an effort to secure lasting peace for men of all nations and all creeds.

Then, one by one, all the protagonists of late fifteenth-century Florence left the stage: Lorenzo died in 1492, Poliziano in 1494, and in the same year, aged only thirty-three, Giovanni Pico, whose last years had been spent in strict religious meditation. For some time now a warning voice had been thundering from the pulpit of San Marco: that of Girolamo Savonarola, calling the people of Florence to penitence and expiation, and announcing, as a forerunner to great reforms, the advent of the Antichrist, bringing great sorrow and tribulation to Florence, Italy and all Christendom. Prophets, monks, astrologers and, it must be admitted, even the most devout humanists, scanned the heavens for signs of coming disaster, and looked for woeful conjunctions of the stars which might foretell unimagined evils. And, in fact, down the slopes of the Alps were pouring the militiamen of Charles VIII of France, soon to be welcomed by defenceless Florence, and Piero de' Medici was driven out by his own people. But the popular Christian republic wanted by Savonarola was born feeble and mistrusted, ushered in by a « disarmed prophet » destined to perish at the stake, who had tried in vain to quell the « vanity » of the humanist world. Only Marsilio was left, dragging out his last years, having long survived his time.

In these hard, gloomy last years of the century, however, the humanist tradition lingered on in Florence. The new Secretary of the Second Chancellery of the Republic was a thirty-year-old who had learned well from his humanist teachers to appreciate the lessons of the past. From his Florentine observatory and in his frequent diplomatic missions, he had discovered

Fifteenth-century educational methods were often fairly strict and consequently the schools run by Florentine and foreign scholars were well attended (Benozzo Gozzoli, detail).

the inner springs which regulate the mechanism of societies and states, the swing of fortune's pendulum, the invincibility of the great Imperial powers, the weakness of unarmed Florence and Italy. His judgment on the tragic political failure of the Italian states was clear, forthright and ruthless. He laid bare the faults of a society incapable of creating either a healthy political organism, or the order and discipline necessary to survive. His name was Niccolò Machiavelli. Hard and cynical he might have been in *Il Principe*, but he never abandoned the ideal of a society of strong free men, or the myth of the classical republics which had inspired Ser Coluccio and Messer Leonardo. His Prince still resembled the ancient dictators of the classical republics, to whom all power was entrusted that the city might live. These hopes and illusions of the Secretary of Florence brought a smile to the lips of another cool, unprejudiced observer of the political scene, Francesco Guicciardini, who in his long career had learned the art of dissimulation and deceit before he committed to writing his bitter reflections and confessions. His *Ricordi politici e civili* is a work in the humanist tradition, but one of the last, if also one of the liveliest, records of a civilisation born on the firm soil of the Florentine Republic. This civilisation became the patrimony of all Western nations, but it was now losing its oldest and dearest ideals.

The academies in the Florence of the Second Republic and the first Medici Restoration were to become centres of political debate, both open and closed, or hotbeds of conspiracy. Francesco Cattani di Diacceto, professor of Platonic philosophy in the Studium, continued the traditions of Ficino, and gathered together in his house a band of affectionate disciples attracted by the subject, which by now had become far too academic, of the theory of love and beauty. At the same time, in meetings in the Rucellai Gardens (behind the palace built [1446-51] for Giovanni Rucellai and designed by Leon Battista Alberti), attended often by Machiavelli himself, the old inspiration of the early humanist returned, and behind the learned discussions on literature and history lay hopes and longings for republican liberty. These aspirations were, however, to be dashed by Medici repression. The leading figures of the circles which frequented the Gardens were imprisoned or sent to the scaffold, and Niccolò Machiavelli himself was jailed and tortured in the old Bargello palace.

PANORAMA OF A CITY

The fifteenth century in Florence ended with an unprecedented spate of building, encourage by the municipal authorities themselves. The various planning regulations exempted new buildings from taxes for forty years. Yet the city had not yet recovered from the effects of the plague of fifty years ago, and the population figures continued to fall alarmingly: from the early fourteenth to the late fifteenth century they were reduced by half, to fifty thousand. This, however, was the time when the most remarkable development took place, encouraged by different, often contrasting, needs in the climate of spiritual renewal which characterised Florence's golden age. Times had changed: the city no longer needed to be a complex of forts connected by streets which were little more than communicating trenches. Its towers no longer served any purpose. Instead the demand was for large town houses and gardens, wide straight thoroughfares which brought in light and showed up the elegant new mansions of the great families, and allowed free circulation within the city and easy access to the gates and markets outside.
Throughout the fifteenth century men searched for the ideal solution for the ideal city: it was the age of studies and projects. It was to fall to the sixteenth century to realise most of these, to transform the « spiky » town of the Middle Ages into a new city, worthy of Man and built to his stature.

What did Florence look like at the end of the thirteenth century? At that time the city was « the fairest and most famous daughter of Rome », a typical medieval town, bristling with the many towers which rose spikily from the mass of its houses, as in Bigallo's fresco of 1342, and with narrow winding streets which scarcely ever saw the sunlight.

The end of the Middle Ages saw the rise of the three centres which were to form the basis of town life: political, religious and mercantile. The centres of production were probably on the outskirts, and it would seem that it was partly to protect these that the third outer wall was built. Here stood the houses of the workers employed in industry, as was evident in the Ciompi uprising on July 21st 1378. This took place « near the town house of Messer Stefano di Broye, canon of the Cathedral », near, that is, to the present intersection of Via Guelfa and Via Nazionale, which were then on the outskirts of the town.

The principal motive for the building of the third outer wall, decided upon in 1284 but not finished (and then not completely) until 1333, was, however, quite different: the city needed more space, much more space, for its increasing population.

Recent research, based on Giovanni Villani's figures and other sources from the city's archives, has shown the trend of the population of Florence in the thirteenth and fourteenth centuries. In 1280 it was 80,000; twenty years later, at the beginning of the new century, it was 105,000. If the increase had been maintained at this rate, there is no doubt that the extension of the city's boundaries would have been abundantly justified. By 1338, however, the figure had fallen to 90,000 and two years later to 75,000. Then came the dreadful plague of 1348 which reduced the population to such an extent that by 1380 it was only 59,747. The census carried out under Cosimo I in 1552 showed that the population had suffered an even further decline, and

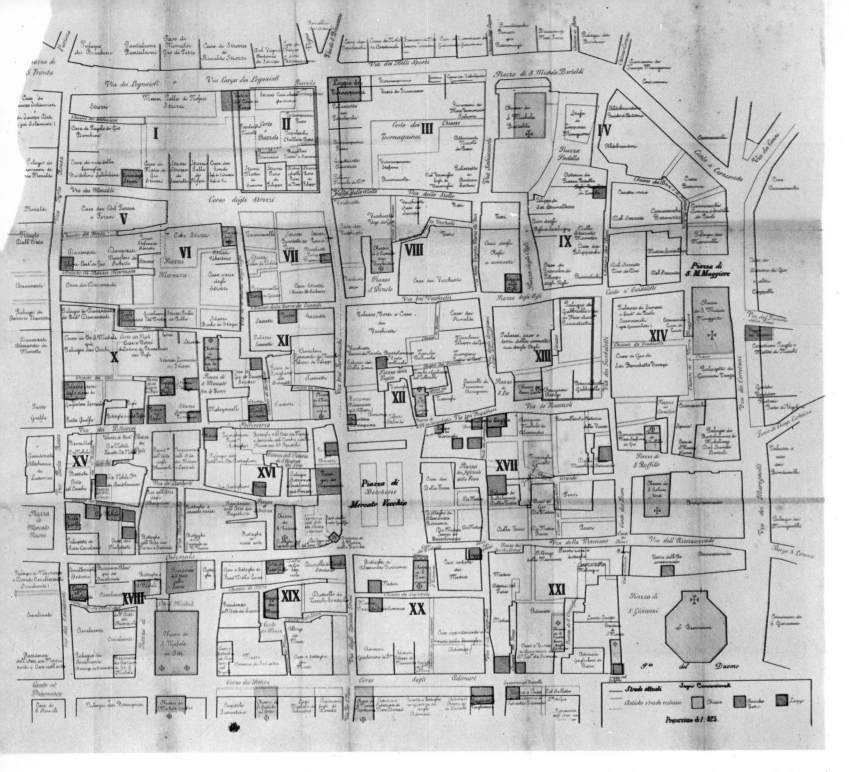

Community life in the Middle Ages evolved around three centres: the political, religious and commercial. Plan of Florence, derived in part from the first land registry drawn up in 1427 for purposes of taxation and to show the ownership of all lands and properties in the city (Studio of Carocci).

it is only in quite recent times that the figure has begun to rise again.

The decline in population naturally caused a reduced pressure on housing and space. The open areas enclosed by the third wall were left largely free of houses and became orchards or small-holdings as, for example, in the Cafaggio district.

It is understandable, therefore, that the policy of the civic authorities should be to encourage good build-ing in every way, as is shown in a document of 1415, the *Statuti Populi et Comunis Florentiae*. These forbid the granting of citizenship to any person who has not undertaken to build a house of the value of at least one hundred florins, or more should the Priors demand it. This regulation is based on a law of 1377, and can be considered to have been in force much earlier, perhaps even in the thirteenth century, when the demand for houses was very great.

A second important document in town planning and urban development is dated May 27th 1489, when the Signoria passed a law exempting all new houses from any « ordinary or extraordinary tax » for a period of forty years. This was plainly aimed at encouraging building, which was, however, now at full spate: in fact, writes the contemporary diarist Luca Landucci, « the men at this time were so over-worked with building walls that there was a shortage of masons and material ».

In addition to wishing to make the city look more beautiful, a general aim of all town-planning regulations, the law-givers clearly intended to discourage all speculative builders and sub-letting, « it being established by the Priors that many would build for their own use, others to let »; moreover, it was stated, there were too few houses in the city, and these were in a bad state.

It does seem, therefore, that the great interest in building in the late fifteenth century was due as much as anything to a desire for new houses, as there had been no increase in population and the old buildings were both dilapidated and old-fashioned, that is to say they failed to meet the tastes of citizens of the day. Among the leading class there was a positive fever for putting up new houses. The 1489 law is a reflection of the new tastes and new needs resulting from the changes in the various social classes, particularly in the higher levels.

From the thirteenth century onwards the urban area increases very little, and as there is so much space available the growth is gradual and apparently well planned. In Stefano Bonsignori's plan of 1584, in the area beyond the second wall, built from the thirteenth century onwards, the streets are nearly all long, straight and relatively wide; there is little trace of the narrow lanes and twisting alleys of the old city centre so characteristic of the medieval town.

THE TOWER OFFICERS

If there was no preconceived plan for rebuilding the city, Florence, during both the Republic and the Principate, possessed bodies of technical experts, whose business it was to put into effect whatever the legislative and executive powers commanded. In this she was ahead of other States which, so far as

is known, had nothing similar until the early fifteenth century.

The first information we have concerning the « officers of the Tower who shall also have control over the property of all rebels » (which was the title of the magistrates appointed to supervise building) dates from October 23rd 1349, when, as a result of the plague, the municipal authorities found themselves having to legislate on property left ownerless after the death of leaseholders, and created this new body. The Officers, in addition to looking after all state property, were also superintendents of public building and road-making, issued the building regulations and controlled everything relating to town planning. Right from their inception they were a body of building and town-planning experts with judicial authority, and it is important to realise that they were one of the first municipal organisations with a clearly specialised function.

Under the Principate the Officers were suppressed and their duties taken over by the Guelf Captains, in a body of nine men (created 1267) who rivalled the Signoria (the supreme magistrature created in 1282) for power and generally exercised tyrannical rule. By the fifteenth century their powers had been considerably reduced. These were soon replaced by special commissioners, as the task proved too difficult and too vast. In 1570 we find one of these commissioners, Cosimo Bossi, in charge of the highways. This organisation fitted in well with the thoughts and practice of the Princes, under whose rule the functions of the Republic were entrusted to specialised bodies of men under a single command.

The building and town-planning policy of Florence from the fourteenth to the sixteenth century can be deduced primarily from the Statutes of the Republic, then from the important legislation carried out by both the municipality and the principate. These show the main lines of the planners' thoughts: the Tower Officers and successive bodies had purely an executive function.

The standards laid down in the Statutes were mainly in regulations of a general nature, and of general application; there were, for example, notable restrictions on types of elevation, on the occupation of public land, on the height of balconies from the ground. Although these many regulations were often aimed at particular cases, they were inspired by the

One of the very rare « views » of Florence which have been preserved from such an early date (1352). With its many tall houses, tower-houses and bell-towers, the medieval town indeed presented a « spiky » appearance (part of La Misericordia fresco, Bigallo Orphanage).

desire, so apparent in all legislation in Florence at this time, to make the city more beautiful, healthier and of the greatest benefit to its inhabitants. The municipal authorities, like the town planners of today, were moved by a sense of beauty and an awareness of the public good. This communicated itself to the citizens of Florence, who seem to have been well informed about town-planning matters. The mid-fourteenth century development plan for the central areas which contained historic buildings was surprisingly modern in conception.

DEVELOPMENT PLANS

The overall design which emerged in the next few decades was already taking shape at the end of the thirteenth century, when there seems to have been a marked effort to control the unrestricted development caused by the rapid increase in population and to

construct to certain aesthetic standards. This would explain the great public buildings and the huge Gothic churches put up by the mendicant orders, all clearly designed to add beauty to the city, as contemporary documents affirm.

In the fourteenth and succeeding centuries this type of building and planning was to become increasingly evident as, first the municipality, then the principate sanctioned enormous and costly development schemes.

The city was planned in successive stages. First the streets were to be widened and straightened; then slum areas, such as the Tintori, were to be cleaned up, or large squares containing public buildings, such as the Piazza della Signoria and the Piazza del Duomo (the political and religious centres respectively), were· to be redesigned to enhance their value and importance.

The desire for wide streets arose immediately when the planners faced up to reality: Florence's narrow winding alleys, described by contemporaries as mean, ugly and stinking, offended their sense of taste and beauty. Modernisation proceeded along two lines: on the one hand an attempt was made to straighten out the more tortuous thoroughfares, and on the other new streets were planned to a standard which had no relation to what had gone before.

On February 16th 1327 the Municipal Council proposed to straighten out what is now the Via dei Banchi. In those days it was dirty, gloomy and evil-smelling, and under the new plan it was to become straight and handsome. A few years earlier, in 1322 to be exact, similar work had been done on the Via della Piazza del Sesto d'Oltrarno (the present Via Guicciardini). In March 1361 (omitting the many streets which had been modernised in the interval) a great amount of work was carried out, at considerable expense to the Municipality because of expropriation of property, firstly on the Via di Parione, said to be « narrow and not straight », then on the present Via del Corso « for straightening and embellishment ». The heavy cost of the compulsory purchase of property soon brought the work on the Via di Parione to a standstill, and only the first part of the street from the Via de' Tornabuoni was widened, as can still be seen today.

The most striking example of street development was the opening of the Via Larga, the present Via Cavour, with a happy combination of beauty and usefulness. « For the greater adornment of the city and its access roads and, in particular, to ease the journey to the Loggia di Orsanmichele for merchants returning from the Mugello or the Romagna with their loads of grain and fodder, it is desired that the new road shall be drawn and constructed as straight and as wide as possible ». Measures such as these, and the forthright language in which they are expressed, bear eloquent testimony to the excellent town-planning of the city authorities in Florence. The words used above imply something more: not only is the new road to be wider than any other in the city (and it will rightly be called Via Larga, Broad Street; evidently its width, compared with the narrow medieval streets had caught the imagination of the people), but it is to have a further purpose in speeding up the transport of grain from the Mugello and the Romagna, the age-old granaries of the Republic, and it becomes a modern supply-route.

In June 1339 the workmen building the churches of San Giovanni Battista and Santa Reparata, under the Guild of the Silk Merchants, which had the supervision

The « Catena Map » of 1470 shows the great change in the appearance of the city in the century or more since the

34

Bigallo fresco was painted. Many of the towers have been demolished, and the « spiky » appearance of the city has largely disappeared.

of the Baptistery, and the Guild of the Wool Merchants, which supervised the building of the Cathedral, petitioned the municipal authorities to reduce the height of the houses in the then Corso degli Adimari (the last section of what is now the Via Calzaiuoli which consisted, in addition to the Via Calzaiuoli proper, of the Via dei Caciaioli, Corso dei Pittori, Via dei Farsettai and Via del Canto il diamante) and the Piazza del Duomo on that side; this was because the

The San Frediano Gate. Through this gate were carried goods which had come by sea, often from distant places.

complex of fine buildings made up of the Baptistery, the Cathedral and the Bell Tower, then still under construction, was partially hidden from view. The buildings stand in a slight depression, still noticeable today, and it is said that « the beauty of all those churches was greatly diminished and hidden thereby ».

What was the remedy for this state of affairs, which the inhabitants of those days considered as great a detriment to the beauty of their city as the narrow winding streets? It was very simple: lower the level of the street and the square, within the limits of stability of the buildings, so that the « dignity of the aforementioned churches shall be greatly enhanced and that they shall appear sufficiently taller thereby ». In this the citizens were plainly moved by aesthetic considerations; the practical and utilitarian aspects do not appear even to have been considered. The fine buildings under course of construction were not being shown off to their best advantage, and this offended their good taste. The money needed was voted by a large majority and it seems evident that this good taste was shared by a great many of the citizens. When we consider that at the time these decisions were taken, there were already growing indications of the economic and financial troubles to come, such as the bankruptcy of famous commercial firms and the consolidation of the public debt by the State, it is all the more surprising that the inhabitants and the civic authorities should have been able to spare time and money on purely aesthetic matters. Measures like these, of course, go far beyond the general desire for order by the mere provision of wider and straighter streets.

From time immemorial there was a kind of market for the sale of « straw, grass or other litter » close to the San Zanobi column on the north side of the Baptistery. It was considered a degrading spectacle which undermined the efforts being made to improve the setting of the famous buildings in the vicinity. In July 1376, therefore, « for the greater embellishment of the city » the market in the Piazza del Duomo was forbidden and the vendors were ordered to move elsewhere. This they did, but sticking to the letter of the law, moved off the prescribed minimum of fifty yards and set up again at the junction of what is now Via Cerretani and Piazza San Giovanni, an area known ever since as the Canto alla paglia (Straw Market).

Work was begun soon afterwards on the development of the Piazza della Signoria, the political centre of the city. This again was aimed at improving the setting of the public buildings, and seems to have been carried out at somewhat greater effort and expense than was the case with the Piazza del Duomo, and the planning seems also to have been more co-ordinated.

A start was made in 1343 by the Duke of Athens, who had all the houses opposite the Palazzo Vecchio pulled down. It was here that in 1363 the prisoners from the war against Pisa were to build that great roof which was named after them. In 1349, to widen the square and improve its appearance, the San Romolo church was demolished and in 1357 a new public building, the elegant Palazzo della Mercanzia, made its appearance on the square. In December 1362, for the same reasons, it was decided « that the houses which stand on the Piazza del Palagio de' Signori ... on the north side shall be moved back ... before the first day of February ». In 1376 the Loggia dell'Orcagna was begun, and just thirty years later all the houses next to it were knocked down to improve its

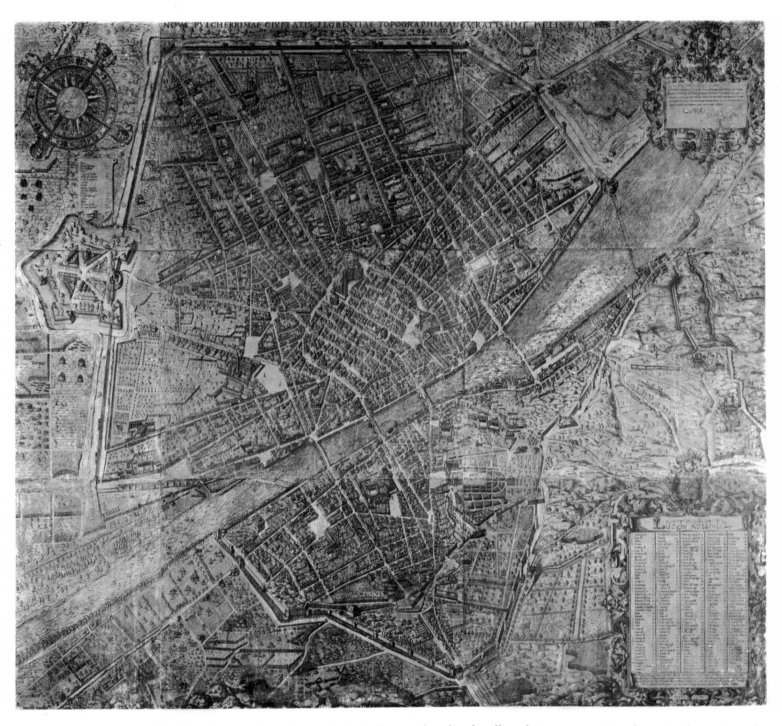

Bonsignori's town plan of 1584. Outside the second medieval wall, enclosing narrow twisted streets, the city is undergoing planned expansion: the streets are nearly all long, straight and relatively wide, and there is plenty of room for orderly growth.

setting. The final touch to the improvement of the square was afforded by the law of December 9th 1385, under which it was forbidden to exercise certain trades, or to expose for sale any goods not conforming to the dignity of the place, or to bring any heavy traffic on to the square. The latter prohibition could well be brought back nowadays.

Whereas the thirteenth century was characterised by a vigorous but unplanned expansion, the fourteenth, with its considerable drop in population figures, was a period of reflection and consolidation, and town-planning at this time was almost entirely concerned with embellishment or practical improvements, rather than with expansion. The striving for order, beauty and usefulness, which is a characteristic of Florentines, reached its height in the fourteenth century, and the whole city, although still looking in panorama like the spiky medieval Florence, was laying a sound basis for future development.

In the fifteenth century Florence did not possess a single new public building which could stand comparison with those of the late twelfth century, or those of other cities such as the massive Ducal Palace at Urbino, or the huge square castle at Mantua; the only noteworthy building was done at the end of the century when, consequent upon the broadening of the city's constitution, the Palazzo Vecchio was extended back and a hall, designed by the architect Cronaca, was built on to it in 1494-5 to house the meetings of the Grand Council. It became known as the Cinquecento room. Simone del Pollaiolo, also known as Il Cronaca (1457-1508), also built part of the Palazzo Strozzi.

The decrease in the amount of public works during the fifteenth century was a direct consequence of constitutional crises and a change in the nature of political power, which slowly became oligarchical then dictatorial.

There was, however, a considerable amount of private building as the rich bourgeois cloth-merchants and bankers rose to the aristocracy and, in the following century, became courtiers. This explained the rich flowering of private town-houses in Florence, and many of these were quite exceptional works of art. The previous period of extensive public building had found the artist of the moment in Arnolfo di Cambio; the man of the new era was Brunelleschi, whose style set the fashion for the remainder of the fifteenth century.

The panorama of the city now showed much renovation and the beginnings of great changes: the new buildings, although fitted into the general design of the medieval town, nevertheless opened up great areas which gradually altered the whole appearance of the city. One example will suffice: when the Palazzo Strozzi was built, together with the square of the same name, not only were many shops and houses, some of them of considerable size, razed to the ground, but the two very ancient towers on the site were pulled down also; this meant the destruction of quite a large area of the old town. Thus Florence came to lose her medieval appearance and took on that air of calm, placid beauty, crowned by Brunelleschi's dome which « rideth high in the heavens and can shelter all the people of Tuscany » as Alberti wrote.

Whilst the Bigallo orphanage fresco shows us Florence as a city of many spiky towers rising from its mass of buildings, the Catena plan in the Berlin Museum, which dates from about 1470, or the miniatures of the contemporary Florentine painter, Pietro del Massaio, almost make us think that we are looking at a completely different place.

In its desire for straight lines and its preference for wide straight thoroughfares, the sixteenth century continued the ideas of the fourteenth, but was able to draw on all the theorising of the fifteenth when, more than once, town planning had sought the ideal solution for the ideal city. Through the practical experience of the previous centuries and the theory of the fifteenth, men achieved a new sense of harmony in building and a perfect relationship between architecture and free open space.

The favourite style of public buildings at this time had graceful features standing out in relief and contrasting harmoniously with the intervening smooth plaster surfaces and decorative motifs. Private houses too, and often the poorer ones, had a certain distinction and elegance which went well with both the more recent developments and the old medieval town.

Another tendency, already evident in the fifteenth century, showed clearly in the sixteenth: the creation of green open spaces and public gardens, and the building of large houses in the midst of great parks. The great garden of Boboli, the green acres of Ognissanti, with their twelve hundred great trees, the costly garden of the Bianca Cappello in Via della Scala, said to be a marvellous sight, and the botanical garden

One of the narrow streets in the outskirts of the city which lead up, through olive and cypress groves, to the Florentine hills. Flanked by high walls enclosing orchards and gardens, they characterise the quiet dreamy approaches to the city.

called the Giardino dei Semplici, created at considerable public expense, were all examples of this new outlook in town-planning.

The fifteenth century was a period of comparative stagnation in city development, and this continued beyond the last years of the Republic for at least two further decades. This is not surprising, as in its later stages the Republic was fighting to stave off one political crisis after another, and the principate in its early years was so heavily involved with pressing problems of consolidation and territorial expansion that it could spare neither thought nor money for anything else.

Part of the city as seen in a detail from a fresco by Gozzoli. Note the entrance gate, similar to those still standing today, the Porta San Niccolò, the Porta Romana and the Porta al Prato.

THE RENAISSANCE HOUSE

Houses built all to the same style, with façades six yards wide; houses which included, within the narrow compass of their walls, a dwelling and a workshop; houses built up against each other in rows separated by dark narrow streets, made even narrower by wide over-hanging cornices; at the back a garden, or more often a courtyard, to let light into the rooms; this was Florence.

The streets which contained shops concerned with the same trade were centres of common interest, and almost had a community life of their own; and when the houses in one block belonged to one landlord (and were then overlooked by a house with a tower, squat and menacing) the streets were merely communication trenches leading to a fortress.

Here and there rose the town houses, which the newly-rich families of bankers or merchants were building, vying with each other in opulence and beauty. They bore the names of their owners, and were the most striking and immediate testimony to their wealth and power. Daily they were being furnished with the books and works of art from the workshops of the copyists, the engravers, the cabinet-makers, the upholsterers, who all laboured to meet the tastes, not only of one class but of all the inhabitants, for the houses, the workshops, the mansions were open to all, and the stream of civilisation flowed through all their doors, so that the whole of Florence was the common patrimony of all her citizens.

Born during the first century B.C. at the only convenient river crossing-place in those parts, Florence still lay, twelve centuries later, within the perimeter of the ancient Roman fortified town, with very few outposts in the area of the ancient settlements outside the walls, either down towards the Arno or up in the hills towards Santa Croce, apart from those lying out along the crucial Arezzo-Bologna and Pistoia-Siena axes and, as decreed by fate, towards Pisa.

These outposts would today be called industrial areas, and this is what they were in those days. The houses were strung out in rows along the streets so that they might be easily accessible to trade. The roads were thus not made to serve the houses, but rather were the houses built alongside them as the streets were extended. This explains the rational arrangement of the road network, and why the houses characteristically open on to the streets, though maintaining their close grouping for community purposes and for self-defence.

Street and house were thus one unit in twelfth-century Florence, as she began her rivalry with Pisa for the leadership of Tuscany. At the beginning of the fourteenth century, apparently aware of her high destiny, she girdled herself with an imposing city wall, within which there were ample possibilities for development along the Via Bolognese, the Via Faentina, the narrow road leading to Fiesole, the Via di Pinti, the road to Pisa and the roads leading out to the smaller gates. Throughout the fifteenth century the suburbs continued to expand, still within the wall. Outside it there was gradual expansion until the early sixteenth century, when some of the outer districts were razed to the ground for the great siege of 1527 when the combined forces of Pope Clement VII and the Emperor Charles V imposed on Florence the restoration of the banished Medici. The Renaissance city did not grow out of a feudal settlement, as seems to have been the case with Lucca, in spite of its Roman plan, but from the

The massive San Frediano Gateway, opening on to the road to Pisa. Florence came into being where the roads to Pisa, Bologna, Arezzo, Siena and Pistoia had to cross the Arno.

growth of houses for craftsmen and the building of warehouses, as in Pisa, both opening on to the streets surrounding the blocks, each street housing its own particular trade. Workshops and warehouses all had dwelling-houses attached. The craftsman's shop was to be the nerve-centre of Florentine life for centuries to come. The city gradually took on the structure we can still see today, a structure determined by the necessities of trade and industry based on the house-workshop unit.

In the building regulations the standard minimum width of every house fronting on to the street was nine spans, that is, some six yards. This would allow for a workshop just over four yards wide, and an entrance with a facing staircase just over one yard wide.

THE WORKSHOPS

Even today there are whole streets in Florence which still show traces of the rows of shops and doorways so characteristic of this period, and some of these have withstood all the improvements made since the four-

City wall near San Niccolò gate. On the right the first houses of one of the districts of the city which have most closely preserved the characteristics of the fifteenth century. This was a secondary gate, defended by the Belvedere fort, some few hundred yards away.

teenth century. Via Romana, Via dell'Agnolo, Via Toscanella, Via de' Serragli, Via S. Maria, Via Ricasoli and il Prato all have three-, four- and five-storey houses with a shop and doorway. The chest-makers lived in what is now the Via de' Martelli, Ghiberti lived in Via Bufalini, Donatello in the Piazza del Duomo, as also did the Grasso Legnaiolo who made the roof ridges in the Piazza S. Giovanni, and Cimabue lived in Borgo Allegre, all of them in workshops opening directly on to the street. None of them would have wished to live or work elsewhere, because to

them the street was more than a road to and from the city, it was the basis of a way of life which could be shared by all who lived and worked on it. Some of the work was literally done on the street, because the shops were often extended by putting workbenches outside under a lean-to roof. The street was variously the place for a siesta, a conversation, an argument, or the place to dry out in the bright sunlight printed fabrics, varnished wood, glue, timber and leather.

It was not uncommon for certain streets and squares, though open to the public, to be privately owned.

Some of these houses, or perhaps a tower, or more rarely a tower-house (of which there are admirable examples still standing in Lucca, Pisa and Volterra, where they were much commoner than in Florence) had basements, which, though splendid for keeping the house dry, were difficult of access and often caused the ground floor to be raised above street-level, so that a short flight of steps had to be built up to the front doors, even of warehouses. These were a great encumbrance. In some cases the entrances to shops had unavoidably to be brought down below street level, as was the case under the Badia church or in the Piazza S. Lorenzo. Trade went on, however, in spite of all these difficulties. Does the fact that the basements and all the upper storeys were in use mean that there was a shortage of space in fifteenth-century Florence? It is impossible to say. The great length of its surrounding wall brought within the one city whole farms and smallholdings. If the Leopolda railway station would have gone completely into one part of the orchards and kitchen-gardens of the S. Maria Novella friars, if whole districts within the walls, such as the present Via Bonifacio Lupi or the Piazza d'Azeglio, had then been newly opened up, if in the sixteenth century it was possible to lay out gardens such as the Boboli, the Oricellari, the Bartolommeo Scala, to mention only a few, then there would appear to have been space in plenty. It is true, however, that those citizens who practised an art wished to live together and have their house in an important street. As a result the houses in certain streets took on additional storeys, and the artists and craftsmen, rather than set up new centres of trade, willingly occupied them. It was but a short step to work, their sons grew up in the trade and took it up almost without noticing it; the house was a workshop and a school, and usually the apprentice lived with the master in an atmosphere of natural domesticity where the master-pupil relationship became that of fathertoson. To make up for its lack of comforts, the house had to be large and the shop had to have many workers.

THE HOUSES

It must not be imagined that these rows of houses did not include larger and richer dwellings. Until the mid-sixteenth century there was, in fact, no exclusively wealthy district of the city, except perhaps the Via Maggio area. The wealthy, the men of learning and the politicians built their houses amidst the more modest dwellings in every part of the city. When the Palazzo Strozzi was built, fifteen houses had to be knocked down, and amongst these was the tower-house of the Counts Guidi da Poppi. The others included the houses and workshops of a stone-mason, a wood-carver, a baker, a farrier, a pork-butcher, a scrap-iron merchant, a wool worker, and a cobbler. Quite clearly certain powerful families, either for strategic reasons, for collective defence, or for trade and economic purposes, combined their interests and bought up whole streets and squares to which they gave their names.

The family which immediately comes to mind, because of its unique position in the city and of the reputation it has handed down of its rapid rise to financial and industrial power, is that of the Peruzzi; but there were also the Albizzi, the Buontalenti, the Donati, the Alberti and others, and later the Guicciardini and the Rucellai. These families owned blocks of buildings with a church or a square in the centre, around which, in the stormy fourteenth century, the houses had been built close together and even, in some cases, equipped for defence. As the troubles passed, however, the houses began to look out on to the world and open their doors to everyone. The same applied to streets or squares which were the centre of the activities of a guild; the common interests of the craftsmen formed a basis for community life, in the same way as common interests in trade linked together the householders dependent on powerful families. When it came to siting the area in which a particular guild would concentrate its members, this was not left to chance, but account was taken of tradition, the availability of services and the distance from large workshops. The Via dei Ferravecchi (Old Iron), the present Via Strozzi, was near to the market because the street itself was an iron and scrap-market and did not need many work-people, whereas the dyers and the finishers of the Corso dei Tintori drew their labour from the adjoining large working district of Santa Croce.

The workers' houses were variously planned inside, but were all designed to fit in the prescribed width of six yards. There was considerable difference in the layout of those houses which had some depth from the road; here it was possible to place the staircase dif-

Via Toscanella, near the Pitti palace. A typical Florentine street, preserving the sequence of house and workshop, as seen by the adjoining doors.

House with façade built within the prescribed limit of six yards' width (from a fresco by Masaccio).

ferently and even to build on additional rooms at the back, or have a garden or an orchard. Where there was little depth of plot, the workshop ran from the street on to a courtyard which it overlooked, and which was often very useful. Next to the workshop, in the front of the house, and usually on the right, there was the house door which opened on to a small area at the foot of the stairs. These were usually straight and steep and led to the top floor or the loggia, which could be open or covered and, used for hanging clothes, could be found in even the poorest houses.

If the plot extended a long way back, the width of the workshop was the same, but instead of the stairs there was a corridor, and the ground floor area was divided in two by a curtain. The stairs rose from the centre of the corridor and could serve both areas of workshop. In the Via Romana there is a group of houses like this, but because of reconstruction after the siege, not all of them have workshops opening to the front. There are occasional examples, however, here and there. The uniformity of these houses was due to similarity in the way of life and especially the earnings of the craftsmen, who usually owned their own houses.

There was as little decoration in the house as there was in the workshop, where everything was spent on the tools for the trade. There were very rare examples of rich ornate frescoes on the living-room walls which, when not roughly boarded over, were seldom light or smooth enough for decoration.

In the fourteenth and early fifteenth centuries the walls might be painted from floor to ceiling with imitations of hanging cloth or squirrel skin, or with geometrical patterns, pictures in a frieze telling a story, or gardens with trees. And if the curved ceiling over the workshop, plastered and whitewashed, was suitably adorned with the craftsman's tools hanging from it, the wooden ceilings of the upper rooms were often decorated with rose motifs which were repeated on the smooth structural members of the walls.

At night the windows were closed by large shutters, both inside and outside. By day they were protected by linen cloth stretched on a frame and varnished with turpentine or oil to make it waterproof and more transparent. This frame was not fixed to the wall but could be detached, like an awning. Some upper windows had awnings attached externally by iron hooks which can still be seen in the walls at the side of the frames.

A craftsman's house might have a workshop on the ground floor opening on to the street and often taking its light from an inner courtyard.

Glass window-panes were rare and the type of round window made in Venice was very expensive. Plate glass manufacture was just starting in Florence in the fifteenth century.

THE PALAZZO

When the power of the great Florentine bankers had been consolidated, their authority was vested in the head of the family who then became a great patron of the arts. This was characteristic of Renaissance Florence, and we shall find these families vying with each other in the luxury and adornment of their great houses.

The greatest rivalry was between Cosimo de' Medici and Palla Strozzi, whose family had been

Typical fifteenth-century view of Florence with crowded roofs of different heights, romanesque and gothic bell-towers with two-bay windows, the Bargello tower with its machicolation, the Cathedral and Giotto's bell-tower, a harmonious combination of masses and colour.

distinguished in politics, arts and letters since the late 13th century. Around 1445, in the same years in which the Palazzo Medici was being built, the Strozzino, as it was called, was being rebuilt on the site of the houses near the Via dei Ferravecchi owned by Palla, then in exile for ten years in Padua because of his opposition to Cosimo. Both buildings are massive cubes of stone with heavy rustication, and their ground floors are shut off from the outside, after the old style of defensive building, with small windows fitted with stout gratings. Geometrically, the centre was the inner courtyard of greyish-blue Tuscan sandstone, and this was also the centre of domestic life. It did not matter that the outsides of the buildings looked out on to narrow streets, as the light came in from the courtyards and gardens.

These great houses were the symbols of their masters' status. Who could change the name of Luca Pitti's palace? Yet he lived in it for only a short time, and when it became the Grand Ducal palace, then the Royal Palace, the name of its first owner might easily have been forgotten. Yet the astonishment, tinged with envy, with which the grandiose gesture of this magnanimous merchant was received by the Florentines, who thought his palace and gardens something of a folly, has indelibly associated his name with the very stones of his palace and its imposing and original design. If we allow free rein to our fantasy and reconstruct in our imagination this palace, which Brunelleschi may have designed, we find, when we compare it with the traditional mansions of the aristocracy, such novelty of design and conception as make it unique in appearance

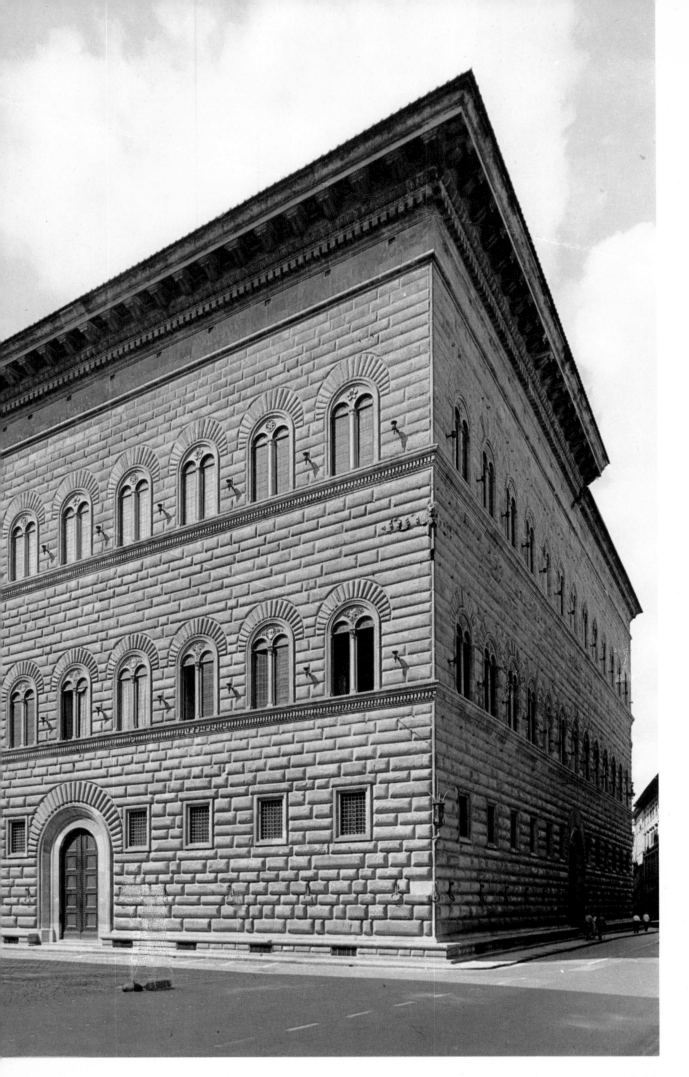

A perfect cube, light and airy in spite of its massive size: the Palazzo Strozzi, probably designed by Benedetto da Majano. Filippo Strozzi laid the foundation stone in 1489. The family, of popular origin, acquired great wealth in trade, and contributed this splendid example of Renaissance architecture to the embellishment of Florence, competing in taste and riches with the other great families of the city.

The Palazzo Pitti and the Boboli Gardens as they were in the sixteenth century. Whilst the palace was one of the most advanced architecturally, the great gardens, with their wide straight avenues, fountains and statues, were one of the most striking examples of the Renaissance concept of « ordered nature ».

The Casa dei Peruzzi, built before the Strozzi and Pitti palaces in sterner days, as shown by its massive fortress-like structure and the two inhospitable little stone benches on either side of the main door.

and construction, and a forerunner in the arrangement of its internal space. In the register of landed property Pitti modestly listed his palazzo as a « house », but, in contrast to other private dwellings, it had three doorways at the front and from the square in front of it, which had been built at the cost of demolishing quite a number of slum houses, one was expected to admire the vast garden which Pitti was having built and which was later destroyed in the siege of 1527.

On the upper floors, and running the whole length of the façade, are stone-fronted balconies; this is a unique feature of the building. In the central area there is a covered loggia which opens on to the front through three large archways; this breaks up the closed-in appearance of the façade and brings the house more closely into its landscaped setting, as the courtyard at the back is open to the garden, which climbs up the hillside behind the house. It is true that some decades later Matteo Strozzi envisaged that his garden would one day reach the Via Porta Rossa, but what other builder in Europe at this time, scarcely out of the grim restrictions of the feudal age, dared to link a house with its surrounding countryside? Even Cosimo, building his villa at Careggi a few years previously, had in mind a rustic retreat, but built a wall right round his small garden and completely enclosed his inner courtyard, and if the Albertis' Paradiso, built in the last years of the preceding century, showed the Florentines' preference for country houses, nothing in any of these villas, which are, admittedly, in a setting of greenery but completely shut off from it, can compare with the originality of Luca Pitti's palace.

It is not in this unique building, however, that we shall find the most typical way of life in a fifteenth-century Florentine palazzo. We must turn to the famous houses in the city itself.

The Medici palace was also cubic in shape, with an inner courtyard and a small, very private garden to the rear. The fear of attack from without was evident everywhere and, once the two leaves of the great main door were shut (this could be done very quickly), the house became a fortress. There was still room for a garden, however. The house as it originally stood was self-contained and self-supporting. There were coach-houses and stables and, adjoining the façade, great gates through which the huge coaches could pass, but none of this can be seen today, as the extensions car-

The Palazzo Medici at the beginning of what was called the Via Larga in Renaissance Florence.

The Palazzo Davanzati, courtyard. Note the steep staircase rising from ground floor almost to roof level, as in many other palazzi.

Above: *the Palazzo Medici, courtyard.* Below: *the Palazzo Bartolini Salimbeni, courtyard. Wide courtyards such as these gave light to the inner rooms which were built in suites round them.*

ried out by the Riccardis took in all the annexes and doubled the size of the front.

All these large houses had adjoining buildings, and required other adjoining space as well. Their owners thus acquired the buildings or the land fronting on the main façade to make a garden and enjoy the view, as Bartolommeo Scala did in Borgo Pinti, or to open up a square, thus bringing light, freedom and elegance and setting off the front of the house. Strozzi had to appeal on one occasion to Lorenzo the Magnificent for permission to buy up some houses belonging to an ancient and powerful Florentine family, the Tornaquinci, which stood opposite his mansion, so that he could demolish them and build a square.

There was also a passageway in all these houses leading to the courtyard, which was like an inner square and usually contained decorative objects reflecting the taste and personality of the owner, such as the round marble plaques in the Medici palace, sculptures, statues and coats of arms. The ground floor was, however, quite gloomy, as there were no proper windows in the outside walls, and it was therefore the part of the house reserved for the servants. This meant that the stairs leading to the first floor were an important feature of the house, as these would be used by friends and important guests. But anyone who has climbed the stairs of the Palazzo Strozzi, which are the original ones, knows how steep they are, and those of the Medici palace must have been the same before they were altered in 1715 by Francesco Riccardi, whose family, arriving in Florence from Cologne in 1520 and originally tailors, bought the palace from Grand Duke Ferdinand II in 1659. In so doing he apparently did not hesitate to break into the wall of the Chapel which contained Gozzoli's frescoes. The stairs of the Palazzo Busini also are steep and narrow, and rise direct from the courtyard; in winter it could be rather unpleasant having to go outside to go downstairs, but less disagreeable perhaps than one might think, as these large houses were very cold inside anyway. The narrow service-stairs were a means of avoiding the principal staircase and keeping the servants out of sight; they led more easily to the mezzanine floors and these, in the palaces of some size, contained not only the servants' quarters, but rooms furnished comfortably for occupation in winter, when it was impossible to heat adequately the great drawing-rooms. The backstairs were therefore the intimate secret passageways of the

Above: *typical large cornice on Florentine house.* Below: *the Palazzo Guadagni, main doorway.*

house and the servants used them only as a privilege.

In the morning when the porter opened the great double front door, he also closed the grille at the far end of the entrance hall. This stood almost up against the portico leading to the inner courtyard, and was made of wood. There is a particularly fine example in the Palazzo Giugni.

Above left: *example of house with projecting upper storey, common until the late fifteenth century, then forbidden when streets were widened and straightened.* Top right: *wall carvings, Via delle Belle Donne.* Bottom right: *the Palazzo Medici, entrance gate to courtyard.*

Outside, there was a stone bench on the pavement on which anyone who had to wait might sit, and sometimes the owner himself might be found there, taking a breath of air and exchanging a few words with passing friends. It was never his wish that the house should be entirely isolated: only in the seventeenth century was it completely separated from the street.

The stone bench outside the Palazzo Strozzi was very long but outside the Palazzo Giugni there were merely two cubic blocks by the front door. As for the drawing-rooms, in Renaissance times there was little of the stuffy privacy demanded by the nineteenth century. The gentleman's house in the fifteenth century existed not only for its master, but welcomed all his friends as

Bath used by Cosimo I de' Medici. One of the first of its kind. Previously baths had been tub-shaped, often large enough to hold two persons.

well. This is seen clearly in the arrangement of the floor space. The rooms lead one into the other; it was not felt necessary to divide them off with corridors. In some houses the big bedrooms were lived in also by day, and the bed was a minor item of furniture. All bedrooms were at least as large as other rooms and had fireplaces. In some cases, though these were rare, as in the Palazzo Davanzati, they had serving-rooms attached. For washing there were deep basins on wooden stands; for bathing there were tubs the size of half a barrel, wide and low, and sometimes large enough to take two people at once.

The bathroom comes in the late sixteenth century and finally the bath gets an outlet. In the Palazzo Vecchio there is still a bath said to have belonged to

Underground room in the Medici villa at Careggi. Rooms such as this, decorated and furnished as living rooms, were often used in the very hot weather, though their lack of ventilation could be detrimental to health.

Cosimo I. It is certainly of his period and has only very recently undergone some alteration.

The principal feature in the reception rooms was the fireplace. When it became practicable to draw up the smoke through the roof, the fireplace replaced the brazier which could either be carried about, or left fixed in the centre of the room. The chimney-piece came later; this was covered with the family arms, then later with sculpture which was sometimes of great artistic beauty. But the fireplaces were considered solely as pieces of architecture, and were of many shapes and sizes, from the simple ones with the fire on the floor and a cowl with a means of drawing up the smoke above it, small but pleasant to sit by, to the huge ones of the sixteenth century in which enor-

mous logs would burn slowly, and which could accommodate a whole row of chairs around them.

The fireplace had its own benches, and other benches and chairs were brought in to make up the circle. Some of the smaller rooms were heated by stoves or braziers, and occasionally had fireplaces, and here one could sit and write without having to put on extra clothes or get chilblains on one's hands and nose. The festivities of the household were held in these smaller rooms in the winter.

The first floor was usually given over entirely to assembly-rooms. These could be cross- or barrel-vaulted, even on the second floor also, as in the Palazzo Strozzi. In this case the rooms were enriched with capitals and lunettes around the windows, giving an

Above: *Chimney-piece (Palazzo Borgherini)*. Below: *The beautiful « lily » doorway in the Palazzo Vecchio (Benedetto da Majano)*.

air of solemnity, and an effect of a solid well-connected structure and great spaciousness, not to be found in rooms with unbroken vertical walls and beamed ceilings. There are many examples of the latter type in the houses and palaces of Florence, not to mention the very rich examples found in public halls from the Palazzo Vecchio to the Parte Guelfa. The private palaces contained rooms of more intimate proportions on the second floor (in Florence they all had a ground floor and two upper storeys) because they contained either ladies' and young persons' bedrooms, or a loggia used for such private purposes as drying the washing or taking a breath of fresh air. Above there was a belvedere, which could be open or covered, work-rooms for the domestic staff, store-places for fruit such as apples and raisins, and attics which were too hot in summer and too cold in winter. There were also basement rooms in which one could keep cool in the height of summer. In the villa at Careggi, one of these basement rooms, which always feels cool and damp, has walls painted with imitation trellis-work and climbing plants. Rooms such as this certainly contributed to the early deaths from gout and rheumatism of some of the more illustrious Medicis.

Although often vast in its proportions, the Florentine Renaissance palace is simple in structure, with its identical rooms repeated on all the floors and arranged in the same sequence around the inner courtyard, whence everything starts and where everything finishes. The stone-work of these houses is sometimes plain and sometimes it is plastered over and decorated with imitation bosses (the only complete example is the delightful Palazzo Busini and there are a few fragments elsewhere). The courtyards are paved with a greyish-blue Tuscan sandstone, grown green with moss in out-of-the-way places, and crumbling where it has been continually used, deadening the noise of the iron-clad wheels of the carts and carriages, growing darker in the rain and sparkling with tiny specks of light in the sunshine. The same stone was used for the columns and capitals in the courtyard, the decoration of the doors and windows, both inside and out, the cornices and the handrail and steps of the staircases.

The inside doors are of polished walnut, usually only one side having a frame. They are polished with oil or wax, and do not have handles with spring catches, but wooden catches and drawbars with little chains. Occasionally the doors and their framework

Beam and coffer roof (Palazzo Davanzati). The beams were decorated by young craftsmen only recently established or by pupils of the great masters.

are painted some simple colour such as red, green or blue, but only rarely do we find them inlaid, as in the Ducal Palace at Urbino. In Florence there must have been many doors inlaid in the fashion of those of Carthusian monasteries, even in private houses, but only very rare examples survive.

Another feature of the Florentine house at this time was the baked clay floor. This was universal, except for structures such as galleries and stairs. It was red, but not the dull red we see today, machine-polished, even in the noblest halls of the Palazzo Vecchio; the earth had been baked until it was a bright glowing red, then it was worked in by hand, and not cut with machines. There are not many of these floors left, though they were the most durable and comparable in wear to stone. The surface must have been somewhat irregular, but could be varied with designs of squares, rectangles and diamonds, alone or in various combinations, and with different colours according to the type of clay used, the bright red from the Arno or the yellow from the Signa.

FLOORS AND THE LOGGIA

The finest and most richly ornamental floor is that of the Biblioteca Laurenziana, Lorenzo's library. This consists of great squares of dark clay, which must have been very difficult to bake, inlaid with lighter clay and perhaps baked a second time. The effect is wonderful, and makes this very poor river-bed clay look as if it were set with precious stones. Very few of these original floors have survived. It would have been an easy matter to keep them clean in the drawing rooms and the bedrooms, and similarly in the kitchens, though here, as also in the entrance hall, the stables and the courtyards, the floors were often flagged.

It was usual to cover the floors with home-made or imported Eastern carpets. The latter are found in use throughout the centuries, and must have been one of the commonest articles brought into Europe through Italy's maritime republics. Every Madonna's throne painted in the fourteenth century has one, and in the rich man's house they were to be found in the dining halls, the reception rooms and the bed-rooms, together with silks, tapestry and leatherwork, the former being common in the mid-fourteenth century and the other

two some time afterwards, in the late fifteenth and early sixteenth centuries.

The rooms were decorated with pictures, wall-paintings and ornaments of terracotta, bronze and glass. Tapestry was still in use in the fifteenth century, though in some cases giving way to the carpet, and other wall-hangings included silks for festive occasions, marriages and funerals.

These ceremonies were held in certain cases in loggias built on or near to the house for this purpose by certain families. Some loggias had been in existence for a very long time: those of the Peruzzi, the Frescobaldi, the Albizzi, the Scali, the Medici, the Rucellai, for example. They were used for specifically public ceremonies and were open to everyone. It was expected that any person of the same rank would join the family in these celebrations, and not to do so would cause open offence. Later, when the ceremonies became more refined and restricted, they were held in private in the houses.

The loggia typifies certain habits of behaviour which determined the social structure of Renaissance Florence. The government itself had its loggia for ceremonial occasions, and thus invested its activities with the maximum publicity, making every citizen aware of the opportunity, nay the duty, of participating. To be seen in the Piazza della Signoria on important public occasions was in itself a political act. Similarly to put in an appearance at a family ceremony in a private loggia was openly to show one's good relations with the head of the family. The fashion of the loggia, however, soon died away with the changing political situation. The loggia in the Piazza della Signoria became a kind of open museum, and gradually the private loggias were put to different uses as the open ceremonies and publicly-held festivities were transferred to palace halls and gardens. The loggia might then be closed in and become another room of the house, as happened in the Medici Palace, or an artist's or craftsman's workshop, as in the Frescobaldi and Rucellai palaces. As its function declined, so did its architecture.

The pattern of daily life in Renaissance Florence, though often disturbed by frequent political upheaval, meant that the house remained the centre of human activity all through the fifteenth century, and the most important symbol of the personality of the politician, the high official, the merchant and the famous artist.

THE NEW STYLE IN FURNISHING

More ornate in design, more precious in materials, more personal in style, as the most famous craftsmen and artists competed to beautify the interiors of the Florentine house, Renaissance furniture reached a standard of elegance hitherto unknown, and even ordinary household objects reflected an outstanding good taste. This was the new style, which gradually replaced the older gothic, and developed from the early years of the fifteenth century to reach perfection in the early sixteenth.

As well as a great increase in the quantity of furnishings made and sold in Florence at this time, there was an equally important development in techniques and materials; majolica and glass-ware were perfected; rich material was widely used and velvet greatly improved in weave and colour; there was an increased demand for rich cloth and tapestry hangings; French and Flemish tapestries came into the great halls of the Florentine palaces, together with precious carpets from the East, porcelain from China and other exotic objects brought by merchants from their travels in distant lands, along with the first « antiques » — implements, sculptures, and coins — found in the first archaeological excavations.

There was also a spread of culture. In the houses of the richer Florentines one large room was fitted out as a library, whilst another quiet small room, the writing room, was set aside for the study of classical texts and for meditation.

We do not know very much about the furnishings of an ordinary house in the fourteenth century, but they must have been very similar to what we find in the early fifteenth. Large bench-chests for the linen, a kneading trough in the kitchen, and benches and stools with or without backs. The straw-covered chair did not come until the sixteenth century. The beds were low: sometimes merely planking with a mattress on top, either flat on the ground or just raised up a few inches. The crockery was of glazed earthenware, some drinking-vessels could be of glass and the cutlery, when there was any, could be of wood, iron or bone.

Walnut and white poplar were the commonest woods for furnishings and utensils, whilst spruce was used more particularly for building, especially in those outside balconies which sometimes ran right round a house or a tower, and, particularly on the upper storeys, were used for defence and attack in battles

between political factions. As civil strife gave way to a firmer central authority, first known as the *Comune* and then as the *Signoria*, the balconies were less frequently used and tended to disappear in the fifteenth century, or to change their style and material to ornate stone. They then became those characteristic projections over the street which served the same purpose as a modern balcony today.

The city grew in size and the surrounding hills were dotted with villas in the brief lifetime of Brunelleschi. At the same time the city took on a new look. In the late years of the fourteenth century there arose a class of industrialists and banker-patrons who were to play a major part in the political life of the city. Wealth became a means of adding lustre to the power of a family; the newly-rich had wide experience of life and the world, and wished to possess and distribute material things, at the same time aspiring to a refinement of the spirit, upheld and stimulated in this by the high

Palazzo Davanzati. Rooms such as this, with their ample proportions, high ceilings and bare minimum of furniture were vast impressive places, yet the oil lamp flickering before the holy shrine added a note of intimate light and warmth. The linen chest, painted, carved, inlaid and embellished with silver high-relief betrays the elegance of the lady of the house and the wealth of the match.

level of culture in Renaissance Florence and its wide contacts in Europe and the Mediterranean.

The Florentine tower-house of the thirteenth century was little more than a fortified lair; the houses at Lucca and Pisa, particularly the latter, were still in Renaissance times often of less importance than the warehouses to which they were attached. By the fifteenth century, however, the Florentine house was clearly the domain of an individual, and he had chosen it as the symbol of his personality in that society of houses, which was the walled city covered with roofs, and as a means by which he would be remembered.

The builders of the Florentine palaces in the fifteenth century taught this lesson to so many other men of their time: that not only did the house bring to its owner the satisfaction of a personal ambition,

*In Renaissance times there was no dining room proper,
even in the richest palazzi, and therefore no dining room
furniture as such. There were, however, many fine examples
of sideboards for the display of crockery and of beautiful
tables as shown here (Palazzo Davanzati).*

but it enriched the city with an illustrious monument
and maintained the supremacy of Florence, a supremacy
born of that individual liberty for which the city had
fought so hard over the years. The fact that almost all
the masterpieces of the Florentine artists: tables, sculpture, goldware, furniture and precious stones, which
have found a home in museums all over the world,
came originally from Florentine houses is clear proof
that these objects were to be found in large quantities
in the palaces, the houses and the convents of the time.

The best clients of the Florentine artists were the
Florentines themselves, who seem to have purchased
regardless of expense and entirely for their own
satisfaction; there was a clear identity of taste between
the artist and the cultured elements in society. Antique-
hunters of the eighteenth and nineteenth centuries pil-

laged the Florentine houses mercilessly, but for all
that some treasures still remain. What must this treasure
have amounted to in the hundreds of great town houses
in Florence at the end of the sixteenth century?

The walled-in industrial city of the fourteenth century was changed by an economic miracle, which
brought with it changes of another nature, mainly
cultural, and the new houses springing up all over
Florence brought a gradual transformation in the
appearance of the city throughout the fifteenth and
sixteenth centuries. It must be added, however, that
whereas the older houses were demolished and many
of the larger ones modernised, little was done to the
smaller houses, except to increase their comfort and
convenience. The wooden troughs, for instance, used
in the kitchen for washing-up since time immemorial,

Four-poster bed (Palazzo Davanzati). These were very common, not only in the houses of the rich, and their curtains and canopy, which in more modest households would be of linen or occasionally silk, gave privacy to the bed when this was installed in the one living room.

were replaced by stone sinks with an open outlet on to the courtyard, and water was brought in by bucket from a tap in the wall. The ornate marble wash-basins still seen in certain monasteries and sacristies give us some idea of what their domestic counterparts must have looked like. Other services improved when the first drains were laid. The streets were paved with jointed stones, and the first pavements were laid around the larger houses such as the Palazzo Rucellai, the Palazzo Antinori and the Palazzo Strozzi.

The house roof became even larger and more ornate, so that it overhung sufficiently to direct the rainwater into the centre of the street and protect both the front of the house and the passers-by. Thought was given to street-lighting, to relieve the gloom, hitherto unbroken except for the occasional lamp burning before a sacred image, or the torches which projected from their holders on the wall of some private house. Caparra's ornate lampholders on the Palazzo Strozzi and the ones on the Palazzo Guadagni were certainly not the only ones in Florence at this time; almost all the larger palaces must have been lit up outside after sunset to relieve the darkness of the street in front of the main door. People usually had an early supper and went to bed at dusk, but there were frequent late gatherings of friends around the table, in the light of an iron-framed lantern with glass walls. If there was no moon at this late hour, the city would be quite deserted; even behind closed doors, and with a watchman patrolling the streets outside, it could be dangerous.

In addition to improved services and better comfort, the Florentines also wanted furniture which was more beautiful, more practicable (the drawer, for instance, dates from the Renaissance) and more serviceable.

Sixteenth-century furniture- and cabinet-makers had a particularly florid style and turned out carved, inlaid and sculptured pieces which were works of art, yet solid enough to defy the centuries, and many, in fact, have survived in use to this day.

Wood was the most widely-used material in the house, from the precious rare woods to the common timber from the forests of Vallombrosa and the Mugello, where there is still today a flourishing trade in rustic furniture. The fixtures, fittings and wall-panelling were of beech, alder or ash; the doors, window frames and the low raised platform on which stood the framework of the bed, were of spruce or cypress, and these were also used for the handrail of the stairs and the stair steps when these were not of stone.

The plain furniture was of beech, service-wood (*Pyrus* [*sorbus*] *domestica*) or cherry-wood; the carved furniture in the houses of the nobility was of walnut, and later, when the furnishings reached their peak of elegance, of precious exotic woods. Then the simple carving and smooth shaping, which had been the feature of domestic furniture until the first few decades of the fifteenth century, gave way to new ornate motifs on the framework of chests and coffers, the edges of high-backed chairs, the covers of kneading-troughs, armchairs, corner-pieces with capitals and supporting brackets with wooden feet in the form of a lion's or a griffin's claw.

THE HUSBAND AND WIFE'S BEDROOM

The basic furniture of the room was the bed with a headboard which was often sumptuously carved and painted, the linen-chest and the wash-stand and commode, fore-runner of the small private closet, then the cupboards for weapons and the wardrobes for clothing, including underwear and the *lucco*, or long gown worn by Florentines.

In the wealthier families' houses the four-poster bed was richly hung with silk and velvet brocade, and laid with embroidered sheets and an impressive counterpane. The latter was an important possession and could be quilted with wool between double silk of brilliant colours, red, green, deep blue, or golden yellow, or

The severe lines of the rather sombre fifteenth-century furniture were often relieved by objects of exquisite taste and superb craftsmanship.

Sometimes when the chests were not large enough to hold everything, clothing and linen were kept in drawers fitted along one side of the wooden frame on which the bed stood.

An elegant and indispensable piece of furniture was the small cabinet which contained numerous small chests and boxes and leather purses for money and jewels, or cosmetics, oils, cakes of soap, face-powder and paste, phials of scent and little bags of amber and musk balls. Nearby were the equally indispensable mirrors, square or rectangular.

In the poorer houses, where the bed consisted of planks and a straw mattress covered with a quilt, clothing was hung over poles arranged diagonally across the corners of the room. More modest chests contained other clothing and rough hemp and linen coverings. But whether the bedroom was in a rich family's mansion or the simple home of a poor couple, artisans or peasants, pride of place was given to the cradle, especially for the firstborn child. This could be neatly made in the shape of a small-scale bed on rockers, also with its painted head-board and a little quilt of silk or wool, or, if the family were poor, it would be a very simple basket-shape of interwoven rushwork. This article of furniture was so important

a double wool blanket stitched together with square, oblong or diamond shapes. In summer it was stored in the linen-chest with rosemary to keep away the moths.

The marriage-chest or *cassone* was still an important piece of furniture in the fifteenth century. It contained, sprinkled with bunches of lavender, the *donora*, or household linen contributed by the bride and sewn, woven or embroidered by her own hand. The linen-chests which belonged to her grandmother, and which were often stored away in the wardrobes, were smooth and painted on both the sides and the rounded lid, sometimes also on the inside. Hers, however, was richly carved with figures and scenes in relief on the sides, the flat lid and even on the corners; it was also not unusual for the chests to be decorated with stucco work embellished with inlaid silver.

On the writing desk stood a variety of inkwells and seals. Some bronze and silver inkwells such as this one (Museo del Bargello) were of great beauty, and had tiny statues often made by famous artists.

that it sometimes figured in contracts for payment as a compensatory item, and not only for labourers and craftsmen but also for merchants' agents, one of whom was, in fact, paid as salary 3 lbs. of pepper, 9 oz. of saffron, 12 soup plates and a new cradle.

The work of the carpenter and cabinet-maker was also matched with that of the iron- and goldsmiths who made the complicated and elegantly-designed metal bosses, locks and keys, for the coffers, safes, chests and cabinets which held money, documents and jewellery. Some of these chests were real strong-boxes, often with iron or silver-plating on the sides, and massive lids fastened with great complicated secret locks. They were usually kept in the master's bedroom, or, if brought into the counting-house or workshop for greater convenience by day, they were always taken back into the safety of the house at night. The biggest, heaviest and most complicated strong-boxes were those of the money-changers. These were never used on the counting-house table, but the money was brought to the office by the clerks and servants in smaller portable boxes a little at a time. One of the many famous smiths working in Florence at this time was Niccolo Grosso, nicknamed « the Advance » because he refused to start work on a commission, or

even to design it, without an adequate deposit. Even Lorenzo the Magnificent had to pay a large deposit when he ordered a pair of andirons for the large fireplace in one of the rooms of his villa at Careggi. The story has it that Niccolo was not satisfied even with this, and, having suffered on a previous occasion from Lorenzo's parsimony, decided to teach him a lesson. He pocketed the money and set to work, but made only one, asking for a further deposit before he would start the second.

TAPESTRIES

The medieval custom of hanging banners from windows and balconies on feast-days, to celebrate the coming of spring or to honour a victorious captain returning from the wars, a noble champion back from the tourneys, a band of cavalry back from a foray against armed invaders, or a new bishop or a saint in holy procession, had emblazoned the exteriors of Florentine houses with splendid ornamental wall-hangings. Curtains as we know them were comparatively rare, except, as we have seen, round the four-poster bed, but there was a great passion for tapestry, that

The work of the craftsmen was often indistinguishable from that of the artists, especially in the design and manufacture of elegant objets d'art. The sculptor collaborated with the casket-maker, creating exquisite little figures, engraved or sculptured or cast. Small casket (school of Donatello) and candlestick from Prato Cathedral.

great art of pictorial representation by needle and loom which had reached perfection in France and Flanders. These represented a story, a landscape or a coat of arms which might be connected with events in the history of the family, or scenes from hunting or the Bible, and were hung everywhere on the walls.

From early Renaissance times Florence too had its tapestry-makers, brought in the first instance from Flanders by Florentine merchants and bankers, though the designing was done by Florentine artists themselves. When Lorenzo's direct descendants were banished, and Cosimo I became Grand Duke, he created the Medici tapestry workshops, where the designers were Botticelli, Perin del Vaga and Bachiacca.

Another product of the craftsmen's workshops, and one which became a speciality of the Florentine cabinet-makers, was the ornate picture-frame. The demand for this grew rapidly with the spread of non-religious paintings and the family portrait. Many of the painted, gilded, carved and sculptured picture-frames of the late sixteenth century are round: this is peculiar to Florence, and some are even decorated with stucco flowers and fruit. This was the type of frame which the Della Robbias put round a Madonna and Child or a group of Cherubim, Virgins or little angels.

Renaissance Florence still had, however, traces of refined gothic in the votive paintings hung on the walls over little altars, chests of drawers, or beside the bed; these often had little flanking pilasters with capitals and cusping and could be simple, in diptych or triptych.

THE TABLE

The Florentine house had no dining-room, properly speaking, either for the family or for guests. The long tables which stood in the middle of some rooms could be used for eating, but they required in addition a sideboard with a high back, a plate-rack and various compartments with doors. The table was usually laid where it was most comfortable: in front of the large fireplace in winter, in the garden or under a porch in summer. It was laid with a long, draped, embroidered cloth, often strewn with fresh flowers and greenery. Those eating usually sat along one side only leaving the other side free for serving the food and wine.

On the tables, sideboards and plate-racks stood the glazed earthenware and enamelled majolica. Jars, plates, mugs, basins, pitchers and amphorae, decorated with scenes from history and engraved with copper,

Piece of sixteenth-century Florentine furniture belonging to the antiquarian Bellini. The workmanship of this type of furniture became increasingly more refined and elegant. The drawer was invented in this century.

The art of picture-framing reached its height in the fifteenth and sixteenth centuries with painting, gilding, carving and sculpture-work on wood and stucco. Not all beds were four-posters. By the fifteenth century the high wooden head-board was common and this, like the foot, was usually carved or painted.

bronze or silver, stood on the table and the side-tables for daily use. The finest pieces were brought out only on special occasions for a family celebration or a public event.

The finest tableware came not only from Faenza, Urbino, Deruta, Gubbio or Spain but also from the workshops of Florence itself.

The Medici wished to have their own ovens for the manufacture of majolica-ware for use by the family and their guests in their palace and villas. They employed the finest craftsmen in the city, and the most famous painters designed decorative motifs from allegorical and mythological subjects and the family crests. The Medici ceramics made at Cafaggiolo were famous for their very deep blues and brilliant orange-yellows.

Correct mixing, colouring, glazing and skill in baking produced tableware of the highest quality, and these miniature works of art, which were in daily use in Renaissance Florence, set a family tradition for fine and beautiful things and were a symbol of wealth and standing. Thus the Florentine household would have

The savonarola, *a characteristic Florentine chair of the fifteenth century, still found today in studios and libraries.*

its decorated crystalware and fine coloured glass: cups and water-jugs of rock crystal, or of crystal set with gold or precious stones; beautiful deep transparent green and blue glassware in the more modest houses, for Empoli glass was traditional in Tuscany for everyday cups and beakers, and as early as the end of the fourteenth century the well-known strawbound Chianti flask was being manufactured at Poggibonsi.

The peasants preferred to drink from earthenware bowls and from jugs, using the spout, as in the inns and the wine-shops. Their plates and bowls were of wood, as also were their spoons and ladles, though the handles might be of carved bone or covered with strips of metal. There were no sets of cutlery as we know them consisting of knives, forks and spoons. Though the spoon had been used since ancient times, the four-pronged fork was a novelty in the Renaissance, and seems to have been first used in the house of the Pucci family in Florence. Such forks as there were in the Middle Ages had one prong only, otherwise one turned one's knife over and used the point of the handle. The knife was usually a personal one, worn in the belt and used also as a weapon. When the custom spread of providing table-knives, these came in various designs. The chief steward's enormous knife, with which he carved up animals roasted whole, was, with its damascened blade, a valuable object in the houses of the wealthy, as also were the table-knives of silver and gold with handles decorated in niello or precious stones. There were also fine goblets of precious marble and little cups of silver and gold instead of the usual glassware.

In the country, in farmhouse or villa, the rich were content to use the same kind of cutlery and crockery as the peasants, as we know from Madonna Isabella Guicciardini, a shrewd housewife married to a rich and noble official of the Florentine Republic. Madonna Isabella, who ruled over the treasures of the sumptuous palace beyond the Ponte Vecchio, and who had brought to her marriage the Sacchettis' taste for practical wellmade household equipment, wrote to her husband in Arezzo: « Wooden tableware will be very useful if you can procure some, for both here and in Florence; of wooden chests, we have enough for the moment ».

Pots and pans were of iron, copper or earthenware, as they are today; the *mezzine*, the typical one-handled Florentine jugs used for collecting water from the well or the fountain, were of copper with bronze feet.

Palazzo Davanzati: first floor drawing-room. The elaborate ceiling, leaded windows, embroidered chairs, heavy carved table, tapestries and pictures reflect great wealth and elegance. Most of the furnishings were made by Florentine craftsmen.

In the houses of the rich there were also vases, amphorae, decanters and boxes which were purely ornamental. These were outstanding for the quality of their silverwork, richly embossed and engraved, and there were some with lids which were never intended to open, as the whole was made in one piece.

THE STUDY

The larger and more important houses had a small room set aside for writing and quiet thinking — Michel-angelo's, and Machiavelli's in his country house, have become famous — and in some cases this study and writing-room became the centre of administration of the household. It usually contained, between two windows, a long table on two supports, almost as wide as the shorter sides, with carved lions' or griffins' feet; the wooden bar joining the two supports would also be carved. On the table, in addition to the usual writing-materials, the dusting-powder, the hour-glass, the sheets of parchment and the seals, there were often antique bronzes and marbles, mosaic tablets and pieces of ancient ivory. Next to the table stood a long torch-holder on cast-iron feet.

A large two-sided rack contained books and papers, and around it were chairs, stools, fold-stools and « savonarolas », folding chairs with low backs. There would also be a high reading desk of wood and wrought-iron. In the study of a lawyer or a man of letters, one wall might have carved and inlaid seats arranged like stalls.

Large libraries were usually found in monasteries. Here the books were arranged on shelves, each volume on its own reading-stand, as in the Laurenziana library. In the fourteenth century there were only manuscripts, and these were collectors' pieces for the wealthy, but public and private papers and notebooks were kept on shelves. Manuscript books were usually kept in cases, like the rare mathematical library collected by Antonio dell'Abbaco. This contained some hundreds of volumes and was left to the Corporation of Florence, who kept it in padlocked strong-boxes and lent out sections of it from time to time to whoever was teaching mathematics in the Studium. Account-books and household papers were stored on shelves, but the library as we know it, where books are stacked in cases with their spines to the front, only came in the late fifteenth century, when printed books began to circulate freely.

The daylight came in through the large windows which, in the wealthy houses, were fitted with glass. This, however, was often removed with other equipment when the house was sold, or even when a room fell into disuse, and refitted elsewhere. In the poorer houses the windows were covered with cloth or paper until after the sixteenth century.

In the evening the family had to dine and retire early. If for any reason they did stay up late, light could be provided by the lantern which could be of iron with leaded glass panes, round and convex like the windows, or of wood and oil-paper with wax candles which might have three or four wicks. A festivity which went on well into the night would demand torches and wooden or silver candelabras, after the women and children had retired to bed with their candles. The votive lamp before the shrine of the Madonna glowed day and night. This burned oil from a single wick, and was similar in shape to the larger ones in beaten silver with three and four wicks which came into use in the sixteenth century. All these lamps smoked badly, and the small wax candle was preferred, though it was more expensive.

TASTE AND DIGNITY IN DRESS

From the extreme monkish simplicity of the late Middle Ages to the sumptuous elegance of the Medici courts, in spite of the opposition of moralists and the sumptuary laws, Florentine fashions, though far from the haute couture we know today, had no rival in any other state or city in their capriciousness and stylish ingenuity. When Lorenzo di Piero brought home a French wife, Florence replied to her clumsy, ostentatious wide gowns with the simplest of flowing robes.

The wool and silk weavers, the shoemakers, the wigmakers, the goldsmiths, were all superb craftsmen and made the name of Florence renowned throughout the world. But their coffers were filled not only with the profits of ladies' fashions: men too had a taste for originality and extravagance in dress, particularly the young ones, who, as might be expected, were much given to flaunting fine cloth and brilliant ornaments, often to the point of affectation. Men of more mature age preferred more sober dress which, although it gave the impression of wealth, also added an air of gravity, circumspection and culture, which reflected its owner's dignity and commanded respect. Machiavelli wore such clothes in his study, out of respect for the spirits of Great Men: clothes such as these were worn among equals.

In Renaissance times the Florentines' style of dress was elegant, well-proportioned and practical, even if it did not match the austere lines of the fourteenth century, when the simplicity of women's clothes was proverbial and when men of all callings, craftsmen and merchants, lawyers and scholars, dressed with great modesty and dignity. Some of the rich young men did in fact imitate foreign fashions, but Florence never saw the slashed doublet and hose or the exaggerated plumes and trimmings which were all the rage in other countries.

The chroniclers and story-writers, as well as the sumptuary laws forbidding over-spending and the extravagant use of material, and the sermons preached against affected and immodest dress, all reveal that by the end of the fourteenth century a certain costly elegance had entered the lives of citizens and their style of clothes.

The typical Florentine garment continued to be, for men, the *lucco*, or long cloak of red, black or peacock blue which reached down to the feet, with no belt, with long wide sleeves and buttoned down the front with a hood attached. At the beginning of the fifteenth century this was worn by old men, doctors, lawyers, great merchants and bankers. The young men preferred a kind of long jacket called the *guarnacca*, belted at the waist, which came down over the hips; over their legs they wore long tight-fitting trunk-hose, called *calze-brache*, which reached up to the waist, and could be of wool, silk or velvet, sometimes with legs of different colours. The wealthy were distinguished by the richness of their cloth and embroidery, and by the various types of jacket-sleeve, which were sometimes so wide that they looked like short cloaks. In winter the sleeves were lined with fur, as also was the *lucco*.

Towards the middle of the fifteenth century the *guarnacca* became close-fitting down to the waist, and below this it spread out in great folds over the tight-fitting breeches. In this form it became known as the *giornea* and was always an item of clothing of great elegance; it could be worn under a wide cloak of brilliantly-coloured silk-lined wool or velvet.

The ordinary man wore jacket and trunk-hose, or trunk-hose and narrow-sleeved doublet, drawn in at the front and widened at the collar to show off the linen shirt. In summer he would wear a sleeveless doublet; in winter a coat padded with hemp. The tradesman often wore a leather coat with heavy metal buttons; his breeches were less tight-fitting and might even have an ample waist for ease of movement, in which case they were called *panni da gamba* and were usually made of heavy wool, grey or deep brown for the old men, green, red or yellow for the young ones. They were worn even under the working tunic or the leather apron. The doublet and coat were attached to the breeches with hooks and cord; the *guarnacca*, however, which came down to the knees, was held round the waist by a thick leather belt.

The servants, like their masters, wore trunk-hose, and every page, valet, footman and groom sported a pair of these tight-fitting breeches under his jacket, or short *giornea* of smooth silk or plain velvet, which could become his livery if it bore the emblem or the arms of his master's family.

In winter the old men wore a cloak or *guarniccione* over the *guarnacca*, and the young men a short woollen cloak with a small turned-up collar. The peasants wore long sheepskin or wolfskin jackets and a large hood of coarsely woven wool, or a short cloak, called a *salta-mindosso*, more suitable for riding. When he travelled, the merchant took a wide woollen cloak as well as his *lucco*, and this was fastened round the waist with a high leather belt to which his purse was attached by a slip-knot.

In the familiar language of the *novelle*-writers a doublet is a *giubbarello* rather than a *farsetto*, and a *giornea*, or short jacket, is a *gonnella* or *gonnellino*; the heavy *guarnaccione*, of coarsely woven wool, pressed like felt, which, together with other items of clothing, was distributed once a year to the poor by the various religious fraternities or the tradesmen's guilds, was called a *coprimiseria* or *pinzocco* (hence, it would seem, *pinzocchero*, or bigot).

HEADWEAR, BEARDS AND HAIR

After the fourteenth-century hood with its long strips of twisted cloth, called *budelli* (« guts ») reaching

Florentine dress in the fifteenth century (from a fresco, school of Ghirlandaio). The girl is wearing a short smock over a gamurrina *of contrasting colour, and her hair is wound up in special plaits called* intrecciatoi. *The men on the right are wearing the traditional* lucco, *which was generally red or black.*

73

down to the ground, after the shorter red or black woollen hood which went with the *lucco* and was worn over a close-fitting white cap pulled down over the ears, called a *camauro*, the typical man's headwear in fifteenth-century Florence was a felt cap with a tall crown or a woollen *mazzocchio*.

The *mazzocchio* was a large cap of cloth wound round in the shape of a ring or, when tightly made, like a cabbage. It had a strip of cloth attached, called a *foggia*. This hung, not down the back like the fourteenth-century *budello* from the hood, but was folded flat and rested on the opposite shoulder, where it hung over the back.

The simple low-crowned cap was worn not only by the ordinary man but by the well-to-do youth when he put on the short *giubbetto*, rather than the longer *guarnacca* or *giornea*, for travelling, riding or playing tennis or football in the square. In addition to the classical tall-crowned cap already mentioned, there was a flatter type which turned up at the back only and pulled down over the ears. At the end of the fifteenth century the sugar-loaf cap came back again; this had a brim which turned up at the back but was long and pointed in front, not, however, exaggerated in shape as it had been previously when worn by page, minstrel, craftsman, student or fashionable young man.

The craftsmen's caps varied in colour according to the trade they practised and whether they were apprentices or members of the guilds of the Municipality of Florence.

In the fifteenth century the ordinary man's cap was universally red, except for the old men, for whom it was black or dark brown and trimmed with fur in winter. The long pointed brim was soon abandoned. Then the cap took on the shape of a hat and was called, in fact, a *cappello*.

Young Florentines of all classes preferred to wear their hair long at the sides, short over the forehead and with a centre parting, from which it was combed down smoothly. It was a sign of elegance to have the hair lightly curled with hot irons at the nape of the neck.

In the second half of the fifteenth century it was common for men to have their hair curled with irons and often dyed blonde or golden, like the women. At the beginning of the century the fashion had been for closely-cropped hair at the front and sides. This fashion seemed to have been set by the painter Pisanello and came to be called the « long mane » or « pudding-basin » cut, as it did in fact look as though the front and sides of the hair had been shaved round a basin placed on top of the head. The rest of the hair was thickened with tight little curls which the Florentines called *alla caprara* (goat-girl) or *alla montona* (shepherdess). Men's hair was curled also in the late fifteenth century, when it was grown so long that it fell on to the shoulders and showed under the velvet caps which were then coming into fashion, adorned with plumes, metal discs and ornaments set with precious stones. Among the many hair-styles of this later period were the so-called *all'angiolesca*, in which the hair tapered down gradually from the forehead to the ears, and the *alla bellina* or « convolvulus » style in which the hair fell in long curls like vine-tendrils from the forehead to the nape of the neck. Tradesmen, craftsmen and clerks, however, wore their hair of normal length, washing it with soap and combing it smooth. Baldness was a mark of distinction in Florence, whereas in Paris and London at this time it was often disguised by wigs. Beards were uncommon, except among priests, pilgrims and the older common men.

THE ELEGANCE OF FLORENTINE WOMEN

It is a mistake to take only the Tornabuoni figures in Ghirlandaio's frescoes in Santa Maria Novella as typical of fifteenth-century feminine elegance. Their dress was, in fact, fashionable in the 1480's, but there was a considerable variety of elegant clothing from the early years of the century to the later years of Medici rule. These fashions, called *portature*, showed great inventiveness in line, embroidery and ornament.

The typical dress was in one piece from shoulder to hem and touched the ground, the more sumptuous ones having a train. It had a close-fitting waist, and full-gathered skirt, and was often embroidered round the hem with cloth of a different colour. At the beginning of the fifteenth century the long dress often had an overdress with open sleeves, like the men's wide-sleeved *giornea*. The open sleeve revealed the close-fitting sleeve of the dress proper, which came right down to the wrist and was of a different colour. The waist was held in by a high belt. The open sleeves of the overdress often became so wide as to form almost

Masculine headwear in fifteenth-century Florence (from paintings by Gozzoli and Botticelli). Top right: *the mazzocchio of cloth with hanging folds, the longest of which rested on the opposite shoulder. Below: three styles of cap in red cloth or velvet.*

a cloak from shoulder to hem, free at the back, but with a high, gathered-in waist. The belt around the dress was embroidered and trimmed with gold and silver buttons, pearls and precious stones. The necklines varied; sometimes they were low enough to provoke harsh rebukes from the moralists, sometimes high enough to form a wimple-like collar under the chin, such as that on the splendid mourning dress of Ilaria del Carretto.

One elegant type of overdress found in the paintings of Pisanello and Piero della Francesca had no sleeves, but fell from the neckline to the ground in close pleats and fanned out over the dress, which was of different colour and material. The dress, however, was held in at the waist with the jewelled belt, and from this hung the purse, called a *scarsella* or *elemosiniera*. The hair-styles worn with these dresses had long plaits wound round the head. Later the hair was cut and curled and worn with a coif, or embroidered head-band, which allowed a tuft of hair to fall over the neck like the modern pony-tail. Later still came the fashion of the *balzo* or *capigliara*, high round headwear supported on a frame of wood, rush or very light metal bent into an arc-shape to support folds of silk covered with pearls and embroidery, precious stones, bunches of little feathers or peacock-plumes. This high head-dress was worn over hair close-cut and shaven almost half-way up the head to emphasise the height and fullness of the forehead, a style called *scorticatoio* which persisted even when the back hair was grown in long

Feminine fashions in Renaissance Florence (from frescoes by Ghirlandaio). The styles were very numerous and the materials excellent in quality, design and colour. Popular styles were those of Giovanna degli Albizzi (second from left) and Ludovica Tornabuoni (fifth from right). The camora, a dress with a long straight line, was becoming increasingly popular and occurs frequently in details of trousseaux for rich weddings. The head was covered often by a fine shawl of linen or light wool.

plaits. These were then held in place with ribbons or a head-band, and wound round the head to make a pointed chignon and ringlets falling down over the ears. These hairstyles verged on the extravagant when made to match the fantasy of the dresses, such as the *uccellatae*, with their vivid embroidery of peacocks, eagles, griffins, doves or hawks, or the *litteratae*, on which were embroidered in silk love-sayings, proverbs or messages in poetry, or the *araldiche*, embroidered with the family coats of arms.

All classes of women wore cloaks which covered the dress and under-dress down to the ground and had a hood. They were made of various kinds of material. The ordinary women wore an overdress, called the *gonna*, which was shorter than the dress itself, called the *gamurrina*, and as the two were of different colours the contrast in the flounce gave the effect of a deep embroidered hem. One feature of the ordinary woman's dress, which also proved popular in other parts of Italy and among the upper classes, was that of the detached sleeve. This allowed a choice of sleeve which could be attached to the dress at the shoulder, leaving a gap through which protruded the embroidery or lace of the chemise. Thus the same dress might have different sleeves for working, for festival occasions, for winter and for summer.

Ladies might wear dresses with horizontal stripes like the hoops of a barrel, called *addogate* in Florence, but only the working-class woman ever wore dresses of one colour, wool or silk with a white chemise and

a dark blue overdress, a few inches shorter. If she was poor and could not afford a *gamurrina* to show up the *gonna*, she might sew a strip of differently coloured cloth on the shorter overdress: this was called a *balzana*. A working overdress for spinners in the cloth factories, servant-girls and washer-women was the *guarnello*; this was made of coarse cloth and might be worn tucked up on one side, as aprons sometimes were, with one corner fastened to the belt. The dress was laced up the front and tucked in at the waist, but sewn into a close-fitting bodice in the upper part, which was again laced up and often had a deep neckline both in front and behind. From the end of the fifteenth century to the middle of the sixteenth, all necklines were generally square and deep and showed off the embroidery and lace of the chemise, whilst the open parts of the sleeves, bodices and dress-tops were puffed out with the linen or white Rhemish cloth of the undergarments.

Instead of the high head-dress of the ladies with its head-bands, plaits and gold and silver embroidery, the ordinary women wore muslin veils or linen head-scarves. The old women wore large shawls over their heads; these were ample enough to cover their shoulders and to be wound round the neck like a nun's wimple.

The ordinary people wore ciantelle *(left), heavy leather shoes with a reinforced sole. Above: typical working-apron with large pockets (from a fresco, school of Ghirlandaio).*

FOOTWEAR

The ladies of Florence wore shoes of the finest leather, silk or velvet, embroidered with pearls, coloured glass and silver and gold thread. White and red leather were the most popular. The ordinary women wore the same type of close-fitting shoe without a heel, slightly cut away at the ankle, of lightly-dressed calfskin and with an upper in one piece. Indoors in the country the women wore slippers called *ciantelle*, and still so called today, and out in the fields wooden clogs. The men wore short boots of coloured leather, close-fitting to the calves; in the house and in town they wore shoes with red tan uppers and soles of heavy leather or wood. The elegant young men wore well-styled boots called *borzacchini*, close-fitting almost up to the knees where they were turned down to show a border of silk or velvet over the fine coloured leather. When at home, at festivals, or in the country they wore shoes of a style similar to women's drawn in at the sides with two laces in eyelets. Military men on war service or on campaigns wore armour to protect their thighs (cuisses) and legs (jambs). Merchants and bankers when travelling wore shoes fastened with leather straps over thick wool socks in summer, and in winter heavy plain half-boots up to the calves fastened with laces and hooks at the side. The ordinary men wore sabots, but the young craftsmen, the pages and grooms wore shoes and *borzacchini*.

ELEGANCE AT THE COURT OF LORENZO

Luxury and elegance were the only way of life for Lorenzo the Magnificent, and this is nowhere more clearly shown than in the procession of the Magi in Gozzoli's fresco, where he appears in « dazzling splendour ». The sumptuous cloak he is wearing is notable not only for the artistry of its weave and the brilliance of its jewelled ornament, but also for the elegance of its cut. It is of the kind known as a *guarnacca ad alie*, or « winged cloak », from the ample upper sleeves which looked like a pair of wings rising from the brocade doublet with its close-fitting sleeves of similar rich and ornamented cloth. This garment was edged with rare and exotic fur, and had precious gems worked into the cloth. The belt is set with precious stones and the neckline with pearls and diamonds to match the

At home young women wore simple dresses. Note the detached sleeve, a popular style in Renaissance Florence (a portrait by Botticelli).

buttons. He wears a hat similar to those worn by elegant ladies, round, high, of velvet embroidered with pearls and precious stones, but with thin pointed strips of gold, where the ladies' hats would have feathers and peacock plumes.

Lorenzo de' Medici's great personality set the style for the second half of the fifteenth century, through the luxury in dress introduced into his court. The prosperity of the city, the great wealth of the Medici family, together with the excellence of the craftsmen's work and organisation, all served to foster and to develop in Lorenzo a profound aesthetic sense and a love of beautiful things. His poems sang of the simplicity of Nencia, but he loved the refined elegance of Lucrezia Donati; he respected the reserved and dignified manner of life of Clarice Orsini whom, he said, « I took to wife, or rather she was given to me as wife », but he brought into the drawing-rooms of his palace in Via Larga or his villas the brilliant Simonetta Cattaneo, gay, witty and elegant, and her cousin Ginevra, the daughter of Piero Vespucci, called « Ginevra of the noble bearing », as well as the daughters of the Peruzzi, the Pucci and the Strozzi.

Vasari's portrait shows Lorenzo in old age; he is wrapped in a long cloak lined with fox-fur, a rather simple garment for someone who, like Lorenzo, was always a lover of elegance and luxury. His style of dressing now is but one of the requisites of a way of life of which he has always been a master, but it is not the least important. His is now a life of measured dignity.

The fine ladies who adorned his court after 1480 continued, however, to wear sumptuous dresses, new in style and design, such as those of Giovanna degli Albizzi and Ludovica Tornabuoni, whom Ghirlandaio painted in Santa Maria Novella between 1485 and 1490. These paintings reproduce, with the accuracy of a fashion-plate, the cut, the design of the cloth and the colour and embroidery of the different brocades which make up the clothes of the two ladies of quality.

In the last decades of the fifteenth century, therefore, women still wore two dresses, one on top of the other. The outer one differed only because it was generally of uniform colour, and simply cut with a shaped bodice and a skirt ruffed out from the waist. It was ample, of rich cloth, velvet, brocade or satin, embroidered with coats of arms, birds and flowers, and simply sewn to the bodice, from which, because it was cut in a circle, it fell in deep folds, as we see in the dress worn by Ludovica Tornabuoni. Giovanna's dress, however, is the new style which will continue to be the height of fashion in the sixteenth century,

Lorenzo's gown, of exquisite workmanship, is inlaid, like his hat, with precious stones and pearls (from « The Procession of the Magi » by Benozzo Gozzoli). He is followed by a procession of people whose elegance seems inspired by his: doublets and cloaks are of the finest satin and brocades, splendid in both design and colour.

called the *camora*. This is open at the front and shows the under-dress, has puffed-out sleeves, straight lines without a bodice, and is cut to fall in widening folds from shoulder to hem; the sleeve, narrowing down to the wrist, was said to be *scalata* or *scesa*, terms still used by Florentine dressmakers today.

These were the clothes of such « dazzling magnificence », which Lorenzo the Magnificent ordered for his daughters' trousseaux. So well were his daughters fitted out that part of Lucrezia's trousseau, for example, was handed down to her daughter Maria when she married the famous *condottiere*, « John of the Black Bands »: chemises of Rheims linen and Lucca silk, hair-bands of brocade and pearls, muslin handkerchiefs and fine gauzes of gold and silver thread, which Lucrezia had never used.

Equally resplendent was the dowry of Medici clothing and jewellery given to the children of Maria Soderini: Lorenzino de' Medici and his sisters Laudomia and Maddalena. Laudomia's elegance was captured in Bronzino's portrait of her wearing black velvet and pearls.

Yet in times of danger, Florentine women could forego these fine materials and sumptuous dresses. This was shown during the siege of 1527, when they proved themselves to be true proud Republicans, scornful of luxury and, like the matrons of Rome before them, gave their rich clothes and jewellery to buy arms for the conquest and defence of liberty, with better grace, be it added, than when urged by the querulous sermons of Savonarola and the public burnings of the tokens of vanity in 1497. This date should, in fact, have seen the end of Florentine high fashion; it did

Textiles are masterpieces of design, workmanship and colour. The designers of brocades, velvets and damasks were often artists of repute and the motifs could be inspired by famous paintings. Flowers and shrubs were very popular, bright and delicate as in the dress of « Spring » by Botticelli.

Sixteenth-century Florentine dress in a well-known picture by Bronzino. Note the joining of the sleeves.

in commissions to tailors, furriers, goldsmiths and jewellers. The pomp and luxury of the Medici court reached its height on the occasion of Lorenzo's marriage to Madeleine de la Tour d'Auvergne. This was celebrated by Pope Leo X, the Magnifico's favourite son Giovanni, who had also married his brother Giuliano to Filiberta of Savoy.

It was the year 1518. Madeleine arrived in Florence wearing a heavy embroidered dress of Lyons silk and Paris brocade, with sleeves puffed out with *bourrelets,* and her head hidden in a coif of starched Rheims linen. The ladies of Florence had waited to see how she would be dressed before displaying their own finery, and so, more perhaps at the festivities following the wedding than at the wedding itself, and particularly at the dances in the Medici gardens and at the performance of a play, they appeared in their most costly *camore* of gold, green and rose-coloured brocade or of coarse watered silk with fringes and slashings of black or dark-brown velvet, with an underdress of scarlet and crimson brocade, white satin or turquoise velvet, embroidered with birds of paradise. All these various rich materials were set off with jewels, pearls and ornamental necklaces.

This was the occasion for the first appearance of an over-dress known as the *sbernia,* a very long cloak-like garment, widening out from shoulder to hem, open in the front with a neckline or closed up to the throat with a little cord attached from one shoulder to the other. It could be with or without sleeves.

An exquisite sixteenth-century adornment to which Florentine women attached great importance was the fan. Many who practised the fine arts painted their own. The fan could be of silk or parchment, either on a wood frame or with little sticks of wood stuck on separately, or « the vaguest collection of colourless plumes and feathers ».

This period also sees a development in men's styles: the trunk-hose is widened and shows a contrast of colour and material against the silk or ermine lining of the cloak. Doublets are longer and, though widening out at the bottom, continue to follow the waist-line.

On the long, smooth, or curled hair were worn elegant soft velvet hats, known at first as Florentine, then as Raphael hats, adorned with a feather or a gold medal on the front. The sixteenth century was also the period in which Florence, together with Naples, produced the finest gloves.

not, however, and elegance returned in the sixteenth century with the restoration of the Medici, more sumptuous than ever.

ELEGANCE IN THE SIXTEENTH CENTURY

This return to the former splendour was due to the young followers of the Medici family who, at the restoration of the family under Alessandro in 1531, immediately took up again the sumptuous way of life associated with the older Lorenzo, now called *il Magnifico Lorenzo Vecchio de' Medici,* and united for this purpose in societies for good living, called *Compagnie del Broncone* and *Compagnie del Diamante.*

The young Lorenzo de' Medici, son of Piero, the Magnifico's eldest son, and Alfonsina Orsini, was equally prodigal in matters of display and dress and

FAMILY, WOMEN, SLAVES

The prototype of the Renaissance family was clearly cast in a wholly Tuscan mould. Inwardly it was the centre of affection, determination and hope, yet at the same time externally it identified itself with the city because the two were governed under similar principles. The family group was founded on tradition, on memories of the father and his forebears (for proof of one's lineage it was sufficient to give the name of one's father and grandfather), but it also had an extraordinary capacity for initiative. An awareness of the past and a faith in the future strengthened and extended the moral authority of the Renaissance family group, which never existed in isolation, but was always well in touch with its own members and with the everyday life of the district in which it lived, with the city itself, the state, and even with distant parts. Yet, fifteen centuries after the birth of Christ, the Renaissance family had slaves. They numbered among the master's possessions, like objects. They came along the trade routes from the Levant, like so much valued merchandise, from Russia, the Crimea, Mongolia and Africa. They were infidels, and for that reason slaves. Even baptism did not redeem them: it made them Christians, but not men and women, a dignity reserved only for those born free.

Generally speaking, the family in the fifteenth century had its roots more or less firmly planted in the city, and was tied to urban life out of necessity and the nature of its work, be it in trade or industry. But the « civic » conscience of the family was not always limited to life in the city and work in the organised labour-force of the guilds: it frequently extended to life in the country, the districts lying outside the town and to work on the land. The Tuscan family group in Renaissance times, and the Florentine in particular, often had this double basis, urban and rural, happily combining a two-fold source of contentment and well-being: work and business in the city, agricultural labour in the country. This was found in families of all classes, from the humblest to the most wealthy: as well as the work in the city there was usually a strip of land, an orchard or a field to cultivate, which would make a useful contribution to the table.

The daily round occupied most of the time and activity of the family. In spite of the great attention paid to public life and politics, the general feeling was that these would not feed hungry mouths, and this caused the family to depend on itself for its means and way of life, which was the first rule of independent existence. It determined the structure of family life, its hierarchy, its inner relationships, its rights and duties and prescribed what lay within its competence.

Here we see the nature and the limits of the authority of the head of the family, the husband and father, who was assumed to administer the patrimony, large or small, to determine how each member of the family should be most usefully employed, and to increase the amount of trade or business carried on, however small. The children were almost unconditionally in his power, particularly when it came to choosing the work they were to do and the part this would play in the general running of the family business. The wife was at the centre of all domestic affairs, ran the household, looked after the children in their early years and was responsible for all the servants, both male and female.

THE MOTHER

The wife and mother played no part in the trading or business activities of the household, which were the sole concern of the husband and father. She saw to it that family life ran smoothly within the home, guaranteed its continuity and sought to maintain that continuity of tradition and custom so characteristic of family life at this time. She was responsible for the cleanliness of the house, the safe custody and upkeep of all goods and chattels, the control of domestic expenditure, the supply of victuals to the kitchen, the care of all clothing and in many cases supervised the

making of garments from wool and linen cloth of her own choosing. This followed the most ancient of customs, exemplified in Dante's image of the housewife, surrounded by her maidservants, busy at the distaff and loom, in which the wife was the symbol of continuity and loyalty and the centre around which all family life revolved. Woe betide anyone who offended against or diminished, even indirectly, the dignity of the wife and mother in her position as keeper of the household, or who attempted to depreciate the moral or material value of the family's patrimony of furniture, materials and other household possessions.

A significant but almost forgotten incident occurred in the early years of the sixteenth century. Florence was faced with the threat of invasion by the King of France, and it was hoped to gain his sympathies by offering him some munificent gift, such as the Borgherini's marriage-bed, which had been painted by Pontormo. The reaction of Margherita, Pierfrancesco Borgherini's wife, to this suggestion was forthright and exemplary, and symbolised the sense of honour and devotion to the family of all Florentine women: « Wretched dealer in trash, dismantler of gentlemen's beds », she called Giovanbattista della Palla, who came to make this imprudent request, « a man fit only to furnish and decorate the houses of our enemies abroad ...; it is I who order that nothing shall be removed from this house; I, a woman, will defend to the last her bed, her house and her family ».

There was nothing new in this attitude. In the fifteenth century Florence had had, as worthy consorts to wise, prudent and strict heads of families, women capable of managing their household with equal firmness and dignity, of educating their children with a due sense of moral responsibility, of training the boys for work, at the bench or counter, and of finding a suitable match for their daughters, after showing them in their turn how to run a new house and a new family. For this there was little need for the women to be educated. In the late fourteenth century a famous preacher and counsellor to Florentine matrons, Paolo di ser Pace, had said and caused to be set down in writing: « If it is a girl child, set her to cooking, not to reading, for it is not meet for a girl to know how to read unless she be intended for a nunnery ». But he added: « Dress the girl well; do not let her grow too fat; teach her to perform all the duties of the household, to make bread, dress the capon, sift the flour, make the bed, spin, cut out linen and woollen garments, darn stockings and perform other similar duties, so that when you marry her it shall not be said that she comes from the woods ».

There existed also a series of « commandments » setting out « what the mother should say to her daughter when sending her away to a husband ». When we read these we find that they do not differ very greatly from the wise practical advice, including how to keep a husband's love and to stop the family from quarrelling, such as any mother might give her daughter today on the eve of her wedding.

Here are some of them: « Be not troubled if he is happy, and if he is preoccupied, do not insist on knowing the reason why. Do not seek to know his secrets and if he confides them to you, do not reveal them to any other person. Try to know his tastes in food, prepare it diligently and do not let it be known if you dislike some dish of which he is very fond. Do not watch over him whilst he sleeps; however, if this is really necessary, do so only with the greatest tact so that he is not angered. Do not concern yourself with his money, nor try to find out where he keeps it; if chance leads you to discover it, do not take any of it for yourself. Neither a borrower nor a lender be without your husband's permission, and remember that a generous man is well thought of, and so is the woman, if she looks after her husband's money. Do not do anything on your own, but first seek his advice, and if sometimes it turns out that he was wrong, learn never to say ' I told you so '. Never ask him for things which require great labour or sacrifice, or which go against his convictions. Be always well-groomed and elegant, but never to excess, and take care not to dress too ostentatiously, lest this raise suspicions which might disturb his peace of mind. Do not be too often out of the house and do not talk too much. To talk little is a mark of honesty, and makes even the stupid woman look intelligent. Be more considerate to his family than to your own ». The advice given by Alessandra Macinghi Strozzi in a letter to her daughter finishes with an appealing image: « Do as I say and you shall be as a crown of gold to your husband ».

It was considered natural that the mother should act so firmly and authoritatively, and sometimes with such apparent harshness, towards her daughters. This tradition continued through the fifteenth century in Florence. It was less common, though the examples were very striking, for a mother to be equally firm with her sons. The same Alessandra Macinghi Strozzi wrote some famous letters to her son Filippo in Naples. She sent him a younger son to look after, a mere boy, not so much to learn his trade as to remove him from a political atmosphere which was generally hostile to the family. Not only did she fear a more open hostility from the Medici towards her sons, but she was very unwilling to see hatred bred in them at such an early age. Alessandra had married Matteo Strozzi, who had been one of those responsible for the banishment of Cosimo de' Medici, and who was in his turn exiled when Cosimo returned. She had thus been left alone, and later a widow, to run the house and the business and bring up five children, the youngest of whom was born after their father had been sent into exile. She succeeded in marrying her daughters well and provided them all with a dowry; she found Filippo a wife, and the right one, after he had been living in Naples with the « slave » Marina, who, however, turned out to be such a fine girl and had such a good influence on Filippo that his mother, after some time writing and speaking about her, came to call her « Monna Marina ».

But the title, « madonna », was reserved only for ladies who were well-to-do and free. This made Alessandra all the more anxious to see Filippo suitably married, yet she did not succeed in getting him Tanagli's daughter, whom she liked. Although she knew that Tanagli's financial situation was not as good as that of another family with an eligible daughter, the Bardi, she nevertheless excluded the latter because her family were mere « clumsy country gentry ». She would have liked him to marry one of the Adimari's daughters, but the ladies of this family were too refined, too concerned with fine silks and velvets and one of them even used cosmetics on her face! One who did not use cosmetics and who had few pairs of shoes, and those mostly simple slippers, was Costanza di Pandolfo, but she was too timid. When she realised that Monna Alessandra was looking at her in church, she averted her eyes and, when they left the Santa Reparata, she disappeared « like the wind ». Such a timid woman would be too feeble a wife for her Filippo. But one of Adimari's daughters was very beautiful, proud and imposing of figure, as fresh as a girl of fourteen. The mother wrote to Filippo that the girl was « growing more beautiful », but she was afraid that the Adimaris, who were very rich, might be seeking an equally rich

A promise to marry was binding and the exchange of rings was an important ceremony requiring the presence of the lawyer for the establishment of the dowry and the exchange of gifts.

husband for their daughter. But Filippo would come into his wealth, the family fortunes would be his, and sure enough, some time after Fiammetta Adimari became his wife, Filippo Strozzi commissioned Michelozzo to build him a fine house as large as a royal palace. He became so wealthy and powerful that he was able to set himself up against Lorenzo and compete with him in every sphere, even in the luxury of his household and the elegance of his living. In this he was aided as much by the distinction and refinement of Fiammetta Adimari as by his own wealth, business acumen and good fortune.

Finding a good wife for their sons was a constant preoccupation for the mothers of Florence, not only from the point of view of the family and the peace and happiness of their children, but also because it was regarded as a civic duty so to organize a new family nucleus that the city would benefit from the stability and continuity of the home-life of its inhabitants. The women, no less than the men, allied themselves to this or that political faction, even though, traditionally reserved in public affairs, they did not often attend public meetings of men, nor did they go out in the streets and squares to argue over civic matters. They did, however, follow developments by listening to the men's conversations indoors, and often took a passionate interest, as the interests of the city and the political parties were their interests also. The

Medici women played a very active part in the policies of Cosimo and Lorenzo. The wife of Piero, Cosimo's son, Lucrezia Tornabuoni, who was superior in culture and intelligence to many women of the day, was at great pains to find a suitable wife for their son Lorenzo, who promised to be such a great power for good in the family and the city, and insisted that whoever he married should be capable of assisting him in his great calling. Whilst Alessandra Macinghi Strozzi had been concerned to find her son a wife from one of the families of Florence, because this would strengthen the alliances of the Strozzi family, Lucrezia realised that the Medici were now so powerful in the city that they could afford, indeed ought, to seek good connections elsewhere among the powerful Roman families which were behind the policies of the Papacy. She went therefore to Rome to find Lorenzo a wife, but the girl she found, Clarice Orsini, was not the kind of wife for Lorenzo that his mother had hoped she might be. She was beautiful, healthy, good and respectful, and an excellent mother to Lorenzo's children, but she fell short of the high standards required of a Renaissance matron in Florence, where it was expected that the woman of the house would have a certain *savoir vivre*, and play an influential part in a court where art and culture were just as important as politics and economics, and where it was essential to foster and extend relationships among the well-connected personages who passed through Lorenzo's many houses and villas. Lorenzo had much affection for her, and acknowledged her gifts as a good housewife and mother, but in the story of his life he could only dedicate a few words to her, and those were hardly flattering: « In the year 1469, I Lorenzo took to wife Clarice, the daughter of Signor Jacobo Orsini, or rather she was given to me as wife ».

The ideal woman, wrapped in an aura of poetry, was for Lorenzo a refined, genteel, cultured and intelligent person, a good talker and a better listener, elegant and fond of festivities, music and dancing. Lorenzo doubtless loved such women and was loved by them: by Lucrezia Donati and Bartolomea Benci, for example, and another, Simonetta Cattaneo Vespucci, was the object of his brother Giuliano's devotion. All these beautiful refined ladies had inspired poets, among them Lorenzo himself, and were passionate creatures of markedly strong personality, whereas Clarice by contrast seemed respectful, docile and passive. Her

very first letter to Lorenzo in January 1469 begs him, in an Italian both badly spelt and grammatically incorrect, « to remember me kindly to your father and mine, to your mother and mine, and to anyone else you please ».

FAMOUS WEDDINGS

The Medici wedding in 1469 had been a grandiose affair, however, and had caused quite a stir in Florence. It had been the finest since 1420, when Baccio Adimari married Lisa Ricasoli, and this was enshrined on that famous marriage-chest with its carved panel showing the procession to the Cathedral. According to eye witnesses' accounts, Lorenzo's wedding-suit, with its fine cloth and precious ornament, was much more splendid than the dress of his bride, who was, however,

wearing the Medici jewels, worthy to adorn a royal princess. The procession of friends and relatives of Lorenzo and Giuliano, with all the ladies of the Torna-buoni family in their finest clothes, was, according to an eye-witness, quite « resplendent » as the colours of the silks and velvets, the sheen of the gold and the brilliance of the jewels shone in the sunlight outside and amidst the flowers in the church and the ban-queting hall.

Another famous wedding, equalling that of the Medici, was that of Lorenzo Tornabuoni and Giovanna degli Albizzi in 1486. The ladies of the Albizzi family were noted for their elegance and gentility, and Gio-vanna was radiant. Like Ludovica, she too had the good fortune to be painted by Ghirlandaio. Young Lorenzo Tornabuoni also was cultured and elegant, a true man of the Renaissance and with a passionate interest in medals, old coins and ancient sculpture.

Lorenzo de' Medici, who had helped to bring about this Tornabuoni wedding, was one of the witnesses. He came magnificently dressed and brought splendid gifts. There were also a hundred fair young maidens in the wedding procession, all dressed in white and deep blue silk at the expense of the Tornabuoni, and fifteen youths, dressed uniformly with the colours of the Tornabuoni house, acted as pages. A Guicciardini and a Castellani were witnesses for the bride and the Spanish Ambassador to the Holy See was also present.

Another wedding which Lorenzo de' Medici wanted to have in great style was that of his young sister Nannina, his favourite, and Bernardo Rucellai, a humanist and a scholar, worthy in every way of his brother-in-law and his friends. The Rucellai were a wealthy family too, although they had made their money by trading, and, as Giovanna Rucellai wrote, they wished to show that « the spending of money is no less a virtue than the earning of it ».

AUTHORITY IN THE FAMILY

The general management of family life and the moral and material direction of the family group were a right and a duty of the man. The husband and father gave his name to the house, the property and all the possessions, and impressed the seal of his virtually unlimited authority on every aspect of the family's activity, whether in the city or in the country.

The father exercised his authority in two distinct but parallel directions: in one his influence was ethical and educational, in that he brought up his children like the father-educator dear to Leon Battista Alberti; in the other he administered the family's economic interests and made himself responsible for its material well-being.

This régime clearly tended to make the family unit autonomous. It was the father above all who provided for the upbringing of the young children up to adoles-cence. As soon as the child left infancy it came gradu-ally under the control of its father, not so much for direct instruction, since reading and arithmetic, though begun at home, could be continued at schools closely connected to the local parish church and convents, as for the long-term process of training for a skill and a job. This was where the father's initiative counted, because the children were gradually drawn into the

father's sphere of activity, or undertook an apprenticeship in a similar calling according to the economic demands of the time. Further study might lead to the professions of medicine or the law, but the practical skills acquired in his early training could fit the youth for any one of the many socially useful occupations: tradesman, money-changer, wool or silk manufacturer, and, in the case of those less well qualified, an infinite variety of humbler trades.

The concern shown by the heads of families in Florence for the education and training of their sons was a source of admiration to foreign visitors, who saw young men following their father's calling and promoting the interests of the family business, not by mere chance, but by careful preparation and apprenticeship, beginning with the very rudiments of the trade, so that the workshop became a school for life. A Venetian ambassador was so struck by this that he reported on it to his government as an example to be followed.

The strict home upbringing and workshop education did not prevent Florentine fathers from showing a tender concern for their young sons. In parent-son relationships there are two examples which show the typical closeness between the two generations. In 1489, when Filippo Strozzi laid the foundations of his great palazzo, a citizen, Tribaldo de' Rossi by name, went to watch the excavations with his children. He was holding on to the little boy by his collar, whilst the maid had the little girl by the hand. It was a wonderful thing to dig foundations so wide and so deep: who could tell what enormous palace might rise from them? And the father told his two little children (he himself relates it in his diary) to throw down into the foundation whatever they were holding in their hands for luck. Guarnieri, the little boy, threw a copper, with the Florentine lily on it, and the little girl a small bunch of Damask roses. « Will you remember? » he asked. « Yes », they said. There is a similar example in Lorenzo de' Medici's letter to his son Giovanni on the latter's nomination as cardinal. « Monsignor Giovanni, with all respect, you are under a great obligation to God and to all of us, and this is how you must regard your good fortune, so as to be worthy of the rank to which you have been elevated and the mission which you are to accomplish ». The son became an important figure at the Papal Court, and eventually was Pope himself, but the head of the family never felt that his duties and responsibilities as a father were in any way diminished.

In the administration of its patrimony the family aimed at the establishment of security of possessions and the well-being of its members. The head of the family strove always to consolidate and improve the position of the group by intensifying its activities in the city and extending the sphere of its labours in the country. The little community had to be established on a solid, secure basis: « in this world he who is poor suffers need and deprivation » was a maxim which justified the repudiation of poverty and the search for wealth. Avoid all waste, save, buy and sell at the right time: this implied a thorough knowledge and appraisal of conditions so as to find the most advantageous moment. Trading in silk and wool was a fine thing, but it was an even better thing to look after the family's country estates, living happily on the land which provided everything and where « all one had to buy was a little salt »; the estate gave food and drink, wood

for the fire and wool for clothing. To be self-sufficient was the ideal. This was both a principle and a warning: « he who finds no money in his own purse will find much less in other peoples' ». Free yourself, therefore, of the bonds of dependence, manage your family affairs to your advantage, so that all the time you act as a free man.

THE SLAVES: « THE DOMESTIC ENEMY »

A traveller to Tuscany in Renaissance times would be astonished at the appearance of the domestic servants of the Florentine *signori*. Small and thick-set, yellow-complexioned, black-haired, with high cheek-bones, almond-eyed, deeply pock-marked and scarred, some-

Domestic work was heavy, without respite, and done according to inflexible standards. Within the small society of the family, therefore, the possession of a slave was of considerable economic benefit. Perhaps the best method of assessing the value of a slave is to compare it with that of other goods and possessions. We know, for instance, that in 1394 Francesco Datini of Prato was prepared to pay up to 50 or 60 florins for a little slave-girl of eight to ten years of age and 30 for a horse, but he spent 60 on his daughter's white damask wedding gown. For Datini, therefore, a good slave was worth twice as much as a horse but rather less than his daughter's best dress.

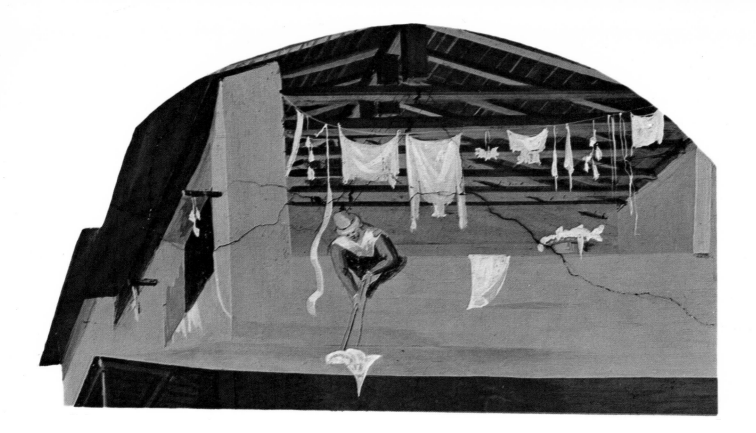

times tattooed, they clearly did not belong to Florentine stock. The lady of the house might sometimes be seen accompanied by a Negro or a fair-haired, white-skinned maid who looked equally foreign. In the Florentine palaces the nursemaids and playmates of the young masters and mistresses were often olive- or yellow-skinned young girls of eleven or twelve years of age, or even little Negroes.

All these servants were slaves, mostly of Tartar origin, but there were also Russians, Circassians, Greeks, Moors and Ethiopians. Many Florentine noblemen and merchants had at least two or three; even the wife of a notary or a modest tradesman might have one, and it was not unusual to find a slave in the households of priests and nuns.

How had these slaves come to Florence, and what part did they play in the domestic life of the time? The answer is to be found in the acts of sale and enfranchisement, in the ledgers of the foundling hospitals, in the unloading receipts of merchant vessels, in the acts and statutes, in account-books and sundry records. There emerges a whole underworld of strange creatures, alienated and uprooted from their distant homeland. *Domestici hostes*, Petrarch called them: domestic enemies.

For at least a century these slaves formed a considerable proportion of the population, enough, in fact, to affect the Tuscan stock. The Tuscans had already inherited characteristics from other peoples: Etruscan, Roman, Lombard and Frank. Here, however, was new blood, vigorous and vital, from the Orient and, later, from Africa.

Domestic slavery was not new, but the great social revolutions of the ninth and tenth centuries had severely restricted it. It had continued only in the feudal castle where there were a few servants or slaves (*servus* in Latin means both), considered part of the lord's possessions, like his furniture and domestic animals.

It comes as something of a surprise, therefore, to see that domestic slavery should be revived in Florence, at the height of Tuscan civilisation, by the importation of great numbers of slaves from the Levant. There are two main reasons for the phenomenon: an enormous increase in Italian trade in the East, and a great decrease in population at home due to the plague of 1348. The years which saw the rise of the great Florentine merchant families, with the increased demands for servants, also saw the decimation of the working population by the plague, brought, tragically enough, by one of the ships carrying silk and spices from the East, or so it was thought. More than half the population of Florence died and other smaller Tuscan cities suffered as greatly: like other epidemics, the plague struck the poor, the dirty and the hungry.

In the country, all who survived were required to till the soil; in the city every trade was short of labour, both skilled and unskilled. There was virtually no-one left for domestic work, and servants increasingly found pretexts for absence. Their mistresses complained, and a remedy was sought by the importation on a vast scale of slave-labour from the East. The Priors of Florence, recognising the urgency of the situation, gave their permission and, under a decree published on March 8th 1363, formally allowed the unlimited importation of foreign slaves of both sexes, provided they were not Christians.

This was the beginning, and with the continued prosperity of trade and commerce, the demand and supply of slave-labour increased. A bride would bring a slave as part of her dowry, and would expect to have more in her new home. Doctors freely accepted slaves in lieu of payment for their services. Priests bought them as personal servants, and even a modest trades-man's family might have two or three. The custom spread from Florence to other towns of Tuscany: to Prato, Pistoia, Lucca, Siena and San Gimignano. The slaves, little yellow-skinned Tartars, great fair-haired

Circassians, Armenians, Bulgarians, Alans, became some of the most profitable merchandise on the Eastern market.

Some of them had been snatched from their homes by Tartar horsemen whilst still babies, others had been sold by their parents. Some, chained together in pairs, had been brought over the mountain passes by merchants of Daghistan or stolen from the Crimean beaches by Genoese sailors and sent to the great slave-market in Alexandria, through which no fewer than two thousand passed every year, or to the ports of Venice and Genoa, where whole shiploads of men, women and children, bewildered and half naked, were discharged and sold to the first comer. The Venetian government collected a tax of five ducats for each slave sold, and over ten thousand were accounted for between 1414 and 1423.

Some wealthy Tuscans had their own agent in the ports to buy this kind of merchandise along with the rest, and, like other goods, the slaves were sometimes

insured. Amongst the papers of a certain citizen of Prato called Datini we find an insurance policy taken out on May 9th 1401 for a Tartar slave-girl named Margaret, whom he was sending from Porto Pisano to a Catalan purchaser in Barcelona. The amount was fifty gold florins.

Let us try to follow the journey of one of these young Tartar girls, aged eleven or twelve, who were so much in demand. Loaded on to a galley bound for Genoa, Venice or Pisa, she would spend the first part of the journey in chains in the hold, suffering horribly from the cuts made on her face and hands so that she would be recognised as a slave if she tried to escape. As soon as she reached her destination, she would be sold to an agent and taken to Florence, where she would be entered on the city registers and sold to a client.

The act of sale for any similar little slave-girl was generally drawn up by a notary, and gave a number of particulars: origin, price, height, features, type of work for which she was suitable (domestic or agricultural), and certified that she was « free of all illness, whether visible or invisible », and sometimes that she was not a thief, lazy, quarrelsome or liable to escape. Any such defects, which would lessen the value of a slave, were to be declared by the seller.

The purchaser's rights were as absolute as human ingenuity could make them: the slave was sold to his master, « free of mortgage, pledge, loan or obligation to a third party, with power to dispose of him as he wished, or to have and to hold him in full legal right ». He could hire him out for profit, give him away or barter him for another slave or for any other thing.

Immediately upon his arrival in Florence, the slave was baptised. His master took him to the San Giovanni Baptistery where the priest blessed him and baptised him (the term was *insantare* and the godmother was called a *santula*) substituting for his exotic name one which sounded more Christian.

In 1421 a great hospital was built, called Santa Maria degli Innocenti « for children whom mother and father against the laws of nature have abandoned, that is children known popularly as i gettatelli *(foundlings) ». Some-times the children of slaves were taken there openly by their master or mistress, but most babies were left secretly at night-time on the stone font, which still exists under a little square window of Brunelleschi's great loggia. The mother laid the child, wrapped in meagre rags, on the font, rang the bell and ran away. The little window opened and another baby was added to the number of what the hospital register called « The Innocents of Jesus Christ ».*

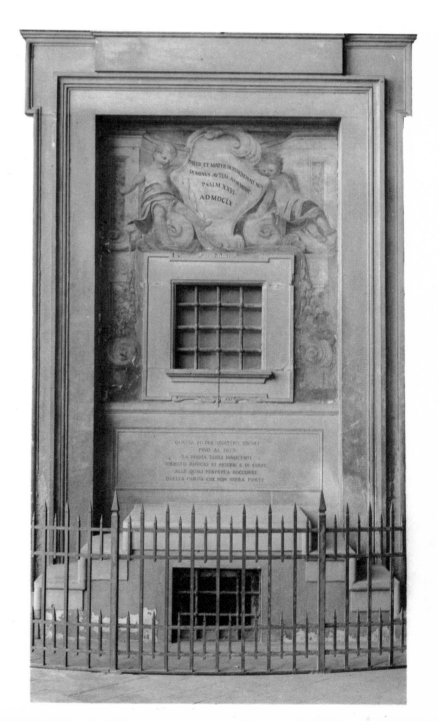

Most slaves had scars of identification or were tattooed « with a cross on the right forefinger » or « marked on the right hand ». Two female slaves (P. Lorenzetti).

But now there arose a complicated moral question. As we have seen, the Priors of Florence had decided to allow the importation and sale of slaves in 1363 *purché fossero infedeli*, because they were heathen. Slavery, they argued, was the just reward of the infidel. In 1367 the Priors added to their original decree that « heathen » meant « of heathen *origin* », to get round the question of whether it was permitted to keep the slaves once they had become Christian. Archbishop Antonino said it was. A good Christian must only *buy* heathen slaves, but he might *keep* them after baptism, because baptism in itself could not emancipate a man from slavery, as it was not asked for with the free will. « For most of them », said Sacchetti, the poet and short-story writer (c. 1330-1400), « it is like baptising oxen ».

It is interesting to examine the registers of the sale of 357 slaves in Florence between 1366 and 1397. The first thing we notice is their diversity of origin. 287 were Tartars, and the rest Greeks, Russians, Circassians, Slavs or « Saracens ». 329 were women, mostly just out of puberty, an age which guaranteed robustness.

In the first half of the fifteenth century there was a great demand for girls with a certain grace and refinement, Russians and Circassians, rather than Tartars. Alessandra Macinghi Strozzi, however, advises her son Filippo to choose a Tartar girl, « for they are peasants and can endure fatigue », but admitted that « the Russians are quicker to understand and more comely ».

What happened to the slaves after their arrival in the civilised and well-ordered Tuscan homes? Basically they were treated more or less like everyone else in the family and it would be mistaken to distress one's self over much at their plight. It is true that a slave came under the *potestas puniendi*, the master's power to punish, and could be beaten, whipped or thrown into jail: so, however, could his wife and children.

Yet the records of the law-courts give such a picture of gloom and violence that it is easy to see how slavery could only be controlled by the severest legislation. There must have been many cases of sullen, uncouth slaves on the one hand, and frightened, suspicious masters on the other. The fear could be justified: in these times, when poisoning was rife, who was in a better position than a slave to administer the lethal dose?

At least one slave in five was pock-marked. Their skin has been described as « white, black, olive, reddish or greenish in colour ». The « domestic enemies » were also distinguished by their strange language: a half-incomprehensible dialect of their own, a kind of bastard Tuscan with many deformed consonants, most of the verbs in the infinitive, and interspersed with some Tartar or Saracen words. Two slaves, evidently painted from life, by Benozzo Gozzoli and Pietro Lorenzetti.

Many private letters complete the picture: slaves quarrelling with freed slaves and amongst themselves, or stealing anything that came to hand. It is clear that some masters were very frightened if Alessandra Macinghi Strozzi, for example, could write to her son Filippo in Milan that she could no longer control her slave-girl Cateruccia unless he came home and gave her a beating.

THE CHILDREN OF SLAVES

It happened sometimes that a slave-girl became a mother: in that case her price fluctuated. Up to the birth of her child it decreased, and her master, if he was not the child's father, suffered a loss. Under a decree of 1366 the Priors of Florence laid down that a man who caused another's slave-girl to have a child should pay her master 30 florins and the entire expense of the birth, in accordance with the custom of the family: if the girl died as a result, her master was to be reimbursed with her full value. We may judge how generously this decree was interpreted by Jacopo's

Memoirs of Giovanni Ottavanti, a Florentine who, in 1459, for the birth of a child to Giovanni Rucellai's slave girl Caterina (his brother Paolo being the father), paid 75 florins and bought a cradle and clothing for the baby and food for the mother for a fortnight, including several pairs of capons, four fresh eggs daily, biscuits and jam.

The children whose parents were both slaves were not considered, under the Justinian code, to belong to their parents, as marriage between slaves was not recognised. « It is wrong to use the words ' father ', ' son ' or ' brother ' when speaking of slaves, as no relationship exists between them in the eyes of the law ». These children belonged only to their masters, who often disposed of them at the orphanage, the Ospedale di Santa Maria degli Innocenti, whose registers contain a wealth of interesting information. Between 1394 and 1487 the average proportion of the children in the orphanage whose parents were slaves was 12 %, but for the period 1446 to 1457 it was 30%. It is likely that the true proportion was considerably higher.

What became of these foundlings when the orphanage door shut behind them? Most of the boys of twelve to eighteen were put out to work in factories or in the arsenal at Leghorn for no pay, whilst the girls, or at least the more fortunate among them, were adopted by private individuals. All were considered free and legitimate, enjoying full rights of citizenship, so that within one generation almost all the children of slaves were absorbed into the rest of the population. Their blood, Tartar or African, Circassian or Russian, mingled with the Tuscan stock, just as that of the Etruscan, the Latin and the Lombard and the Goth had done. Their descendants are still to be found in the cities and fields of Tuscany.

The Statutes of each city took for granted the principle in the Justinian code by which any slave who escaped was a thief, because he robbed his master of his person. If a slave did run away, a proclamation was read in the principal squares of the city, giving his name and description; it was the duty of every citizen to hunt him down, capture him and restore him to his master. Every coloured person and every foreigner then became suspect, as also did anyone with a scar or a stigma, or anyone with a foot or hand missing.

EMANCIPATION

Under a decree of 1452, anyone who stole a slave and hid him for more than three days was liable to be sent to the gallows, and when the slave was eventually recaptured, the justices of Florence took proceedings against him, tortured him, then sent him to prison.

It was almost entirely impossible for a slave to escape. His only hope lay in eventual emancipation, and this was often granted, especially when the master on his death-bed asked for a remission of his sins. Sometimes the slave was also given a gift and allowed to keep whatever bits of money and clothing he had accumulated during his years of service. In Lorenzo and Filippo Strozzi's diary, under Easter 1523, we find that they freed their father's old slave, « a Moor from Portugal », adding that it was their mother's wish that she should receive every year « provided that she leads an honest life and conducts herself worthily » twelve bushels of flour, six barrels of wine, half a barrel of oil and a quantity of firewood.

The emancipation ceremony, which had been a complicated ritual in the Middle Ages, had become a simpler affair in the fifteenth century. The usual proce-dure was for the master to take his slave before a notary, who set it all down in writing. A complete description of the ceremony is to be found in the act of emancipation of the slave Maddalena da Caffa, on September 3rd 1441 in Siena. Master and slave went before a notary and here Maddalena, whose freedom had been granted because she had served « with solicitude and according to the law », knelt down before her master, placed her hands between his, in the feudal act of homage, and begged him « with the greatest veneration and humility » to free her « according to the Roman custom ». The master opened her hands and said « be free and a citizen of Rome, liberated from all servitude to me ».

Not all slaves obtained their freedom at once, in spite of an act of emancipation. A very common form of ceremony was the *Manumissio sub conditione*, by which the master specified that the slave would be freed only after further service without pay to himself or his heirs for a number of years, a formula which allowed unscrupulous heirs to exploit the slave without mercy. But these slaves were perhaps not the most unfortunate, for when eventually a slave gained his freedom, what kind of life awaited him? The *peculium* referred to so solemnly in the act of emancipation was often a few coppers and the clothes he stood up in. He was un-trained for any job, and in some towns it was even forbidden to employ freed slaves in many of the guilds. What could he do? Often he went to join the bands of rogues and vagabonds who roamed the roads of Tuscany.

DAILY LIFE IN THE FAMILY

Daily life for the Florentine family in Renaissance times was striking in its simplicity. Everyone rose early, as work at the bench, on the estate or in the market began early, though later in winter than in summer. The whole family group first gathered for a frugal meal. The men then left for work and the women would go to the mother, who allotted household tasks for the day. In addition to tidying up the house, there were clothes to wash, repair and put away in the ward-robes, and there was spinning and sometimes weaving to be done. In some households the women's labour was a little industry on its own, but solely for the benefit of the family. The preparation of food was important

It was considered a civic duty to provide clothing for the needy, for those, that is, who would be ashamed to appear in dirty rags. Many guilds and fraternities made it a statutory duty for their members to provide linen and clothing for the poor once a year: the fraternity of the Buonomini di San Martino, under a legacy of Benedetto Giorgini, had to provide habits and cloaks for decayed gentlefolk and a dowry for impoverished girls about to marry. Detail from a fresco in the San Martino ai Buonomini Oratory.

and demanded its time. There was a meal at about mid-day, even though some might not be able to partake as they worked too far away from home. Many workshops were part of the house, or adjacent to it, but many others, for reasons of trade, were some distance away, at crossroads (called *trebbi*) and along the main streets, where the greater affluence of people and a heavier traffic gave greater opportunities for business. Sometimes certain members of the family, even including the head, would be away on business. This was particularly the case with the merchant families, large, medium or small, who were scarcely ever all at home together at the same time: their absences could last whole seasons or even years. But these families were enlivened by the visits of other travelling merchants and business acquaintances, whose company enlarged their horizons and brought them wider interests, not only material but spiritual and moral as well.

Supper was taken late in the evening, and was more frugal than the mid-day meal. Then the family retired to bed. There was virtually no going out in the evening, either in the fifteenth or sixteenth centuries. There were very few amusements or entertainments in the course of the day, except for the tavern, where the principal attractions were the wine and games of chance, such as dicing. These were frowned upon as a temptation by the moralists of the time, particularly by Sant' Antonino, the mid-fifteenth century bishop and acute observer of Florentine life.

CONCESSIONS TO VANITY

There were, however, festivals and banquets, at which those who had the means could vie with their neighbours in expensive finery. This was particularly the case with the women, who knew endless recipes for preparing scents and toilet-powders, for washing and dyeing the hair and encouraging its growth, for putting on weight or taking it off, for « driving away the vapours », for disguising bad breath, for keeping the hands soft, removing warts, keeping one's hair, eyes and teeth beautiful and for « keeping a healthy colour in one's cheeks ».

Cosmetics, never completely neglected in Italy, became widely used from the fourteenth century onwards, and by the sixteenth they were being used to excess. Books of prescriptions were written in profusion. A simple prescription for freckles had been handed down from a fragment of Ovid: it contained one or two ingredients mixed with honey or gum. This was now not enough; a great variety of substances was added: white lead, nitre, ceruse, verdigris, sublimate, ammonium salts, cinnamon, nutmeg, and even some precious stones, all to make the skin smooth and beautiful. In Venice it was an ancient custom for women to dye their hair a most attractive golden colour, and to make their hands artificially white and delicate; in the times of Vecellio they smeared smoothing cream on their faces, necks and breasts. These, and other delicate customs from the East, spread to Florence and other Italian towns. There were prescriptions for making one attractive to the opposite sex, many of which have been preserved in manuscripts in Italian libraries; prescriptions for dyeing the hair, for « making the eyes bright », for making « medicinal water for the skin », scented soap, pomades and perfumes largely based on spikenard, sandal, orris root, aloe and roses. With his instructions for making up a preparation for the face, in which there were twenty-three ingredients, including « fresh bread and a good malmsey », alum, a white hen, lemons and twenty-five eggs, the gallant inventor of the prescription adds a warning to the lady in love and jealous of her beauty « not to consider at the same

There were no school text-books, but the children of wealthy families had their tutors who compiled, designed and sometimes illustrated for them arithmetic and science books. The illustrations were often ingenious and made for easy comprehension. Illustrated pages from the arithmetic book used by the children of Lorenzo the Magnificent.

time the Psalm of David, that is the Miserere », and « not to let it pain her to spend money on making herself beautiful ».

No woman could turn a deaf ear to these suggestions, of course, and, in any case, the use of make-up was long-established in all Italian towns. San Pier Damiani spoke of Florentine women of his day who were « comely and painted », of men who used cosmetics, and he reproved a hermit for using a pomade to simulate the pallor of an ascetic. Boncompagno, a *magister* of the early thirteenth century, reported that young men were « very preoccupied with comb and mirror », and « made up their faces as women do », that men were taking to wearing wigs, and some women adorned their hair with tresses cut off corpses. By the mid-thirteenth century the fashions had changed; some women painted their faces and necks, others, both young and old, wore short hair and clothes almost as close-fitting as men's, with skirts above the knees.

FAMILY FESTIVITIES

Life in a Florentine Renaissance family was not all work, however. The famous bell-tower on the Badia church, as Dante said, chimed « terce sext and none », marking, that is, the passing of the work-a-day world, but it also announced times of rest and relaxation.

Family celebrations usually took place on Sundays, or on the many saints' days consecrated to the Virgin Mary, or to one of the patron saints of the guilds, the district or the town. They constituted by far the most memorable events in the life of the family.

There were the christenings, the engagements, the weddings and other events which brought joy and marked great changes in family life; there were also sufferings and death which brought grief to everyone.

A christening was a happy occasion. The family gathered round the mother and child to pay their respects and to bring gifts. There was a tendency to celebrate the event with a certain amount of solemnity and display, although this was frowned upon at certain times by the authorities (« children brought for baptism and their wet-nurses are allowed to wear clothes worth only five pennies and silks to the same value »). Attempts to level down the spending on dress at christenings did nothing to reduce their importance in the eyes of the family. Whatever the restrictions on dress, once back in the privacy of their homes, those families who could afford it put on a good feast, with plenty of sweets and delicacies. To the family a christening marked a new member to be welcomed, a new responsibility to be taken on, and a new hope for the future: in every way the new child was seen to be a blessing from God.

Yet more than the births and christenings, it was the weddings which most profoundly affected family life. The exchange of promises, or the engagement, was a formal act, and the family regarded it as a sacred pledge to begin a new family group, at once a branching-off from the parent stem and a guarantee that the family would develop and be renewed. Here too, there were differences at times between the near-austerity imposed by the authorities, especially in the matter of dowries, and the tendency, within the privacy of the family, to celebrate the event with a degree of pomp and display.

A wedding was the most splendid and the happiest of family festivities, and it has been preserved for us in some of the glorious Renaissance paintings which transmit the sense of joy and thanksgiving evident in the privacy of the family celebrations, but also overflowing into the wider world outside.

THE LAST FAREWELL

As well as the joyful occasions, there were the sorrowful ones. The web of life had its dark as well as its golden threads. Death was then, as indeed it still is, a terrible thing, and grief found its expression in mourning and obsequies, though it was tempered by hope and Christian faith. The observation of mourning differed very little in Renaissance times from what we see today. The body was laid out in a downstairs room near to the front door. In many small Tuscan towns it was customary to have a special opening in the wall, called *l'uscio del morto*, through which the body was carried out of the house; this was then sealed up and not used again until there was another death. It was less commonly found in Florence, but the custom emphasizes the rather special nature of the mourning ceremonies in Tuscany. Most people wore black, although persons very close to the family, and some members of the family itself, might wear red.

When the dead person belonged to one of the leading families of Florence, the whole city went into mourning and took part in the ceremony of honouring the departed. On the day of the funeral workshops and banks closed early and people lined the streets along which the cortège was to pass, to « enjoy the spectacle », as one chronicler of the period puts it. Towards midday the body was taken to the church on a catafalque draped with a rich red cloth embroidered with gold. Carried on the shoulders of members of a fraternity of bearers, who were dressed in white for the occasion, it was preceded by priests intoning psalms and followed by horsemen, some bearing the coats of arms and weapons of the dead man, others representing a guild or a family taking part in the mourning. After its journey past the two lines of the populace buzzing with subdued conversation, the procession came to a halt in front of the church. Here the funeral sermon was preached. Then the body was taken into the church which, notwithstanding the brightness of mid-day, appeared dark and sombre with its great windows draped with heavy dark-coloured cloth, allowing only a pale sad light to filter through into the aisles. The body was placed in the centre of the church, so that anyone who wished might kneel and pray at the catafalque and offer a last farewell to the dead man. At a poor person's funeral a collection was taken for the offering of prayers of intercession, but this custom was waived by the wealthier families, who bore the entire cost of the funeral themselves. This could be considerable, and a contemporary chronicler records one funeral which, with its hundred large torches and heavy ceremonial dress, cost some three thousand florins, not including alms to the poor, a large sum when a well-to-do family might consider it was treating a daughter generously to give her five hundred as a dowry.

After the religious rites had been performed, the body was taken down into the crypt of the church and put in the family vault, reached through an opening in the floor covered by a stone or marble slab.

It was this method of burial, different from that used today, which gave rise to the singular episode of Ginevra degli Almieri who was declared dead during an epidemic and buried in the crypt of the Santa Reparata church. During the night after her burial the young wife recovered from her apparent death and, with a superhuman strength aided by despair at her situation, succeeded in raising the heavy marble slab covering

Those who could not afford private tutors sent their children to schools, of which there were many in the city. Here the educational system was not marked by excessive indulgence. Detail from a fresco by Gozzoli.

the opening to the vault. She came up from her grave, walked out of the church and, at dead of night went to her husband's house, then to her parents', then to her relatives', begging at each to be welcomed in and recognised as living. Rejected by all, she then turned to her former lover, whom she had had to renounce at her family's request. She knocked on his door, and, such is the power of true love, had no difficulty in convincing him of the strange thing that had happened to her. She was warmly welcomed and, so as not to give rise to gossip, entrusted to his sister until they were able to marry. Permission for this was granted after an ecclesiastical court had declared her husband to have forfeited his rights over her because he had not been able to distinguish his wife from a ghost.

THE FAMILY AND MORALS

The Florentine family in Renaissance times was not an abstract entity, an ideal « principle » in an empirical, untypified society. On the contrary, the very « theory » of the family which emerges in the fifteenth century, especially in the philosophy of Dominici and Alberti, and becomes a subject for speculation in itself, arises out of the impact of a solidly-based, practical institution on the new culture.

Vespasiano da Bisticci had spoken of the sanctity of the family, and the fifteenth century, with its increased sensitivity to ethics and culture, placed the family on the same plane as the priesthood, as a religious institution which was the source of grace and perfection. Firmly based on earth and rooted in the wider society of men, the family was seen by the great Leon Battista Alberti as a fundamental reality and the nucleus of all larger forms of society. Its morality and its permanent value lie in its being the source of the *ethos* and the reality in which a code of ethics can be fulfilled.

Thus Alberti regarded the family as a nation in miniature, an organism in the process of developing, though with institutions which would last forever, into the larger and more complex associated forms of the city and the state. The structure of family life depended on order and a hierarchy, which determined its moral authority. Marriage was said to be a vocation, the wife and children to have a mission. Gioviano Pontano considered the family to be a political institution, and as such one of the pillars of public life. Because of the insistence upon the sanctity of the family's mission in society, it was possible according to Renaissance ethics to permit, or even to expect, the family group to have also an economic function, to be « a small capitalist nucleus », the capital being, of course, not only that of accumulated wealth handed down, but a whole complex of reputation, prestige, well-being, power and position in society.

This confirms the ancient image of the family found in Dante, whose exile caused him to judge bitterly the great families of his time. These were not simple nuclei or groups within society, but great powers who exercised often tyrannical rule, not gatherings of honest men, as in the good old days, but forces bent on the conquest of earthly possessions, under the banner of a morality at once confused and identifying itself with the physical laws of the universe.

IN THE KITCHEN AND AT TABLE

Paolo da Certaldo's Libro dei Buoni Costumi *recommends « cooking once a day only in the morning », keeping « the cooked food for the evening » and particularly eating only a light meal before going to bed. This was the rule for the very poor, who considered a rasher of bacon a luxury, who scarcely ever drank a glass of wine and for whom the commonest flavours were garlic and leek.*

But the merchant, the banker, and every rich Florentine kept a good table and looked upon the banquet as a symbol of successful good-living or a show of wealth. Here the traditional boiled or roasted food, cooked in the good old ways at home, was discarded in favour of fancy spiced dishes painstakingly elaborated by whatever chefs happened to be in fashion. This style of cooking must have had its points, though, as the two Medici women who became Queens of France both took their chefs with them to Paris, as well as their tailors and perfumers.

A meal was also an opportunity for talking and listening to conversation, possibly also away from home. Florentines of any station in life who had the necessary money and wished to relieve the monotony of the daily round, could, and often did, frequent certain inns, detested by their wives, where good food and wine loosened the tongue and predisposed them to the most amiable conversation.

Giano della Bella's *Ordinamenti di Giustizia* were the common man's statutes and guide to living: they contained, albeit among the minor trades, the names of the bakers, butchers, greengrocers and wine-merchants.

Many a name now resplendent among the Florentine aristocracy can be found in the list of bakers: the Allegri, Berti, Manni, Buonavolti, Corsini, and so on. The centre of the bakery trade, before Vasari built the Uffizi, was in San Pietro at Scheraggio, in a group of houses between Via Lambertesca and the Lungarno.

The trade had its union restrictions, and no-one who was not a member could open a bakery. Every baker had to stamp his bread with his own special mark, and show in his shop a wooden loaf similar in size to the ones he baked, with its price clearly indicated. The price was fixed by decree by the Greater Council of the city, which also determined the quality of the flour, the quantity of yeast and salt and the

method of leavening. The conditions for bread-making were very stringent and detailed, and their infringement brought punishment which might vary from a fine or a period in the stocks for a minor offence, to prison or banishment from the city for hardened offenders found guilty of adulterating the bread of their fellow-citizens.

The guild of bakers also included the so-called *pistori*, more modest brethren who merely baked the dough prepared by others into large loaves called then, as today, *pane casareggio* or country bread, or *pane sciocco* because, being without salt, it tasted insipid (*sciocco*).

Which were the most famous bakehouses? At the beginning of the fifteenth century the Vecchiettis' in Via dei Ferravecchi, the present Via Strozzi; Borghese's in the Case dei Sacchetti adjoining the church of San Piero Buonconsiglio; Burella's behind Sant'Apollinare (Via dell'Acqua); Palagio's in the Case di Neri di Lippo del Palagio (Via dei Servi), patronised by the Medici; the Riccis', perhaps the best known of all,

The kitchen of the Medici villa at Poggio a Caiano, a fine example of spaciousness and symmetry. Its size, exceptional even for the times, made possible the preparation of the many courses served at the banquets which the Medici, by then the leading Florentine family, gave on special occasions.

in Via dell'Oche and the Santa Maria degli Ughi (between Via Monalda and Piazza Strozzi).

Just as important was the Corporation of Butchers, whose emblem, a goat rampant black on a field of gold, can be seen in a fine glazed terracotta outside Orsanmichele. Their characteristic was trouble-making, and when Pecora was Prior they broke out in revolt against the city fathers. They were centred on the Ponte Vecchio when the arcades built by Gaddi were closed and turned into workshops. Later, under the Medici, they were transferred to the Market.

THE TWO MEALS OF THE DAY

The day's activities in Renaissance times were regulated by the rising and setting of the sun. They began early when the woman of the house rose first and wakened the family, and ended round the supper table as night was falling.

It was customary to eat a slice of bread and drink half a glass of wine before setting out for work. Apart from this there were two meals a day: the *comestio*, or dinner, taken at the latest at 11, and the *prandium* or supper, taken just before sunset. When the day's toil was over, it was customary to linger at table after the evening meal chatting with friends and relatives.

The ordinary man's meal was inadequate and frugal, and he still obeyed the precepts in Paolo di Messer Pace da Certaldo's *Libro dei Buoni Costumi* advising him to « cook once a day only, in the morning », to keep « the cooked food for the evening » and « to eat little before going to bed ».

An ingenious system of water supply: it may be brought into the room by bucket from the well beneath. The closed window gives on to a gallery from which other members of the household may draw their water without disturbing those at table.

Scene from a fresco in the San Martino ai Buonomini Oratory, showing flasks, jugs, a pitcher, vat and a cask for wine. The figure on the left is carrying typically shaped wheaten loaves.

A simple homely table with a metal plate on which the communal food was served, flask and glasses for the trebbiano (a white wine), water jug, knives (the only cutlery) and rolls of light bread, reminiscent of the meagre suppers described by Pontormo in his bleak diary, a moving human document. (Detail from « The Supper at Emmaus » by Pontormo).

His basic food was wheat-bread and wine, beans, millet porridge and, in winter, chestnuts. There were also soup, macaroni and various forms of salad. Anything to go on the bread, such as a slice of bacon, was considered a delicious luxury. Pork or fowl went into the pot on a suitably solemn occasion.

There were two meals a day theoretically, but in fact people ate on the whole very little and, what was worse, irregularly. When Paolo da Certaldo prescribed fixed hours for eating, he was trying not only to achieve greater frugality, which in many cases was necessary, but to regulate meal-times.

The rich man's table was quite different, and here there was frequent over-indulgence. The Church intervened by prescribing days of fasting and abstinence, and the Priors tried to limit, by their ordinances, excessive luxury and revelry in certain circumstances. The Sumptuary Laws respected the intimacy of family life, however, and did not attempt to control food and drink consumed privately. On the other hand, with commendable circumspection, they did restrict meals served when outside guests were present to two main dishes, one boiled and one roasted, and, on meatless days, to two portions of fish. It is true that the boiled course could contain three kinds of meat and the roast four, provided that the course was served on the one plate. Naturally the Florentines found an easy way round these laws. Strictly observing the correct number of courses and their content, they contrived to prepare for themselves and their guests certain « pies » which, though constituting strictly only one course, nevertheless contained enough ingredients for five or six with, as we should say nowadays, the appropriately high protein content. The Priors were prepared to grant exemptions under certain circumstances, but anyone applying for these had to swear that the honour done to his guests was « for the greater glory of the city of Florence, and not for any other cause ». Faced with a possible fine of twenty-five gold florins each for the master of the house, his cook and his servants, the Florentines of those days only did, we like to think, what their descendants today would do: avoid the snares of bureaucracy with a « pie ».

FLORENTINE MEN AT THE EATING-HOUSE

The phenomenon of people going out for their meals is partly the consequence of scarcity and monotony at the family table. After business the men preferred to spend a few peaceful hours with friends and enjoy the specialities of the house designed to attract lovers of good food, men of letters and artists. The desertion of the family table for the local hostelry was such that during the Republic the women of Florence, concerned at its effect on family life, turned to the public authorities and succeeded in getting ordinances published forbidding the provision of sumptuous food and delicacies such as *tortellos, fegatellos vel pullos, vel aliquod genus avidam, vel aliqua alias pertinentia ad gulusitatem vel ghiottoneriam* (« fritters, pig's liver, chicken or any other fowl, or any other dish which panders to greed or gluttony »). The Latin, though grammatically incorrect, was easily understood by all concerned.

Among the company at these eating-houses might be found gentlemen such as Lorenzo the Magnificent, men of letters such as Machiavelli, academicians such as Crusca, artists such as Masaccio, Michelangelo and Bronzino, politicians such as Capponi and Ferrucci, to mention only a few of the most famous.

Above: *Majolica jugs with the symbol of a fraternity and glasses in a bowl.* Below: *flask and glass in a wall-shelf. (Two details from frescoes in San Martino ai Buonomini).*

Two hammered bronze plates, normally used to decorate walls or sideboards, and large glazed terracotta bowl for flowers or water scented with essence of orange-blossom for washing the hands. (Property of the antiquarian Bellini).

Majolica amphora with the arms of the Strozzi family in the centre, and two small jars in pietra dura. These were given away as presents at festivals and banquets.

The « *Lorenzo* » *cup in* pietra dura *and silver, bearing the owner's abbreviated name: Laur. Med. (Museum of Silverware).*

The great families held their banquets in loggias. The crowds would gather round: in addition to the spectacle they might also enjoy an unexpected distribution of food. (Loggia Rucellai).

We also know the names of some of the best-known eating-houses, both within and outside the city walls, from a list read out by Bastiano de' Rossi at a meeting of the Accademia della Crusca, an Academy of letters founded in Florence in 1582. They are: the « Michel Del Bello » near the Porta alla Croce, the « Giardino » in the Via de' Pilastri, the « Vinegia » in the street of the same name, the « Baldracca » in San Piero at Scheraggio, the « Frascati », in the ancient ghetto, the « Bertucce » near the San Martino Church, the « Moro » in the San Pietro Market, the « Macine », « Sandracca », « Piovano », and « Trave torta » near the Ponte alla Carraia, the « Panico », « Fico » and the « Neghittosa » under the Tower of the same name.

Anton Francesco Grazzini, called il Lasca, recalls in his « Lezione », on « The chapter of the sausage », that in the Osteria del Porco there was a certain cook called Suria who prepared pig's liver so well that in a few years he made a fortune, and his product earned universal fame: « as well as Ricci bread and Amidei wine, one spoke of Suria pig's liver ». He was so well appreciated that the City Council wanted him at least twice a week in the Palazzo Vecchio to cook his speciality.

KITCHEN AND PHARMACY

Treatises on medicine and pharmacopoeiae of the fourteenth and fifteenth centuries often contained culinary recipes. This was because of the wide use in cooking of spices and herbs also used in pharmacy, and because the apothecaries of those days also made and sold cordials, julep and sweetmeats prepared in their own kitchens or laboratories.

The *Ricettario Fiorentino*, or official prescription book of the Florentine apothecaries of 1498, put together by the best-known doctors of the time, gave recipes for the preparation of numerous candied foods, syrups and preserves, all very varied and most appetising, and a discreet number of « restoratives », or tonic foods, such as partridge, turtle, « extract of capon » and « essence of chicken ».

Florentine, Genoese, Venetian, Roman and Neapolitan apothecaries were experts in the preparation of sweetmeats. They made not only simple candied fruits and flowers, cakes, pastries, tarts, flat cakes of dough cooked in olive oil, biscuits and pastries, but symbolic sugar statues, scenes from mythology, centre-pieces for the table several feet high, scenes from country life, and so on. They made sweets and sugar in lump, powder and loaf form. It was not only the private apothecary in the city who indulged in this side-line, but the apothecaries in hospitals, convents and monasteries also made sweets. Florentine and Genoese *confetti* (sugared almonds) were particularly well-known. The city authorities often made presents of some of their finest sweetmeats to Popes, Emperors and other famous persons.

The Florentines were very sweet-toothed and usually ate these delicacies after meals; but there were many other occasions, even journeys of penitence and pilgrim-

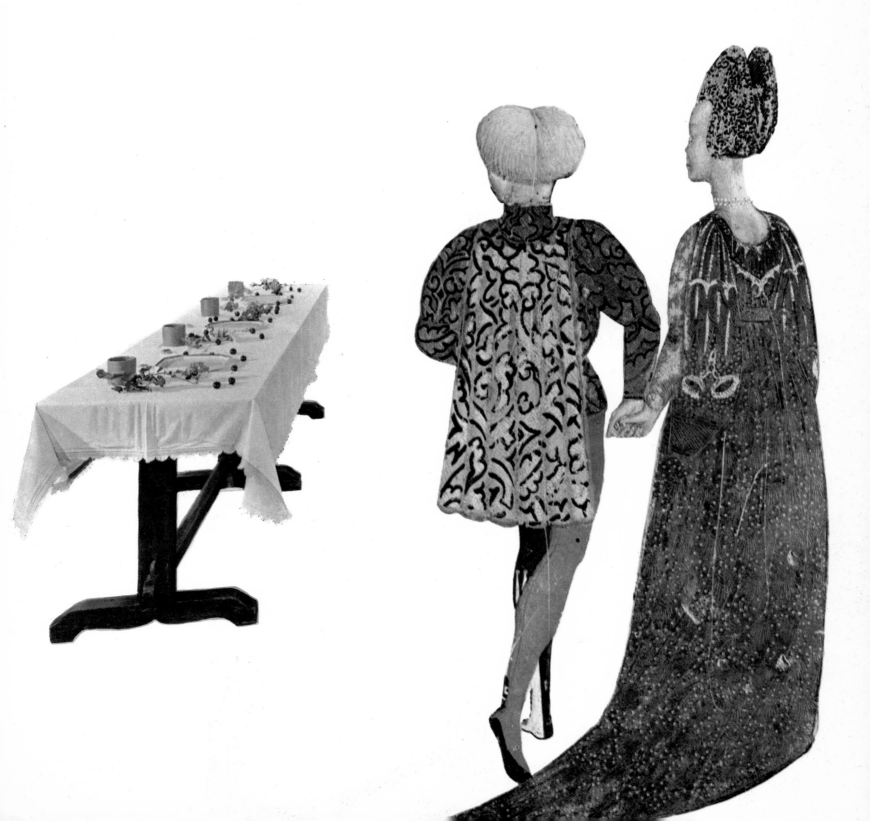

ages, when they indulged their passion, and on festival occasions, such as weddings and christenings, this indulgence became so excessive that the authorities had to intervene to limit consumption.

The account-books of the Alberti, the Cavalcanti, the Peruzzi and the Valori families, not to mention that most extraordinary and interesting book of family housekeeping, Tribaldo di Amerigo de' Rossi's « Libro dei conti », and many other contemporary Florentine documents, show copious records of jellies, *confetti*, candied fruits, creams and many other delicacies on which the confectioners exercised their skill and fancy.

Sugar and honey were used equally. It was a general principle not to eat anything that was not sprinkled with sugar. Spices could have the strangest ingredients such as sumach, a substance now used only in the dressing of skins, gold dust, crushed and powdered precious stones, and could serve either to add flavour to the food, as an infusion with the full-bodied Aegean wines, or in sauces, to which they were added liberally.

Particularly famous was the *peverata*, a broth of meat, fish, pepper, cinnamon, ginger, nutmeg and other similar hot spices, coloured with saffron. Some Tuscan towns devoted whole chapters of their statutes to rules for the making of *peverata*, a costly preparation which graced particularly the tables of the rich.

It was rarely seen on the plate of the poor man, who had to make do with leek or garlic sauce, a dreadful mash of pulped substances which we find described in, amongst other works, that encyclopedia of botany and manual of popular medicine called the *Thesaurus pauperum* by Pietro Ispano (later Pope John XXI), who wrote with the intention of bringing to the poor a knowledge of the commonest and cheapest plants and herbs used in medicine and cooking.

The consumption of spices reached such proportions that on special occasions they were sent out to the millers for grinding on a large scale, as the household cooks and servants could not cope with the demand. This happened, for example, at the wedding-feast of Bonifacio, Duke of Tuscany, and Beatrice, the mother of Countess Matilde.

The abuse of spices was thought by Arab doctors to have brought on leprosy and other diseases which were common in the Middle Ages, but which have now fortunately disappeared.

To prevent the unfortunate consequences of an excessive consumption of spices, several Italian town

A banquet with a simply-laid table against the wall, and a sideboard with high back and shelf for the dinner-service and containers of water and wine. (« Assuero's banquet » by Jacopo del Sellaio).

authorities tried at various times to control their use, just as they had tried to limit over-indulgence in sweet-meats, but with as little success.

To relieve attacks of indigestion from eating too many highly-flavoured delicacies or dishes which only a stomach of iron could assimilate, the doctor resorted to blood-letting to drive away the evil humours and the apothecary to enemas, purgatives and other medicinal brews.

THE BANQUET AND THE TABLE

The Renaissance banquet seemed to revive the Greek love of the « Symposium », a happy blend of the pleasures of the body and the mind, which reintroduced the art of conversation and the delight of a display of dancing during the meal. The new Renaissance society also looked upon the banquet as a symbol of status, and a favourable opportunity to impress friend and enemy alike with the wealth and power of one's family.

Banquets were held on particular occasions, which might vary from family to family, but which nevertheless had common characteristics: they celebrated public and religious festivals, family anniversaries and particularly weddings.

Renaissance chroniclers in Florence have described ingenuously, and sometimes with a vivid imagination, some of the feasts held to celebrate famous weddings, official visits, the arrival of ambassadors, and the like. Shrewd merchants have recorded in their family annals the principal events celebrated with banquets, and have even given precise details of the courses served. The overall impression which emerges from these sources is that of an enthusiastic round of gay music, colour and dancing.

Banquets varied according to the season. In the hot summer evenings people preferred to eat out of doors, whereas in colder or more inclement weather the tables were laid in the great halls of the palazzi.

The more important Florentine families had loggias constructed next to their great houses. These were slightly raised above street-level and there were about forty of them in Renaissance times. They were used for receptions; here the master of the house welcomed the distinguished foreign guest; here the official visitors from another town were received: Popes, reigning sovereigns and princes; here parents and friends were feasted; here also the ordinary people sat to enjoy the cool of the evening in summer or sheltered in the winter to catch the weak rays of the sun, protected from the rain and wind. When there was a banquet in the loggia, these same people stood around at a respectful distance to enjoy the convivial spectacle. They were thus able to watch the dancing, listen to the gay music and gape in wonder at the brilliant apparel of the guests, the rich dinner service and the sumptuous food. They also benefited from the food and drink which was freely distributed on such occasions, so that the town itself could be said to participate in the festivity.

How was a table laid for a banquet?

The walls of the room or the loggia were gaily hung with cloths and tapestries, silk and fine lace, laurel wreaths intertwined with flowers and fruit, and shields painted with the family arms hung from fancy ribbons. Against the main wall stood a sideboard stacked with bronze and silver plates, majolica ware fruit-stands and drinking-cups of fine stone.

There were usually three tables arranged along the three other walls and laid with several embroidered table-cloths or *mantili*. This was because they were liable to get dirty quickly, as each guest helped himself with his fingers from the large dish of food handed round.

Everyone was invited to wash his hands before sitting down at table, and for this purpose, in the room most commonly used as a banqueting hall, there was a washstand of marble, stone, earthenware or even silver, either fixed to the wall or on a portable stand. During the meal each guest had a number of napkins called *truccabocca*, and from time to time the servants came round with basins of water perfumed with orange blossom called *acqua linfa*.

The only cutlery was a very sharp knife with which the food was cut up; the food was then conveyed to the mouth by using the other end of the knife, which was made pointed for this purpose. Forks were still a novelty at this time: perhaps this tool was still held to be the *instrumentum diaboli*, against which San Pier Damiano had inveighed in the cause of simple homely customs.

The table equipment was completed by a glass or metal drinking-vessel.

The kitchen — the harmonious Renaissance kitchen — was rightly considered fundamental to the success of any banquet. It was a spacious room, the domain of the chef, who was then, as now, an important personage. The most famous chefs were held in high esteem, and the wealthy families would compete for their services. Both Catherine and Marie de' Medici, who married Kings of France, took with them to Paris not only their perfumers but their Florentine chefs, because they could not get used to the « barbaric » cooking of the French capital.

For the great banquets and wedding-feasts, the work in the kitchen and other adjoining rooms began some days before the event. Often, from designs of famous painters, sculptors and architects who did not disdain the pleasures of the table, the chefs designed elaborate configurations of dishes which we can scarcely imagine today, and which have a parallel only in the extravagant courses served at the most sumptuous Roman banquets.

The table acquired in Renaissance times the value of a status symbol and everything was done to create *magnificentia*; a good banquet might determine the success of a family alliance — marriages were considered only in the light of wealth and power — a peace treaty or a pact of friendship. This lent a certain importance to the staff concerned with the preparation and serving of a banquet: the stewards, wine-waiters, carvers, valets, pages, heralds, and so on, not to mention the chefs.

It was a pope, Julius III, who considered it right to offer the cardinal's hat to one of his carvers. Just as the chef was absolute master in the kitchen, so the table in the banqueting hall was under the complete control of the *senescalco generale*, a kind of major-domo with considerable responsibility, who supervised first the organisation, then the long and complicated business of serving the meal.

Reconstruction in the antiquarian Bellini's villa of a setting for a Renaissance banquet, with authentic pieces arranged after contemporary paintings. The flower and fruit decoration is copied from Ghirlandaio's « Herod's Banquet » in Santa Maria Novella. The centre table, also called the high table, was reserved for the head of the family and important guests. The ladies sat at the table on the right and the gentlemen at the one on the left, both sitting on the outside only. The centre space was used for service and short plays or dancing. On the sideboard the carver cut up the food and arranged the dishes for presentation to the guests.

It would be too difficult to enumerate all the famous banquets held in Florence in Renaissance times, together with all the details as recorded by contemporary chroniclers. The most important were Cardinal Arnaldo Pelagrua's banquet for Pope Clement V on April 30th 1308, the official banquet offered by the Republic of Florence for Pope Paul II in April 1459, the feast at the wedding of Bernardo Rucellai and Nannina de' Medici on June 8th 1466, the banquet given by the City Council for Gian Galeazzo Sforza and Bona di Savoia in March 1471, and that given by Benedetto Salutati for the children of the King of Naples on February 16th 1476.

Giovanni Rucellai described in his interesting « Literary Miscellany » the wedding feast for Bernardo Rucellai and Nannina de' Medici. He « thanks God for having made him a relation of the great citizen Cosimo di Giovanni de' Medici, as Nannina is now the wife of Bernardo his son », and adds that the feast cost 6,630 florins.

Such a sum might imply a gargantuan feast, but in fact the food was distributed over three days at two meals per day, and the variety and style of the dishes were reasonably limited: the total consumption was of the order of 3,000 head of poultry, 70 bushels of ordinary bread, 2,800 loaves of white bread and 4,000 thin curled wafers, 50 barrels of white wine and 70 of red, 1,500 grapes and quantities of bacon, sausage and fish.

BANQUETING ETIQUETTE

The guests sat down at table, the women separate from the men. At the high table sat the master and mistress of the house and the principal male guests. The drinking cups were handed out and the guests took first a glass of light wine and nibbled at the *pinocchiati* (sweet pastry with pine-seeds), which were already laid on the table. All this took place to the accompaniment of music. Then the waiters came in bearing the main dishes, which were so arranged and dressed as to excite the admiration of all. When these had been presented, the carver began his difficult task. The major-domo graciously accepted the expressions of praise and admiration for his work. The banquet was the testing-ground for his skill. The portions of meat were then artfully carved and arranged on the large dishes to be placed on the table. Between each two or three guests there was a wooden or glazed earthenware dish called a *tagliere* « whose beauty consisted in being white, not of good wood, nor well made, but full of good meat, well cooked and well carved ».

Any unwanted food or remains were thrown under the table, sometimes into a bowl provided for the occasion.

During the intervals between courses the table would be tidied up, some of the top cloths would be removed and there might be a display of dancing, a musical interlude or even a short play.

The banquet was not complete without a selection of wines: these could be light or heavy, local or foreign, and served au naturel or spiced.

DOCTORS, APOTHECARIES AND THEIR PRACTICE

The Renaissance opposed the Medieval and scholastic concept of illness as a punishment of the body with the principle of « disturbed harmony » which nature herself must cure. Anatomical studies were revived and the terror of death gave way to a study of its causes, so that life might continue: dissection became common practice and it became possible to make a serious study of the human body. Medicine, it is true, still resorted to strange and sometimes revolting practices, some more harmful than the illnesses they aimed to cure, but apothecaries were experimenting on the ancient prescriptions based on herbs, and doctors were critically examining classical treatises to refute some of the long-established errors. Although the charlatan still operated alongside the doctor, sharing his rewards and prestige, and although the apothecary, in addition to his normal trade in medicines, dabbled also in cosmetics, by 1498 regular medical and pharmaceutical practice was officially recognised and encouraged in the publication by the officers of the appropriate guild of a list of prescriptions which the law required to be observed. The doctor belonged by right to the world of learning as it was understood by the fifteenth century: his professional equipment included philosophy and dialectics which according to Galen's precepts must accompany the required knowledge of surgery, medicine and natural sciences. He could practise only after long study and a public examination before a most select commission of doctors and surgeons.

From the late thirteenth century, the doctors in Florence, together with the apothecaries and haberdashers, formed one of the seven major guilds. They had a privileged position with the apothecaries within the guild, and in the political representation of the municipality, which they gradually lost in the fourteenth and fifteenth centuries under pressure from the haberdashers, who became stronger within the guild itself and virtually ousted both the doctors and apothecaries from the municipal council.

New trades and greater numbers of craftsmen and workshops brought an increase in the numbers of the haberdashers, and the progressive industrialisation of the town, with its expanding international trade in spices, greatly improved the economic position of the apothecaries. Yet the doctors continued to enjoy the highest authority and prestige, as they were then the aristocrats of culture and knowledge, esteemed even above the lawyers by Dante.

In Florence and elsewhere at this time the field of medicine was much larger than what we understand by this today. The doctor was required to have firstly a philosophical training, and his courses of study qualifying him for admission to the profession included not only medicine and surgery, but also dialectics, which Galen considered the queen of the sciences, philosophy, physics and natural sciences. This is because the distinction between medicine and philosophy was not as clear in the Middle Ages as it is today.

Medicine was based on ancient formulae and prescriptions derived from the classical authors, and in many cases the medical student was simply required to annotate ancient texts. Thus logic and speculative philosophy were compulsory subjects in a medical course; professors taught equally philosophy, medicine and surgery, and philosophy and medicine came within the same faculty and led to the same degree in « arts » and « grammar ». This would explain why Villani

greeted the Florentine Dino del Garbo as « doctor of physics, natural sciences and philosophy », and why Dino's son Tommaso, together with many professors of medicine, translated and wrote treatises of philosophy and natural sciences. It was not unusual to find in Florence doctors of medicine who were also « doctors of grammar », and the records show that in 1320 the Priors made a grant of money to a Doctor Guicciardo of Bologna, professor of « grammar » and « other arts and sciences », resident in Florence for the exercise of his profession and director of a *hospitium* situated in his own house.

A famous example of a man who wrote treatises of both philosophy and the healing arts, whose work was widely read in Florence and many other centres of learning both in Italy and abroad, was Pietro di Giuliano, known as Pietro Ispano, who was born in Lisbon in 1226 and became Pope John XXI. His *Summulae logicales* were a compendium of formalistic logic, after the principles laid down in Aristotle's *Organon* and reinterpreted by Porfidius and Boethius. This was acknowledged far and wide as an authoritative work for several centuries, used as a text-book in schools, translated into Greek and, after being printed for the first time in 1474, ran to forty-eight editions in the next hundred years and was eventually printed no less than eighty-four times. He was judged by the chronicler Salimbene as a most excellent sophist, logician, debater and theologian, who enjoyed great public esteem. In the Annals of the Dominicans at Basle he is called *magnus*. This same Pietro Ispano was just as famous as a doctor. He was medical consultant to princes and cardinals, principal physician to Pope Gregory X, taught medicine in Siena from 1247 to 1252, and wrote no fewer than seventeen medical works, commentaries and treatises, including the *Thesaurus pauperum*, which continued the Greco-Arab traditions brought over to Western Europe by Constantine Africanus. This was a manual of popular medicine, offering simple remedies within the reach of all. It ran to seven translations into Italian, and was one of the first works to be printed in the late fifteenth century (the first edition is dated

Antwerp 1472 but was really 1497). He also wrote a short treatise on ocular therapy called *De oculo* which was popularised by the Florentine Zucchero Bencivenni, and was still recognised as authoritative over two and a half centuries later, as Michelangelo Buonarroti saw fit to copy some of its prescriptions in a manuscript now in the Vatican museum.

This close connection between medicine and philosophy may also explain why Dante, held to be a great philosopher and a distinguished layman in his day, was registered in the major Florentine guild of doctors and apothecaries. His name appeared under the letter D on the roll for 1297, the oldest in existence, and now preserved in the Florence State Archives.

THE « STUDIO FIORENTINO »

Any doctor who had not followed a regular course of study and had not been *conventato*, or admitted after examination, had to go before a special commission before he could practise in Florence. This body was set up by statute in 1314 and consisted of officers of the guild of doctors and apothecaries, two Minorite (Franciscan) friars and two preaching friars. As time went on the commission became progressively more strict; the ecclesiastical members dropped out, and the examination was held by six doctors, two of whom were officers of the guild, and the others freely chosen from among the practising doctors of Florence, though one had to be a surgeon. The guild's lawyer was also present.

In view of this stringency, it would seem that a high standard of knowledge and technique was demanded of medical practitioners who, with a few possible exceptions, could not have been as ignorant as we might be led to believe from the scurrilous attacks on the profession by Petrarch, or the salacious stories of Boccaccio, Sacchetti and other writers, who were pleased to comment on the « great stupidity » of the doctors of their acquaintance and of their city. Such criticism of Florentine doctors, implying as it did that all were badly trained and ill-equipped for their job, was arbitrary and exaggerated. It was, in fact, Florence which provided the leaders of that revival of medical studies, and brought that serious appreciation of medical practice which gradually spread to the rest of Italy from the second half of the thirteenth century. One man

who was responsible more than most for reawakening an interest in medicine, and who was regarded in his time as something of a rebel, was Taddeo Alderotti, a Florentine. In the doctrinal field it was his great achievement to have broken through the arid philosophical systems under which medicine lay buried, by reverting to the pure Greek and Latin sources, and the search for factual knowledge, and in the practical field to have brought the doctor back to the study of the patient and the investigation and classification of symptoms. His work was continued by another Florentine, the famous Dino del Garbo, mentioned above, called in his day *medicinae delucidator*, and praised by Giovanni Villani, who recorded his death on September 30th 1327 as one of the most memorable events of that year, saying that he was « a most famous doctor of physics and natural sciences and philosophy, the best and most sovereign doctor in Italy ».

Further evidence of the contribution of Florence to the revival of medical studies is that, following the examples of Naples, which inherited the Salerno school, Bologna and Padua, all of which attracted the most famous teachers and a student body from all over Europe, Florence, « a kingly city and excelling in other things », set up by decree of the Priors in May 1321 a Studium for the teaching of medicine, so as not to be left behind and so that her students should not have to go elsewhere to complete their courses.

This was reorganised and enlarged after the plague of 1348. With praiseworthy energy and youthful enthusiasm, the city of Dante saw to it that her school was second to none: privileges and advantages were given to students from outside Florence, the best teachers were sought and generously paid; courses and programmes were so arranged that two professors took the morning lessons, two more the afternoon ones *ad practicam* and one in the evening; two taught logic, one surgery, one rhetoric and one law. There were public discussions and debates on certain days, which provided stimulus, not only to the course, but to doctors already practising in Florence.

Doctors and apothecaries belonged to the same guild, and in Florence had the same patron saint, the Virgin and Child, as painted by Luca della Robbia in that delicate terracotta preserved in the Church of Orsanmichele, which also contains the arms of all the craftsmen's guilds. There was thus considerable co-operation between them in all professional matters.

THE DOCTOR-APOTHECARY, THE APOTHECARIES AND THEIR TRADE

Medieval doctors often continued the ancient practice of preparing medicines and selling them to their patients. Frequently the doctor would have a garden behind his house for medicinal plants, or he would run a shop, either by himself or with the help of an apothecary, and would receive his patients there. The reverse was sometimes the case: an apothecary might have in his shop a surgery where one or more doctors could attend their patients. When Frederick II refounded the famous Salerno School of Medicine in 1224, he prohibited any collusion between doctors and apothecaries, and prevented doctors from running their own pharmacy. Naples, Parma, Cremona, Venice, Verona, Nice and Pisa all did the same. In Florence, however, statutes of both the city and guild established the legality of collaboration between doctors and apothecaries, allowing the latter to have doctors in their pharmacies to treat patients, and the former to run their own shop in which they might have a surgery and employ an apothecary. They were, however, forbidden to agree between themselves to sell certain medicines and divide the profit.

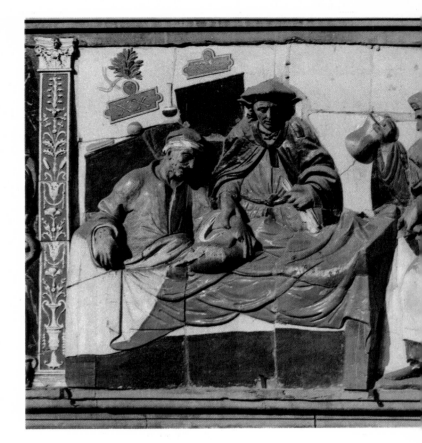

The oldest recorded example in Florence of this type of collaboration within a single shop, where patients were treated and medicines sold, goes back to 1279. The following two centuries saw many more, even when in some cases the apothecary had ceased to specialise in medicines, but had become a retailer or wholesaler of drugs, spices and other colonial goods.

It is well known how in the Middle Ages the workshops of the various trades were concentrated in a few streets so that they might compete better for customers. This arrangement suited both the city authorities, as it made for easier control, and the craftsmen, who were protected from illicit competition in the supply of raw materials and the distribution of the labour force. From the earliest days of her history Florence had a « Via degli Speziali (Apothecaries) », near the old market place, where the apothecaries' guild had its headquarters in a tall building. This was the business centre of the city, where the apothecaries would find all the best-stocked warehouses and the most accredited retailers of the materials of their trade.

But very soon, owing to the increasing demands of their clients, apothecaries grew in number, and in addition to the old-established shops in the centre of the city, new ones sprang up on the outskirts, both inside and outside the wall. From the first decades of the fourteenth century, there were noticeable differences in apothecaries and their shops, according to the district where they practised. The State Archives of Florence, which provide a mine of information from registers of landed property, masses of lawsuits involving officers of the guilds, and countless other documents, contain the record of many apothecaries' shops, the value of their stocks and the amount of their turnover, from the modest establishments mainly on the outskirts, to the large concerns belonging to some of the most distinguished Florentine families, whose value exceeded several hundred or even thousand gold florins. Some of these shops were run by men well-known in the city, such as Antonio di Pietro Toscanelli, a wholesale apothecary, and his nephew Paolo, the famous traveller and writer, who both had businesses in the Via San Martino near the Abbey, and Anton

In the Middle Ages hospitals were founded and run almost entirely by religious bodies, but by the time of the Renaissance several new institutions had been started entirely by private benefactors. At the end of the thirteenth century, Folco Portinari, the father of Beatrice, founded the Ospedale di Santa Maria Nuova and at the beginning of the fifteenth Simone di Piero Vespucci founded the Ospedale di Santa Maria dell'Umiltà, now the San Giovanni di Dio. The illustration shows a ceramic panel by Giovanni della Robbia.

Francesco Grazzini, called Il Lasca, who, together with his associates, practised in the Straw Market. Other famous apothecaries' shops were the *taberna officina aromatum* (herb shop and manufactory) at the Santa Maria Nuova hospital, recorded as early as 1288, and the one on the Rubaconte bridge in Florence whose sign was « a large fat piglet ». There was also an apothecary's shop in the Old Market with a melon as its sign: this was a joke thought up by Boccaccio to satirize the monumental ignorance of a doctor who visited his patients there. One fifteenth-century pharmacy had a sign showing a doctor administering an enema: no joke was intended here.

The statutes of the City of Florence were prepared to admit a less intensive training for apothecaries than that demanded of doctors. Every apothecary worthy of the name had to have undertaken a course of study which would enable him to distinguish herbs and antidotes, with their beneficial and harmful qualities,

to prepare syrups, beverages and enemas, after which, by paying the relevant dues, he was allowed to practise.

We should not assume that all apothecaries were quacks and charlatans. Some of these there might have been, but there were some who measured up to the professional standards we might expect today, men of sound culture, highly trained and animated by the spirit of enquiry. The various statutes which governed the practice of pharmacy recognised degrees of competence. In Naples, for instance, apothecaries were divided into « manual » and « medical » and this distinction applied until the late eighteenth century. Clearly these two categories implied a difference of duties and functions.

The authentic apothecary of Renaissance times was the one who ran his own establishment, usually overlooking the street. We must imagine him at work surrounded by shelves with rows of majolica jars (some of them of the finest ware, the pride of Italian ceramic work), bottles of sweet-smelling essences and perfumed water, scales, retorts, stills, little furnaces, ancient books, paper and notebooks (apothecaries were known to sell books, paper and writing materials: in Florence they were called *stationerii*, and this gave the English word *stationer*) and a hundred other things. Behind the bench, usually opposite the glazed entrance-door, the apothecary presided over the scene, seated in an oak-panelled embrasure on which was usually to be seen a statue of Aesculapius or Hygieia. He was the *deus loci*, the purveyor of remedies made by himself, alchemist, virtual wizard. In the pharmacy, together with the apothecary and his assistant, were the doctor and the patients waiting their turn to see him. The apothecary's shop was for a long time in Italy the meeting-place for men of letters, scientists, politicians and idlers.

Not all apothecaries had their own laboratory, nor were all of them authorised to sell all the medicines named on the official list of the time. Some could sell only certain remedies, and were called *ciurmadori* (quacks) or *ciarlatani* (charlatans), the meaning of which is obvious, or *cerretani* (perhaps from Cerreto near Spoleto in Umbria, in the same way as surgeons were sometimes called *norcini*, because many came from Norcia) or *saltimbanchi* (mountebanks) because to advertise their goods in the city squares they used criers and musicians, and put on a little show or a mock fight. These apothecaries were able to obtain a licence from a Medical Faculty and the State authorities, and were sometimes even included in the official lists of doctors and surgeons.

In Florence they were called, not without malice, *ciurmadori* (quacks) and licensed to sell theriac and mithridate (antidotes against poisons) and *terre sigillate*, a fine ferruginous clay good for snake bites, provided they declared where it had been bought and produced proof of its efficacy, that is, as Varchi, the Florentine historian (1503-1565), wittily remarks, provided that they told a whole pack of lies and led everyone up the garden path. In this they would resemble their Roman colleagues, who claimed to descend from Saint Paul, or to belong to the Marsi, a people who claimed to have special protection against snake-bites, but whose quackery had been unmasked by Galen. They were allowed, under licence from the senior doctor of their district, to sell snake-ointment and Saint Paul's pills. In Pisa, apothecaries were perhaps more fortunate, as they had merely to take an oath before the officers of their guild that they were true practitioners of their art.

Amongst apothecaries' collaborators there were also herb-specialists and snake-charmers. The former, though lacking advanced medical knowledge and skill, were nevertheless experts in medicinal plants. Boccaccio, who described so admirably the customs of his day, often mentioned how herb-specialists and, indeed, ordinary people as well, would go out into the woods and fields in the appropriate season to pick roots, flowers, leaves and wild plants, either to sell or to use as medicines.

The snake-charmers, on the other hand, caught vipers to sell to the apothecaries, who then rendered them harmless by extracting the poison sac from their mouths with special tweezers, cut off their heads and tails, which were of no use, and kept the middle part. Out of this they prepared a substance for making poultices, or a tonic for serious organic debility.

THE PRACTICE OF PHARMACY IN THE FIFTEENTH CENTURY

It is true that in the thirteenth and fourteenth century, chemistry in Florence, as elsewhere, was in its infancy and still confused with alchemy. Pharmacy was still empirical, like medicine, which as yet was not based on anatomy and a study of symptoms. The monasteries had done a great deal to advance knowledge with treatises on plants, precious stones and animals and the first practice of pharmacy imitated from Arabic countries was to be found in monasteries also, from whence it spread to wealthy fraternities, princes' courts and finally became available to ordinary people. From the late fourteenth century and throughout the fifteenth the best of pharmacy was instilled with a spirit of research and a desire to find the truth. As with medicine, practice improved and advanced hand in hand with a growth of theoretical knowledge, so that by Renaissance times pharmacy seemed to have come a very long way since the days when Giovan Gualberto concocted medicaments for his monks in Florence and its surrounding districts, when a monk from Vallombrosa cured inflammation of the eyes with hot cowdung or a Camaldoli prior treated wounds with salt.

As also with medicine, pharmacy started in the cloisters of monastic orders, but gradually spread to the lay world. In 1216 the monks of the Vallombrosa Order were forbidden to go about treating the sick, and, as the practice of pharmacy was taken up by laymen, more rigorous standards were applied. This was reflected, for instance, in the great increase of literature on private hygiene which came out after the great plague of 1348. In the wake of the great cultural movement of the Renaissance, when much of the advance in scientific thinking was due to the medical profession, the development of anatomy and the study of the human body had their counterpart in a renewed interest in the great classical writers, especially Pliny and Dioscorides, in a wealth of exposition and commentary of Latin, Greek and Arabic texts, and the publication of some of the first illustrated books. Among these were the ancient botanical works still in use in the monasteries, designed to instruct the monks in the recognition of useful plants, their medicinal value and the places where they might be found, with a chapter devoted to each and arranged alphabetically; the old treatises on precious stones, with alphabetical lists and the characteristics of each one; the many « bestiaries » with their descriptions of animals, whose flesh, blood and, in the case of dogs, the nauseating so-called *graecum album*, supposedly rich in calcium, were long used as restoratives and cures.

The first books were transcriptions of classical works, particularly the treatises on herbs, and their medicinal properties were often confused with the magical, especially in the case of precious stones. In time, however, the texts were increasingly annotated, and there was evidence of a clearer understanding of the properties of certain medicaments and their effects on the body, as remedies for the digestion, as laxatives, emetics, diuretics, diaporetics, constipating agents, and so on, until the magical element came to be almost completely ignored. The magic and superstition which had attached themselves to the art of medicine were not evident in the early classical treatises, but seem to have been an accretion of later ages. This progress was in keeping with the spirit of the age, and due in no small part to the apothecaries of Florence.

The first maternity hospital, the Spedale degli Innocenti, was established in Florence in 1421 for girl mothers. The babies were kept wrapped up in swaddling-bands until after the first year.

MEDICO-BOTANICAL LITERATURE

In the abundant medical literature of the fourteenth and fifteenth centuries, alongside the writings on medical theory and practice, on the principles of hygiene and the pseudo-Aristotelian letter to Alexander the Great, all taken in the main from Arabic sources, there existed a flourishing literature on medico-botanical subjects called *horti* or *hortuli*, originating in and developing from the manuals used by monks. The most famous of these was the *Hortus sanitatis* by Giovanni da Cuna. It was published in Latin, German, French and Italian, and became widely known in Italy and throughout Europe. It dealt not only with plants, but also with animals, stones, the examination of urine, and covered all that was known at that time of medicine and pharmaceutics. It was a true encyclopaedia of pharmacy and the art of healing.

The fifteenth-century scholars were not merely concerned, however, with discovering and propagating ancient Latin, Greek and Arabic texts, in which humanism had awakened such lively interest. As with the literary texts of Ancient Rome, the interest, once aroused by the discovery and exposition of old manuscripts, extended to the critical examination of their content, so that medical science progressed by the late fifteenth century to the preparation of manuals and treatises which, though utilising the materials and the teaching of the previous centuries, were more in touch with contemporary life and aimed to widen the whole field of culture.

Thus many works were published in the fifteenth century for the training of pharmacists. Amongst these were the *Antidotario* by Nicolo Salernitano, the official text-book of the time on pharmacology, which ran to five printed editions before the sixteenth century, and the *Regimen Salernitanum* which had twenty editions be-

Apothecary's table, balance, pestle and mortar, phials and jars as used in Renaissance times (Galleria Comunale, Prato). The apothecary made up the medicines; the crushing of the ingredients was done by youths. Some apothecaries' shops were meeting-places for men of letters and artists. The Crusca, a Florentine Academy of letters founded by Anton Francesco Grazzini in 1582, started in the apothecary's shop known as Il Moro (The Moor's) owned by Grazzini in the Straw Market.

fore the same date. Both were used by practising doctors who taught pharmacy at the Studium in Florence. Other works were: the *Lumen Apothecariorum*, by Ciriaco di Tortona, the Duke of Savoy's doctor, printed in 1492; the *Thesaurus aromatariorum* by Paolo Suardo from Bergamo, dedicated to the pharmacists of Milan; the *Compendium aromatariorum* by Doctor Saladino Ferri or Ferro, from Ascoli Satriano in Foggia province, who flourished in the mid-fifteenth century and whose work may be regarded as the first treatise on *materia medica* dedicated to pharmacists.

It was not, therefore, merely a matter of honouring the great Ancients such as Pliny and Dioscorides. The return to the study of nature, a characteristic of humanist culture, and in particular the observation of plant-life, also led to an awareness of the errors of the old classical writers, who until then had been acknowledged as the indisputable authorities. It was no longer received opinion but a painstaking study of the facts, and this spirit of enquiry laid the foundations for all further advances. Nicolo da Lonigo, or Leoniceno, for example,

who was born in 1428 and lived to the ripe old age of 96, and who had devoted himself at first to enthusiastic studies of Pliny, finally rebelled against him, and against Serapio, Avicenna and other classical naturalists. At Ferrara, where he had set up a school, soon to become famous by its own merits, he published a treatise with the significant title of *Plinii et aliorum auctorum, qui de simplicibus medicaminibus scripserunt errores notati* (concerning Pliny and other authors who wrote significant errors concerning medicinal herbs), a work which, by its unbiased judgment and its wide humanist culture, ensured its author's fame perhaps even more than his well-known *Libellus de epidemia, quam vulgo morbum gallicum vocant* (Treatise on the epidemic commonly known as the *morbum gallicum*), published in Venice in 1497, and one of the earliest medical works on syphilis.

Works such as this criticising Pliny implied a new outlook and a new approach, soon to be noticed by the new men of letters in the fifteenth and sixteenth centuries. « The study of botany » wrote Castiglione (1478-1529) in his *History of Medicine*, « is one of the

earliest and most important manifestations of the coming revival of medicine in Italy, not only because of the real progress which it makes possible in *materia medica* and healing, but also because it gives rise to that impassioned study of nature, that habit of observation of natural phenomena, that search for analogy between the life of the vegetable and the animal kingdoms, and that criticism, reverent indeed but sharp and well-founded, of the ancient writers, all of which prepare the way, in all areas of science, for the great Renaissance ».

MEDICINES AND THEIR AUTHORISED USE IN THE FIFTEENTH CENTURY

The most expensive items in an apothecary's laboratory were generally the spices and drugs. Both normally came in powder form. In the National Museum there is a huge marble mortar, over one foot high. It dates from the beginning of the twelfth century and was almost certainly used by an apothecary for grinding pepper. In some cities, Venice for example, the grinding of pepper and other spices was considered such an important operation that those who performed it organised themselves into a profession distinct from that of the apothecary. In Florence, where the traffic in spices was not as important, the pepper-grinder generally worked under the apothecary, and Melozzo made him the sign for a pharmacy. He is shown as a young man, and again working inside the pharmacy, both in the fresco on the walls of the entrance hall in the Castello di Isogne (Valle d'Aosta), which depicts a fifteenth-century pharmacy, and in the fresco in Francesco I de' Medici's study in the Palazzo Vecchio in Florence by Giovanni da Stradano, which dates from 1570 and depicts the alchemist. Pepper-grinding was not light work, as we can see by the taut leg-muscles of Melozzo's sturdy youth, his tense manly face and his outstretched arms holding the heavy pestle. When the work took several hours, some relief was afforded by suspending the pestle by a rope to a kind of flexible bow fixed to the roof, which, as it sprang back, would take up some of the weight.

After the spices came sugar in order of cost, then balsam, saffron, herbs, fruit and so on. In the Middle Ages the apothecaries used fruit more extensively than we might imagine. Who would think, for example,

An albarello, *a pharmacist's ceramic jar (History of Science Museum, Florence).*

that the fig, our homely modest fig, could be used to cure haemorrhoids, warts on the nose and fingers, gout of the hands and feet, and that it could be at one and the same time an emollient, an emetic and a purgative? Yet from the Arabs onwards this was medical doctrine and practice in Italy and throughout Europe.

As for herbs, a Venetian proverb sums up what was then their reputation: « No herb groweth but what hath its value ». A remarkable variety of herbs occur in Florentine prescriptions, the commonest being betony, stellate, agrimony, celandine, wild hemp, honeysuckle, pimpernel, sage, verbena, couch grass and barley. Yes, even barley!

In 1405 the tertiaries of the Third Order of Saint Francis, who ran the S. Paolo Hospital with thirty-five beds for the poor and needy, applied to the Florence city authorities for exemption from the taxes to which their supplies were liable as they came through the city gates, declaring that the average consumption of barley at their hospital was thirty bushels for making barley-water. No herb, however, had such properties as rosemary: some books of prescriptions give it eighteen, others twenty-two, and a Palatine manuscript in the Florence National Library gives it no less than seventy-two.

Some medicaments were recommended as being successfully used by Popes, sovereigns, princes, and other well-known historical or contemporary persons. Others had the approval not only of all the doctors in the world but also, no less, of all the saints, male and female, in Paradise! The *Thesaurus pauperum*, for instance, quotes a « precious ointment, as used by Mary and Mary Magdalene, for all fevers and kidney complaints », another ointment is said to have been used by Mary Magdalene, Mary and Lazarus « whom the Romans took from Jerusalem at the time Jesus Christ was crucified », and to have required no less than twenty-two ingredients and more than fifty days to prepare. The barefaced chicanery of the rogues who did not shrink even from quoting the Holy Scriptures was encouraged by the simple-mindedness of the public who, then as now, apparently believed anything. Some herbs were said to be good for whole categories of illnesses, such as a certain poultice, for example, which contained woman's milk and could « purge any humour, cleanse the gums, provoke happiness, drive away melancholy, heal deafness, cleanse fluid from the ear, and clear any obstruction in the head ». The thistle (*centaurea benedicta*) which produced a milk-like fluid in its roots, was said to cure all ills and was therefore called *chatolicon* « which is of universal interpretation, useful to all stages of man, from childhood to old age, and for all infirmities ». Many other medicines were effective only if certain precautions were observed in their use. This was the case of goat's blood, which was difficult to prepare, as the official Florentine list of prescriptions states, with a wealth of detail, and of theriac, an antidote, especially to snake bites, the preparation of which in Venice was under the direct control of the Republican authorities.

The preparation of medicines, entrusted entirely to the apothecaries, was a complicated affair. Often the apothecary would not trust his supplier of herbs, and first of all had to go out into the fields and woods to collect them. This alone demanded a certain skill. Herbs were supposed to be influenced by the stars, and had to be picked in certain ways and at certain times.

The apothecary therefore had to have at least a nodding acquaintance with astrology. Having successfully completed the first part of his task, he could then shut himself up between the four walls of his laboratory and begin the complicated process of making up his prescriptions.

Medicines ran to ten, twenty, or even thirty ingredients. Some had even more, and one kind of Mithridate is said to have contained forty-seven.

Not only drugs and herbs were used in plenty but also, as recorded in numerous manuscripts and in the official list of prescriptions in Florence, iron and steel were used in pills, and other medicines might contain mercury, burnt hair, cabbage-juice, litharge, pig's lungs, nightingale's eye and heart, cocks', asses' and pigs' fat and entrails, « milk of a woman breast-feeding a girl-child », wax, urine, especially of a young boy and ... but that is enough: « an infinity of devilish ingredients », said Redi, the experimental scientist (1626-1698), « fit to undermine a tower, let alone the intestinal canal ».

Although many fifteenth- and sixteenth-century prescriptions are worthy of attention even today, and others were much ahead of their time, there was nevertheless a great deal of superstition in the pharmaceutics of those days. In glaring contrast to the scientific principles of the School of Salerno, belief in magic and astrology was such in the fifteenth century that it was commonly held that « to drive away a fever, let it be sufficient to say a few prayers, make the sign of the cross and articulate strange and incomprehensible words ». « To cure epilepsy carry the names of the Three Wise Men in writing », says the *Thesaurus pauperum*, « id est Gaspar, Balthazar, Melchior ». Other popular superstitions were that the bite of a serpent could be cured by an incantation; the whistling of a basilisk could cause a man to fall down dead, and the blood of an irascible red-headed man, a leper and a woman was poisonous. « Ancus Bernardus », declares the same *Thesaurus*, « says in a *Summa* that if a man touches an aching tooth with the tooth of a dead man, he will be cured without fail ». It continues: « Take care that there are no pears in the house when a woman is in childbirth, as they bring misfortune ».

The *Thesaurus* gives equally empirical remedies, whose efficiency was due less to their therapeutic value than to qualities we can only call occult: a wolf's foot tied round the neck would cure colic, the web of a white-backed spider applied to the temples in a poultice would cure the fever, a wood-lark « placed in front of the patient so as to be able to look him in the face, would cure him of all manner of ills ».

So, as the world has never been short of quacks and charlatans on the one hand or simpletons and fools on the other, here are all the remedies: how to know if a woman will give birth to a boy or a girl, how to make up sleeping-draughts and anaesthetics, including the popular magic candles which, when burnt, induced love and drowsiness, how to be always alert, how to find something stolen, how to see a star by day, how to bring a roast chicken back to life ...; here are the « secrets » for making « ice of antimony or sublimate for the tinting of emeralds and rubies », « extracting oil from a bar of gold », softening steel, making a mixture that will look like silver, discovering the philosopher's stone. Here is magic, the cabalistic, astrology, the negation of the alchemist's real researches, which were making the study of pharmacy truly experimental; here are incantations, wizards, the superstitions of good-for-nothing idlers, the songs of birds, good and bad encounters, the ridiculous remedies described so aptly by San Bernardino da Siena in one of his sermons in Florence in 1424; finally here is the recipe for a certain « most excellent water », of « such virtue that it maketh the old young and the dead living » so that he who drinks it for some time « if he be seventy years old shall seem but forty ».

Among the many remedies current in the Middle Ages were pearls and precious stones. They were taken ground, crushed or treated with certain chemical reagents, in food, syrups of honey and roses, milk or warm water. The *Ricettario Fiorentino* of 1498, the oldest official list of prescriptions known in Europe, puts them with the substances which an apothecary should have in his shop. These lists of permitted prescriptions and remedies, as well as treatises on medicines and precious stones, which appeared in the fourteenth and fifteenth centuries, are full of the wonderful properties of pearls and precious stones, and were believed not only by the ordinary people but by famous doctors such as Dino del Garbo. It was not always necessary to take them internally. Often it was sufficient to carry them about in one's pocket, round the neck, in the mouth or even simply to look at them. Not only did they cure and preserve from ills, but they assisted in the affairs of civic life, preserved one from the danger of death, the evil eye, ghosts, bad dreams, thunder-bolts, misfortunes and bankruptcy. What more could one wish? Finally they freed the body and soul from what for centuries was the unknown evil: the devil.

THE « RICETTARIO FIORENTINO » OF 1498

The officials of the guild of doctors and apothecaries in Florence, « to prevent inconvenience and danger to sick persons and to protect the reputation of doctors from abuse arising from the existing freedom to make up new medicines and to vary the doses of those already allowed », took the initiative of drawing up an official list of prescriptions which apothecaries would be bound by law to respect. This was the origin of the *Ricettario Fiorentino* of 1498.

This manual, which all doctors and apothecaries had to possess, is divided into three books. The first contains general information on the position of pharmacy in the scientific world, a bibliography and lists of the herbs, flowers, tree-bark, simples, stones and other substances which it uses. The second book deals with antidotes proper in eighteen sections: electuaries, soothing medicines and laxatives, medicines in the form of candy, syrups, julep, pills, collyrium, ointments, poultices, oils, cordials, etc. In addition to the remedies specifically listed, many others were allowed « according to the wishes of the doctor, to be made up at his discretion according to the needs of the patient ». These the *Ricettario* declined to list officially, as « the variety of doctors and their fantasies was so great », and also because « some ignorant and presumptuous apothecary might take upon himself the making up of medicines without the expert advice of one doctor, and this would give rise to unending scandals ». The keen apothecary was then invited to read the third book of the *Ricettario ufficiale*, wherein he would find the fullest information concerning the preparation, washing and correct dosage of spices to be used in medicines, and the solution to some problems of practical pharmaceutics.

When we examine the terminology used in the *Ricettario ufficiale* and in the numerous collections of prescriptions found in manuscripts of *materia medica* and pharmacology in the fourteenth and fifteenth centuries, as preserved in the three principal libraries in Florence, we find a preponderance of terms from the classical authorities. Authors consulted by the compilers of the *Ricettario* of 1498 were Messue, the two Niccolòs (from Salerno and Alexandria), who in their turn had drawn on the greatest masters of medical science, the works of Galen, the *Liber medicinalis Almansoris* of Rhazes, the *Canon* of Avicenna, and authors such as Dioscorides and Serapio. There was also a marked influence of Arabian medicine, shown in the quality of the ingredients, their names, often deformed, and the way in which certain electuaries and poultices were to be made up.

This is not to say that contemporary authorities did not contribute. The famous Florentine doctor Dino del Garbo himself made several contributions to the *Ricettario ufficiale*; Maestro Frosino contributed an ointment for « those suffering from madness », and other prescriptions were supplied by a Florentine, Maestro Domenico. Bernardo Trane, an apothecary at the Santa Croce in Florence, contributed an « elixir vitae » and an oil « for pains ». Among the laxatives listed in the *Ricettario Fiorentino* are the *dyasena fresca* of Tommaso del Garbo, widely used in Florence, the *dyapolipodio* of Ludovico da Prato, the *dyasena* used in the Santa Maria Nuova Hospital in Florence, two electuaries by Gentile di Foligno, an « ointment for the bones », and « imperial pills » made of aloes and spices by the « doctor of medicine » Cristoforo di Giorgio, whose name occurs among those who drew up the statutes for the doctors' and apothecaries' guild in 1391 and 1424, and who was one of the officers of the guild in 1406. Other medicines included pills by Dino del Garbo, Maestro Antonio di Scarperia, Niccolò Falcucci, Pietro d'Albano, Giovanni da Lucca, Guglielmo da Piacenza. There were prescriptions also from women doctors, such as those contributed by a certain Caterina, a « woman home doctor », which stood the test of time so well that they were reprinted in part in 1515 for use in the pharmacy at Santa Maria Nuova; others were taken from prescriptions by a « lady doctor Jacopa » who « worked with poultices in the year of great mortality 1374 » to « bring sicknesses to a head ».

The *Ricettario Fiorentino* was repeatedly reissued and brought up to date. Successive editions incorporated the most recent medical discoveries, and appeared in 1550, 1567, 1574, 1597, 1670, 1696 and finally in 1789, on the threshold of modern pharmacy. These show the gradual development of pharmaceutical practice in Florence, as it gradually freed itself from the errors and dross of Arabic doctrines, until by the mid-sixteenth century

The apothecary's shop kept common drugs and medicinal ingredients in albarelli *such as these; they could be of white wood or porcelain.*

we see, with a sigh of relief, that it has begun to abandon the revolting practice of concoctions made from excrement and to draw upon the culture and experience of the best Italian and foreign doctors. The many editions of the *Ricettario Fiorentino* bear witness to its high reputation and show that it was taken as a model by other nations. One of the best botanists of the sixteenth century, Clusius, wished to have it translated into

Latin, so that it might be more easily available to other countries beyond the Alps. The *Ricettario* must have proved very useful and beneficial, since a Franciscan friar, Filippo da Firenze, who was also a notary from the Pian di Ripoli, wished to add his own contribution and make it more accessible to a wider range of the population. In 1572, therefore, he published, in the vernacular, a « compendium of knowledge » dedicated to Cosimo I, in which he explained the herbs and drugs most commonly used in medicine, and many other terms not usually found in popular books.

In conclusion it seems that many scientific habits of thought, including the dogmatic and scholastic associated with the Middle Ages, were still current at the end of the fifteenth century. The great flowering of critical thought in the Renaissance brought a spirit of enquiry into the arts of healing, which was decisive for future ages and for human relations. In the wake of the Renaissance came new concepts and values. The Christian concept that sickness was an evil and a punishment to be expiated gave way to the hedonistic concept that life was good and to be enjoyed, and that any illness was the result of a disharmony within the body, which nature herself should cure. The principle that death was a release from the burden of the body and the beginning of a new, more exalted life, gave way to the idea that life was worth living and enjoying for itself.

Magic and astrology continued, but their destiny clearly lay away from that of medicine. The theory and practice of healing advanced together, the training of the apothecary became more intense and his culture broadened; his work became less manual and more intellectual, a decisive step towards modern pharmacy.

« The Alchemist » (G. Stradano). Alchemy was a more serious science than is commonly supposed. Although it had its magical and occult practices, it was in many ways a forerunner of modern science.

RELIGIOUS LIFE

Fifteenth-century Florence was not only a city of merchants, bankers, humanists and artists: it was also a lively centre of the religious life of the time, a city which participated to the full in the spiritual struggles of the age. Together with the workshops of its expanding industry, the city saw the rise of the Oratories of the Compagnie, *where men of all types and classes joined together in a common act of worship, and where organised charity often brought their labours into contact with civic and political life. But above all Florence was the worthy meeting place of that Council which seemed at last to be opening a way to the spiritual unity of* Christianitas, *and the city where divines and scholars put forward the concept of brotherly concord in Christ. The saintly bishop Antonino, the platonist Marsilio Ficino, the learned scholar Giovanni Pico and the apothecary-philosopher Matteo Palmieri are the men who, with their diverse cultural and theological training, gave the clearest expression to this religious tradition. Then, at the close of the century, whilst the very civilisation of the humanists seemed to be crumbling, the dramatic sermons of Savonarola, the monk of Ferrara, warned of the coming of an age of privation and suffering, an age of penitence and reform. This « disarmed prophet » was to pay with his life at the stake in the Piazza della Signoria for this ideal of a purified Christianity, and the ardent piety of his followers, the* Piagnoni *(the « wailers »), was to bring hope to Christians for centuries to come.*

In the early years of the fifteenth century the moral atmosphere of Tuscany and Florence was reflected in the phenomenon of the pilgrimage of the Flagellants. Long processions of penitents dressed in rags passed through the Tuscan countryside chanting the ancient words of the *Miserere*. Men and women, clerics and laymen, all clad in rough monastic-style clothes, proceeded in long white files, two by two, as is the custom in processions, with unbelievable ardour and devotion, calling for peace and compassion, intoning praises and hymns in Latin and the vernacular, and in particular that chant said to have been composed by Gregory: *Stabat mater dolorosa*. With these words, translated from his racy popular Latin, Saint Antonino, the future Bishop of Florence, ends his account of the « Bianchi », or white-cloaked Flagellants who moved in procession through Florence and the surrounding countryside. They created an unforgettable impression, with their crowds of attendant faithful, on the religious conscience of the citizens.

The land of Tuscany, and particularly the city of Florence, had been for a long time inured to spiritual disquiet. It did not seen very long since the so-called « War of the Eight Saints », against the Avignon popes who were trying to extend their dominion over Perugia (1375-8), and the revolt of the Ciompi (1378), which brought about a form of democracy, albeit transitory, to Florence. There were now stirrings in the heart of the city, indicating a widespread need for political reform, and this carried with it a questioning of contemporary religious institutions.

The religious life of the city found its expression particularly in the public celebrations of feast days, and these were intimately connected with the daily lives of the citizens, from the craftsmen and their guilds, each with its patron saint, to the great congregations of all manner of men which celebrated the festival of John

Members of the Confraternita dei Buonomini offering assistance to victims of political persecution and visiting prisoners in jail.

the Baptist, the patron Saint of the city, when all Florence ceased work and dedicated itself with loving fervour to its protector. On the few days on either side of June 24th, the processions which wound their way through the streets of the city brought every kind of imaginative and inventive display to bear on the theme of Saint John: prayers and singing, games and tableaux, and especially miracle plays in which the « mystery » of Jesus, the Madonna, their Patron and other Saints, was played out before a crowd which became both spectator and participant as the drama was acted before it in the streets. One writer of these mystery

plays, with their immediate popular appeal, was Feo Belcari. The emotion aroused by this spiritual experience even reached Lorenzo the Magnificent who, amongst his manifold literary activities, wrote some very fine religious plays.

The festival of Saint John the Baptist leads us to the religious centre of the city, to the Cathedral church of Santa Maria del Fiore, brought to completion in these years when it was crowned by the wonderful dome of Messer Brunelleschi. The inauguration took place on March 25th 1436 with an immense festival of the city and all its people. The music at the ceremony

The Confraternita supported the liberal elements in the city and chose its members particularly from opponents of the Medici (from frescoes in San Martino ai Buonomini by an unknown pupil of Ghirlandaio).

was directed by Guillaume du Fay, who came from France for the occasion, and those present were able to hear the motet for four voices *Nuper rosarum flores*, traditionally a hymn to the Madonna, but popularly considered a musical tribute to the city, Fiorenza, to its unquestionable greatness and its inimitable charm.

THE BROTHERHOODS AND CHARITABLE ASSOCIATIONS

The Cathedral was the centre of a religious life which spread to every corner of the city every day

of the year. It is impossible to give even an approximate idea of the devotional fervour of the times. One aspect of it was the phenomenon of the *Confraternite*, or the many charitable associations which sprang up, born of a desire to put religion to practical effect, inspired by the figure of some Saint and linked with the name of some particular church. These formed a close bond between citizens of all walks of life.

In fifteenth-century Florence the *Confraternite* were very numerous, and some had ancient traditions. Back in the days of Dante, two at least were very well known: the *Compagnia dei Laudesi* and the *Compagnia del Ceppo*,

A group of cardinals at the Ecumenical Council of 1439 meeting in the Cathedral for a service of propitiation (from an illuminated manuscript in the Laurentian Library).

to mention the first that come to mind. They performed their charitable labours, the one assisting the poor whilst also propagating the liturgical chant and hymns of praise (*laudi*) in the vernacular, the other collecting alms for the poor in a large tree-trunk (*ceppo*), the first example of a collection-box for the needy. Many monasteries, convents and oratories continued their assistance in gifts and healing. Pilgrims, invalids and beggars went to the Institutions of San Procolo, San Remigio, San Pancrazio and San Gallo, and the great hospital of San Paolo run by the Franciscan Third Order. Nor should we forget the *Compagnia del Bigallo*, also devoted to helping the poor, and the *Confraternita della Misericordia*, which provided for the sick poor to be looked after in hospitals.

Other associations were new. The Prior of San Marco, Antonino Pierozzi, founded the so-called « *Buonomini di San Martino* », whose real title was « Protectors of the bereft poor ». The title eloquently indicated the aims of the new association. Many citizens had fallen on evil days for political reasons following the return to Florence of Cosimo de' Medici. Some had been sent into exile, their goods and property had been confiscated and their families reduced to a precarious state, all the more distressing because they were usually people totally unaccustomed to accepting charity. The association was founded in 1442, eight years after Cosimo's return to Florence, to offer such people material and moral assistance. Chosen deliberately from the movement opposing Cosimo, and all of them supporters of the liberal cause, the members of the association wished to make, within their religious activities, a definite political stand.

Another Fraternity, whose work was more striking and imaginative, was the *Compagnia di Santa Maria della Croce al Tempio*, founded in the fourteenth century, but developing only in the early years of the fifteenth, when it began to be known as the *Compagnia dei Neri* (*Blacks*), from the colour of the gown and hood worn by its members. The association was formed to assist those condemned to death, from the moment the sentence was announced to the execution. Food, drink, comforts in word and deed, and the assistance of religious rites were provided. When the condemned person was led from the gloomy Carcere delle Stinche to the Porta alla Giustizia outside the walls, where the execu-

Part of the bull « Laetentur Coeli », preserved in the State Record Office in Florence, by which the Council of 1439 proclaimed the reunion of the Latin and Greek churches. The text, drawn up in both languages, was solemnly read in Florence Cathedral on June 6th by Cardinal Cesarini for the Latin church and by Bessarione for the Greek. The formula for union had been drawn up by a mixed commission of twelve prelates. After the Greeks had left, the Council continued to work for union with the Armenian and Coptic churches. The union with the Greek church lasted until 1472.

The patriarch Joseph, representative of the Eastern Church (from the « Procession of the Magi » by Gozzoli).

tion took place, along the Via de' Malcontenti, as it was popularly named (aptly describing the usual road taken by the prisoners and their guards) the « Neri » walked in front, praying to God for pardon for those about to die and calling on all sinners to repent. When the execution was over, the Fraternity took charge of the mortal remains. The activities of this association show how extensive was the network of private charity in Renaissance Florence.

THE COUNCIL OF 1439

The good deeds of the Fraternities and the charitable associations were part of the ordinary routine of religious life in fifteenth-century Florence. There were also exceptional events, such as the Ecumenical Council of 1439, which left a deep impression on the spiritual life of the city.

The dome of Santa Maria del Fiore, as it appears today. The cathedral was inaugurated, with its dome completed, on March 25th 1436.

Florence then became the focal point of national and international unrest in matters of religion, which dated from the schism between Eastern and Western Christianity and the dualism of the Avignon and Roman Popes, and which had its repercussions even at a popular level throughout Europe. Florence had entered the struggle with the reforming zeal of the Dominican order led by the Blessed Giovanni Dominici, and in 1418 had welcomed the end of the schism by acclaiming as the legitimate Pope Martin V, in honour of whom the City authorities built the Santa Maria Novella hall, and adopted the deposed John XXII as Cardinal of Florence. The Cardinal lived in retirement in the city, and was given dignified burial in the Baptistery, where a magnificent monument was made for him by Michelozzo and Donatello.

Now, twenty years later, the City and its ruler Cosimo received the new Pope, Eugenius IV, the Byzantine Emperor Johannis Palaeologus and a multitude of Roman and Greek prelates. Over the Council hung the shadows not only of the internal disputes over the government of the Catholic Church, but also of the threat of an Ottoman conquest, now a very real and imminent danger.

The Council met in the great hall of Santa Maria Novella, and immediately began discussions of the dogmas of Christian belief. After long debate and much hard bargaining the differences between Latin and

The interior, solemn and serene, of Santa Maria del Fiore.

Greek were smoothed over in the cause of unity and the need to present a single front in the face of political threats.

A solemn ceremony in the Cathedral sealed the reunion of the two Churches, and the city authorities had a stone set into the wall of the sacristy to commemorate the event.

Today we regard the bull by which the Council ratified the reunion of the Latin and Byzantine Churches as of mere documentary interest only, yet between the formal lines we can read, in addition to the historical significance of the act, its meaning to the city of Florence, which was profoundly influenced by the Council. The ancient, archaic world of the city was thrown open to strangers speaking different tongues, and professing beliefs at once heterogeneous and sincerely Christian. The fabled wisdom of the Greeks assumed a recognisable form, and the intellectual stimulus it generated had far-reaching effects on the growth of the Renaissance.

THE CHURCHES OF FLORENCE

The fact that the Council was held in Santa Maria Novella conferred on this great Dominican church immense renown and prestige. We must not, however, forget the other church with an illustrious past, the

Franciscan Santa Croce. It was not by chance that these two churches belonged to the Mendicant Orders, which at this time still had men of fervour and vision. In addition to being a famed centre for preaching and acts of charity, the church of Santa Croce was well known for theological studies, although these fell somewhat into disrepute at the end of the thirteenth and the beginning of the fourteenth centuries.

Yet there were many Florentine churches which were distinguished for their industry and the high quality of their work and were noteworthy centres of Christian enlightenment.

In addition to churches of ancient foundation, such as the Badia, which founded charitable institutions like the Ospedale di San Niccolò, or the churches run by monks of the orders reformed after the year 1000, such as the Santa Trinita, run by the Vallombrosani, and the Santa Maria degli Angioli by the Camaldolesi, both devoted to hospital work and poor and sick relief, there were other illustrious churches: San Lorenzo, Santo Spirito, the Carmine and the Cafaggio church of the Servants of Mary.

San Lorenzo and Santa Maria del Carmine were being rebuilt in the fifteenth century, and their transformation from small parish churches to huge basilicas gives some idea of their importance. Santo Spirito, run by the Augustinian Friars, also had an active life in the fifteenth century, if only because it witnessed the first stirrings of the humanist movement. The church of the Servants of Mary, the Annunziata, was perhaps the most genuinely Florentine foundation. This order established itself on Monte Senario in a spirit of penitence, and built in the city a church which became a centre of devotion to the Madonna and of inexhaustible activity.

We cannot leave out the last great arrival in the company of the great: San Marco, the church which incarnated the spirit of the Dominican reform, the renovator and inspirer of the religious life, not only of the order of the Preachers, but of the entire city of Florence.

The Prior of San Marco monastery was Antonino Pierozzi, who aroused from that institution and from the pulpit of the church an enthusiasm for acts of charity (we have mentioned the Fraternity of the Buonomini di San Martino) which augured well for the great pastoral work he was to perform in the following years.

SANT'ANTONINO, BISHOP OF FLORENCE

In the early days of 1446, after some months of a vacant see, Florence had its new bishop: Antonino Pierozzi, Prior of San Marco. His choice by Pope Eugenius IV, urged by several parties and particularly by the governing council of the city, was, however, quite unforeseen, but nonetheless pleasing to the citizenry: « a Brother well deserving of the poor, most learned in government and fearing God », says Vasari in his life of Sant'Antonino.

The interior of San Lorenzo (Brunelleschi).

Manuscripts belonging to Sant'Antonino, now preserved in the San Marco monastery. The bishop fought in his sermons and writings for the defence of republican liberties against the power of the oligarchy.

Florence had already experienced the new bishop's charity, humility and piety, but as yet could not know of his power to govern. What a wise ruler and teacher he turned out to be! His resistance to his nomination, not out of false modesty, but from a genuine reluctance to accept high office, showed his true Christian spirit, further exemplified by his resolve to accept the Pope's decision and undertake the high responsibilities of the spiritual leadership of this difficult city which he knew so well.

Sant'Antonino's Florence was a city of unrest and uncertainty, at the mercy of passions and opposing factions, but he was truly its Bishop, its guardian and keeper and the protector of the faithful in the period of great difficulty which preceded the change under Cosimo de' Medici from a republic to a principate.

The defence of the clergy, the guardianship of the rights of the Florentine church not to submit to taxation by the civil authority, the administrative capabilities of the Bishop, all these were but the external aspect of a pastoral activity which continued unabated for nearly twenty years, firmly, resolutely and inspired. Sant'Antonino was a true « pastor » in that the care of his diocese meant for him watching assiduously over the souls of his flock, and understanding that these souls were very close to the earth, exposed to the dangers of daily life and its ever-changing pattern of good and evil. The Bishop followed assiduously the daily life of the city, observing and interpreting at all levels its uncertainties, its mistakes and its difficulties, drawing from this work information and inspiration for his great *Somma morale*, his masterpiece and a work of great psychological penetration, which touched men's minds and hearts.

It is particularly in Antonino's activities in the events of 1458, the year of the accession of Pius II, when Antonino intervened against the Medici, which profoundly affected Florentine political life, that we see the Bishop's true Christian spirit. He stood uncompromisingly for individual liberty in the difficult field of local controversy. For some years now the increasing power of the oligarchy had made a mockery of elections to public office by controlling or manipulating the votes under a formal, but quite ineffective, guarantee of liberty. The Bishop denounced this malpractice in his sermons and pastoral letters, and called for a return to the traditional system by which voting was secret, the powers of the city authorities were firmly controlled, and a man's word his bond. It was a clear call to keep faith with the statutes, and a bold interference in the world of politics.

On the morning of July 26th 1458, when the faithful citizenry of Florence read, affixed to the door of the Cathedral and other churches, a letter from their Bishop denouncing the elections as fraudulent, calling those responsible perjurers and threatening them with excommunication, the public reacted enthusiastically to his intervention, regarding it as an act in support of their liberty, rather than an unwarranted intrusion.

TWO RELIGIONS: THE LEARNED AND THE POPULAR

Fundamentally, the pastoral work of Sant'Antonino tended towards the « edification » of the city, to indicating the main lines of a Christian conduct such as the ordinary people might understand and follow. In different ways, though not entirely divorced from this, another great religious influence was beginning to make itself felt in this period. It was centred on a rarefied culture and restricted to an élite, the Florentine Platonic Academy, which, out of philosophical speculation, built an ideal of a highly inspired religious life.

In effect there was a very wide range of religious interests in Florence, from the aristocratic to the popular. The religious experience which the masses found in pulpit sermons could never be the same as that sought in the refined meditation of the Academy. There were two distinct traditions: that of the Holy Word preached from the pulpits of Florentine churches and turned into a scourge by Savonarola, and that of the Platonic Academy, of which Marsilio Ficino and Pico della Mirandola were, between 1470 and 1490, the most celebrated members. Whilst the word of the preachers came to the people insisting on the perfection of the Christian life and on fidelity to the evangelical spirit, the learned members of the Academy attempted to evaluate the Christian message in the light of Platonic idealism. This was what Marsilio Ficino called the *docta religio*, that is the life of the spirit, exalted as the final and perfect moment in the development of the human person, recognised as divinely created and the centre of the universe, in which the dignity of man is the touchstone of the creative work of God.

The *docta religio* thus brought the intellect to the threshold of faith, and showed to the intellect its supreme function. Popular religion, on the other hand, nurtured by the sermon, regarded faith as attainable only by the traditionally biblical mortification of man's earthly attributes and by spiritual exercises.

Two different and apparently incompatible points of view. Yet Renaissance Florence found room for both, and the phenomenon of its religious life cannot rightly be understood if they are not seen as two threads of the same story. In painting and sculpture, (essentially religious arts), from Masaccio to Botticelli, it is evident that these two types of religious belief could coexist; together with the search for an intellectual basis to faith, there is the emotional approach, pressing, fundamental and undeniable. The Florentines saw and venerated works such as Masaccio's *Trinità* in Santa Maria Novella, a severely controlled and almost impenetrable picture, or the fresco of the *Tributo* in the Cappella Brancacci del Carmine, with its clear plasticity and mysterious charm in the presentation of the miracle,

Detail of Girolamo Savonarola's cell in the San Marco Monastery, Florence.

The consuming fires which riveted the gaze of all onlookers, cleric and lay, rich and poor, lord and commoner, formed the lurid, terrifying background against which the drama of Savonarola was played out. His story was typical of the religious life of Renaissance Florence, a story of passionate sincerity and public-spiritedness which reached out beyond the confines of his century and the boundaries of his city.

The central character of the story, Girolamo Savonarola, a Dominican friar, was born in Ferrara in 1452 and became a Florentine by a kind of forced choice. The worldly city, so closely involved in business and the acquisition of wealth, devoted to material gain and the pursuit of pleasure, seemed to the Friar well set on the slippery path to idolatry, and this inspired his famous sermons of bitter, provocative admonition.

His first stay in Florence, from 1482 to 1483, was a disappointment to him, and he withdrew to prepare himself further by prayer, study and meditation. He returned in 1489, and shortly afterwards was elected Prior of the San Marco monastery. From here, where the words of Sant'Antonino were still remembered, he took up again his preaching, which culminated in the famous Lent sermons in the Cathedral.

His words were like the lash of a whip, his argument was ruthless, implacable: « your wickedness, o Italy, o Rome, o Florence, your impiety, your fornication, your usury, your cruelty, have brought these tribulations upon you ... You deceive yourself, o Italy, o Florence, if you turn away from these words of mine; nought but penitence can avail you ... ».

This was not only a violent denunciation of corruption, a declaration of hatred of sin, and a demand for penitence and a return to the scriptures. It was the « reform » of Christian living, radical and unconditional, which the Friar's threats demanded, implying a revolution in civic as well as religious life. It is easy to see how incompatible this attitude appeared to the ethos of the Medici who, however, were not insensitive to religious stirrings. The complex personality of Lorenzo the Magnificent created, as well as songs for carnival time, passionate religious lyrics.

Tradition required that this stark message should be taken out into the streets of Florence, and particularly along the Via Larga which linked the Medici palace to the San Marco monastery. Savonarola's followers, the

or the almost contemporary frescoes of Ghirlandaio in Santa Maria Novella, which tell a story at once courtly and popular. We are now close to the religious climate in which Matteo Palmieri portrayed, in a poem still largely unknown today, the legend of the « neutral » angels, attempting an interpretation of the roots of the human race as lying between God and Satan. Another of his poems, the *Città di vita*, on the dangerous theme of universal redemption, was publicly burned in 1475 after its author had been posthumously excommunicated.

Above: corridor leading to monks' cells in the San Marco Monastery. Profile of Savonarola (Fra' Bartolommeo c. 1474-1517?). Below: Savonarola's cell with relics. Note the large rosary and the hair shirt.

« Piagnoni » made the streets ring with their cry of « penitence », as they marched behind a standard bearing the words *Nos praedicamus Cristum crucifixum* (we preach Christ crucified). Hatred of sin thus became « the burning of vanities », and from the ashes there was to arise the new religious and political order of the city, its reformed government.

After the death of Lorenzo the Magnificent (1492) and the banishment of Piero de' Medici (1494), it began to look as though Savonarola would indeed realise his dream of a new republican government based on Christian ideals. Tension in the city rose with the now open conflict between the Piagnoni and their opponents, the followers of the Medici, called the « Palleschi », from the six *palle* (balls) on the Medici coat of arms. There was also increasing reaction from the pontifical authorities in the person of Alexander VI, the Borgia Pope, who felt himself directly involved in Savonarola's polemics against the church, or rather against the Roman Curia.

With the banishment of the Medicis, Florence was about to enter on one of the most exciting chapters of her history, and her new-found liberty was held to be due in some measure to Savonarola, who now urged the city on to greater efforts and played his boldest card. In a message preached from the pulpit of San Marco he demanded the translation into legal terms of the newly-won liberties and virtually dictated a constitution.

In the critical period 1494 to 1498, Savonarola, aided by his followers, strove for the realisation of that republic which had been taking shape in his mind over the years: an organised, democratic community, with a two-tier government empowered to control the city's affairs, and a reformed administration and penal code, the whole based on the firm rock of a secure Christian faith: « And I announce this good news to the City ... glorious in the eyes of God and of men shalt thou be, o Florence, reformation of all Italy ».

Savonarola's « reformation » was too strong for some people, and it aroused furious reactions from the Medici faction, growing daily more enraged, from the high clergy, who were cut to the quick by the sharp language of the sermons, and by Pope Alexander VI, who, in good or bad faith, saw in Savonarola's doctrines a direct contradiction to the political line of the Roman Curia. The opposition took decisive and united action, not stopping short of treachery. Accusations of incit-

May 23rd 1498. The voice which had denounced, threatened and condemned was choked into silence by the noose of the « secular arm ». The bodies of Girolamo Savonarola and his companions were then burnt at the stake. The Roman Curia and the Medici faction had closed their ranks: against the hopes of those who followed the call of the Friar stood the halberdiers of the City Council.

146

ing the populace to rebel, of heresy, of excommunication, of provoking the «judgement of God», followed each other and progressively hastened the friar's downfall until finally, on the tragic night of April 8th 1498, the San Marco monastery was broken into and Savonarola was taken prisoner and thrown into jail.

His period of imprisonment was short; no time was lost in drawing up the case against him and sending him for trial. He was found guilty of rebellion and heresy by the Ecclesiastical Court, and handed over to the secular arm. This amounted to a condemnation to death. On May 23rd 1498 Savonarola, with two of his most faithful companions, mounted the scaffold in the Piazza della Signoria, in full view of the public which had once looked on him as their liberator. He was hanged and his body burned. The adventure was over, and another chapter in the history of Florence was ended.

THE RELIGIOUS SPIRIT AT THE TURN OF THE CENTURY

Popular tradition has it that when Savonarola was about to be hanged and the bonfire was being lit, a defiant voice in the crowd called out blasphemously, « Prophet, the hour has now come to perform a miracle! ». The miracle did not come then, but it might well be asked if it is not after all to be found in the obstinate survival of Savonarola's ideal of liberty, which was implanted in the people of Florence and which, in spite of great difficulties, is still alive today.

After Savonarola's death the city faced new unrest and new problems. In the confusion and despondency which followed the disappearance of their leader, the « Piagnoni » found it difficult to carry on his work. Once the prestige of the great Dominican's presence and the power of his voice was lost to them, it seemed that his disciples disbanded, and public opinion, which had supported his republican ideals, turned to other

personalities and to other methods of solving the problems of the day.

This uncertainty lasted for some time, during the whole period, in fact, when the State of Florence was struggling against many external enemies and with an unsettled government at home, as the Medicis were alternately banished and restored several times.

It was during these years, from the end of the fifteenth century to about 1525, that Florence saw the growth of other attitudes towards religion. We should not attach too much importance to the clerical enemies of Savonarola, whose preaching had a mystic and prophetic vein of doubtful quality. Amongst these men were Pietro Delfino, a superior-general of the Camaldolensian Order, the hermit Agnolo Vallombrosano, who « wrote and prophesied many foolish things » and inveighed against Savonarola, calling him « Sathana perfidissimo under the cloak of a lamb and a false religion », the Franciscan Domenico da Ponzo, the creature of Ludovico il Moro, Duke of Milan, and an

Huge whitewashed refectories, long rough deal tables: meal-time for the friars, a simple scene repeated every day in every monastery.

accomplice of the pro-Medici fanatics, who brought about Savonarola's downfall, and finally the Augustinian Fra' Mariano da Gennazzano who, in front of Pope Alexander VI, demanded that the « monster » Savonarola be cut out of the Church of God.

Such opposition to Savonarola as this had no truly religious foundation. The more sincere believers took their stand on different spiritual and cultural premises, and strove to uphold the sacred theme of liberty, threatened by the attempted, and later successful, return of the Medici. The Piagnone movement, under the austere Girolamo Benivieni, eventually came to an understanding with the Medici when the latter returned to Florence in 1512.

There is a fine account by Luca della Robbia of the sudden deaths of Pietro Pagolo Boscoli and Agostino Capponi, who played a leading part in the anti-Medici conspiracy of 1513, in which they were moved by the classical example of Brutus, the beloved slayer of a tyrant. Boscoli went to the scaffold proclaiming his republican faith after a night of prayer and meditation.

The conspirators of February 1513 were moved by pagan rather than Christian example, and we find the same thing in 1514 in the groups which met in the Rucellai Gardens, the famous « Orti Oricellari », for culture and meditation. Machiavelli was occasionally to be found among them, and other members included Cosimo Rucellai, Zanobi Buondelmonti, Luigi Alamanni, Alessandro de' Pazzi, Francesco Cattani and Iacopo da Diacceto. Inspired by the renewal of interest in Plato, they were searching for a secular, virtually lay religion, which could also serve political ends in the design for a new constitution for the Republic. The Group began to decline about 1525, after the deaths of Buondelmonti, Diacceto and Machiavelli, just about the time when the Piagnone tradition was reviving.

THE « PIAGNONE » TRADITION

In the period 1525 to 1530, when the political tension, both nationally and internationally, was rising (these were the years of the Franco-Spanish struggle for hegemony in Europe and Italy), there was a marked sharpening of the civic and religious conscience of Florence, and a renewed interest in the republican liberties proclaimed thirty years earlier by Savonarola. There was a revival of the Piagnone movement towards the end of 1525, after many years of stagnation in the backwaters of public life. Again the initiative came from San Marco in the form of sermons by Fra' Bene-

detto da Foiano, which seemed to echo the biting attacks of Savonarola. The movement gathered momentum after the sack of Rome in 1527 by Imperialist Lutherans supporting Charles V of Spain. This clearly showed the need for decisive action. In 1529, after the fall of Niccolò Capponi, the new governing council of the city was headed by Francesco Carducci, and included Piagnoni of the old guard: Lutozzo Nasi, Gerolamo Cambi, Francesco Guardi, Agnolo Doni, Giovanni Gucci, Giovanni del Nero, Simone Ginori and Giovanbattista Bonsi.

It is interesting to see how the Piagnone movement tended to exclude or eliminate other republican groups such as that of the Orti Oricellari. These two were, in fact, entirely different in spirit and opposite in their religious outlook. The Oricellarian was realistic, aiming to reform the Republic in the classical manner and in strictly political terms, and calling Savonarola the

« false prophet » and the « disarmed prophet ». The Piagnonian thought that the State could only be reformed through a reformed religion.

The siege of 1530 by Imperialist forces under Philibert of Orange to reinstate the Medici and the last desperate struggle against tyranny brought some reconciliation to internal factions, and raised again the vital question of republican liberty, which had recently received its religious sanction in the proclamation by the Florentines of Jesus Christ the King. On the day of February 9th 1527, Septuagesima Sunday, on the proposal of the Gonfalonier (chief magistrate) Niccolò Capponi, the Greater Council of the Republic voted by an enormous majority (1084 out of 1102) the proclamation of « The Lord God, our greatest King and Governor of this City » and of « His Immaculate Virgin Mother Mary as Queen », and recorded its decision to « inscribe in letters of gold their holy names on the door of the city hall in perpetual memory of this act ».

This consecration of the city and its liberty, and the terrible trials which followed it, the siege of 1530 and the glorious end of the Republic, set the seal on a century of religious life in Florence, and mark the end of its part in the history of the times.

SCHOOLS AND EDUCATION

Education in Florence in the fifteenth century, for those citizens who were able to go to school, was substantially modern for the times. Teaching had freed itself from rigid tradition and found a new set of values in the rediscovery of the classics and the new concepts of the dignity of man. This spirit of reform was evident in all types of school, from the so-called scuole basse, *corresponding to the kindergartens and elementary schools of today, to the* Studium, *or university faculty. The young people of Renaissance Florence were being led, for the first time since the Middle Ages, into a new world. From the first steps in reading to the study of the philosophical systems of the great classical thinkers, education and teaching were humanistic, that is they were not conceived as a study of dead languages or a training in logic and grammar, but as moral training by example from human experience and character-building through a consciousness of historical perspective. The new society arising from the merchants, the scholars, the bankers, the craftsmen and the artists consisted, in fact, of those men who had passed through the elementary schools and the schools of higher education, men who, in a word, saw, felt and acted differently. This was perhaps the truest and greatest merit of Renaissance education in Florence, both in the public sector and in the family where children were taught at home by private tutors.*

Just when the Renaissance in Florence had reached the height of its triumph, the Dominican friar Girolamo Savonarola was writing and preaching violent attacks on the teaching and education based on « the humane letters », and particularly on classical poetry because, he affirmed, these base lies and no less iniquitous-idolatry were perverting the innocent minds of youth and making guileless children the servants of the devil.

The over-zealous friar proposed violent correctives and punishment rather than a free and liberal system of education. The humanists replied that a happy and integrated system of training could only be ensured if the tender minds of the young were moulded to the perfect good taste and harmony of the literary monuments of antiquity.

Florence meanwhile was in fact enjoying the luxury of freedom of thought brought about by the permitted exercise of every physical and spiritual faculty, but the new ideals in education had to struggle with the traditionalists, who opposed with increasing violence the liberal schools which would form free-thinking men capable, in the immediate future, of speaking a common language, above and beyond all divisions and factions.

The struggle had begun a century before Savonarola, in the early days of humanism, when Coluccio Salutati had opposed the preaching of another Dominican, Giovanni Dominici, a cardinal of the Holy Roman Church, who also fought against the classical ideal and liberal education, denying, in fact, that kindness and respect towards the young scholar and an understanding of his needs were at all effective or even desirable. According to the Dominican, children were to listen in humility and to sit passive and silent before their teachers. They were also to be flogged frequently, because a good beating never did anyone any harm and could, in fact, prevent a child from starting on the slippery slope to perdition.

This strange system was not to be confined to children of four to six years of age, but was to continue until the late teens or even early twenties. Masters and parents were encouraged to flog their charges liberally and frequently, without scruple, whether it was necessary or otherwise and whether the punishment was deserved or not. Flogging at school and at home was always useful: if deserved, it was an act of justice; if undeserved, it developed in the boy a sense of patience and forbearance, and when administered regularly it was a great aid to character-formation.

What was all this? A barbarous, cruel, infamous system which reacted against the now vigorous « new humanity »? No; there were simply two conceptions of education, each of which had borne and was still to bear its fruit, both for good and for evil.

In contrast to the heavy discipline of Cardinal Dominici, there was the teaching of Leon Battista Alberti, the universal genius of the early Renaissance who, in his writings, speech and the example of his life, strove to impart every precept with persuasion, gentleness and love.

How did the schools and the home react to the two opposing conceptions of education? Did they follow tradition, or did they look for new light and hope in the liberal reforms? It is very difficult to say. Which of the two systems was pre-eminent in practice? Perhaps first one, then the other. Education was largely liberal and humanistic, but not without its sacrosanct discipline by flogging and caning, practices which continued until the early years of this century, and are still to be found today in isolated cases. Teachers and educators in the fifteenth century did in fact aspire towards the education and training of a generation of free men, masters of themselves and their destiny.

Those to whom children were entrusted, or those who limited themselves to theorizing on education, such as the great Guarino of Verona and Leon Battista Alberti, did not want the pupil to be trained merely for a vocation but wished to train him for life, teaching him the difficult secrets of being a man, entertaining him gently, moreover, with reading adapted to his age and encouraging him to take part in games to strengthen his body and relax his mind.

It should be realised, however, that the schools and the education which had its origin in the humanist revolution and which grew up with it, were, in fact, the privilege of the few. The children born and brought up in the lower class environment belonged to that category which Cardinal Dominici wished to have brought up to a trade with the aid of beatings and other energetic measures. There were, however, children of rich merchants, whose families were already on the road to bourgeois ease and luxury, and finally, the sons of aristocrats and princes, who were given a thorough humanist education. The sons of Lorenzo the Magnificent were brought up and taught by Agnolo Poliziano, a great scholar and a celebrated poet, and a man devoted to life, love and beauty. He alternated his grammar and Latin lessons with walks in the open air, ball games and even trained his charges to hunt with the hawk. The Medici children learned effortlessly and, by having both formal and recreational lessons in due proportion, came to consider grammar as much a recreation of the mind as physical exercise was of the body.

It does appear, however, that Poliziano had on occasion to fall back on at least some of the reprehensible methods advocated by Cardinal Dominici as the only valid ones for the true education of youth. Perhaps Poliziano, exasperated by some mischievous pranks of his small charges, had given one of them a good spanking to reinforce his argument. Nothing very grave or irreparable, naturally, but Madonna Lucrezia, the children's grandmother, who admired Poliziano nevertheless, thought that he was too free with his beatings and complained to her daughter-in-law Clarice Orsini.

In the Palazzo de' Medici Museum we can still admire the marvellously illuminated text-books used for the education of Lorenzo the Magnificent's children, their notebooks with arithmetical exercises and the Latin passages dictated by Poliziano, as well as the rough copies of the letters they wrote to their father to inform him of the progress they were making in their studies.

This was something of a closed world, even if the humanist spirit was, so to speak, in the air and affecting every stratum of society. It is quite evident that the children of the ordinary Florentine families could not possibly have specially illustrated books for study or notebooks of the finest parchment such as little Piero de' Medici used. These privileges were unknown to the very large majority of pupils and it is almost certain that their reading and arithmetical exercises were done aloud, encouraged by beatings from the master, who might be anything but wise and learned.

Poliziano was a brilliant exception to the general run of teachers, in that he was able both to instruct

Reading stalls in the Laurentian library, designed by Michelangelo, carved by Battista del Tasso, Antonio Carota and Battista del Cinque. With their high backs and steeply inclined shelves for easy reading, they ensured privacy and favoured quiet meditation and study. Below: *A lesson in dialectics by Saint Thomas (Domenico di Michelino).*

the children of his prince and teach Latin and Greek in the Studium.

＊＊

On February 25th 1455 the City Council of Florence debated the appointment to the Studium of two lectors in oratory and poetry. This was in response to a demand from many young men who wished to study Humane Letters and to specialise in these two subjects. The salary proposed by the City Council, however, was so paltry that it aroused the indignation of Donato Acciaiuoli, Alamanno Rinuccini and Andrea Alamanni, three students who devoted themselves passionately to their literary studies and who, with others, met daily for private oratory exercises. The University at this time was seriously short of staff, and many posts were vacant owing to deaths and the wars.

Their complaints led to quarrelling, confusion and mud-slinging, and the Councillors were blamed, not only for the low salary attached to the posts, but also for the mediocrity and presumptuousness of the applicants, who were supported by the Chancellery, where it was well known that many had publicly declared their lack of confidence in the University faculty.

The question was more serious than it might at first seem, as it brought into open conflict the differing attitudes to knowledge which the humanist movement was determined to resolve.

The humanist school and its teaching was still largely unaware of the living world about it; its own world was pagan, and its scholars moved in an aura of myths and legends. Their interests were Venus and Cupid, the laughter of the satyrs, the choruses of the Bacchantes, the pipes of Pan, whereas others might be interested perhaps in the Christian world of Saint Francis's *Cantico alle Creature*. They were still obliged to study philology, epigraphy, numismatics, paleography and the other archaeological sciences, and Latin was gradually reduced to a language of imitation, condemned to wither away to formulae and clichés in the Ciceronian manner.

The schools did, of course, turn out a few Latinists who, wishing to express a rational or fantastic world of their own, continued gaily the study of the despised grammar, lexicography and stylists of the early fifteenth century. Nevertheless, literature, poetry and philosophy could from now on only be taught adequately through the vernacular, and the new movement in thought, which humanism represented, could only be taught in the schools. It would seem, therefore, that any dream of a real and practical revival of the ancients was doomed before it started. Incredible though it may seem, it was really the teaching of the scholastics which, in spite of its discontinuity and contradictions, succeeded in the enormous task of welding together the breach between the three ages of history, of uniting Christian culture to the culture and civilisation of Greece and Rome. From now on the schoolmasters were less anxious to see a complete return to the past, because their teaching of the classics and the Church Fathers was based on a new humanist experience, in which the classical tradition and the Christian message were kept quite distinct.

To illuminate the mind, free it from vague superstition and purify religion: these were the tasks undertaken by the humanist school, and, unknowingly, intuitively, magnificently, it forged a new world, laying the foundations and the principles of the civilisation we have today.

In the Studium at Florence and in the humanist schools, philosophy and history ceased to be centred on religion and became, as was then said, secular, concerned not with the eternity of religion but with terrestrial time, with the *secolo*, meaning the world where time is measured.

This is not to say, however, that the schools denied the value of religion: the humanists removed from theology the accretions of the medieval chroniclers, and substituted an account of the passions and ideas with which men had begun to reconstruct history. It was thus no longer necessary to distort events to suit a vision of history modelled on the great example of Saint Augustine.

There is a meticulously exact representation of a humanist school in Renaissance Florence in a bas-relief by Antonio Rossellino from Settignano on the monument to Filippo Lazzeri in the San Domenico Church at Pistoia. It shows the schoolmaster seated in a high-backed chair with his hands on a book resting on a lectern; his scholars are seated on benches, four on each side of him; one is listening, others are following the lesson in a text-book, and one is writing, perhaps notes. The work is full of life, although representing a rather solemn occasion, as there is a wonderful suggestion of

A page from an illuminated manuscript, showing teachers of law. The fame of some « legum doctores » was such that students travelled great distances to hear them, often following their masters as they journeyed from one Studium to the next.

Bernardo Cennini's printing shop (a model in the History of Science Museum, Florence).

movement, not only in the positioning of the figures and their attitudes, but in the play of light over the whole scene.

But how ancient are these medieval words *scuola* and *Studio*, compared with the new style of lesson and the new concept of education: these new concepts will enter history under the name of Renaissance. There will be Renaissance schools and Renaissance studies. And what will they be like? What sort of people will the school-masters and their pupils be? They will be, the schools, the masters and their pupils, all of them, the reflection of a remarkable phenomenon which occurred in the flowering of the second millennium after Christ, and then the phenomenon was called Giotto and Dante, and in the Purgatorio of the Divine Comedy we hear, from the voice of Statius, as he kneels before Virgil, the first song and the *first lesson of humanism.*

Now in fifteenth-century Florence we have reached the age in which that new outlook on life has spread like a luxuriant growth through the whole of education, from the elementary school to the Studium, when Cri-solora and Poliziano, among many others, are breaking down the barriers of that misunderstood classical culture based on a veneration and imitation of the ancients, and founding a classicism and study of antiquity which recreates the personality and the living image of those great men, revealing the originality of their thought, discovering their feeling for man and for life, and es-tablishing both the prestige of their remoteness in history and the imminence of their message to the contemporary world.

The school was, therefore, where one spoke with famous men of classical antiquity and understood them, learning their rule of life and appraising their know-

When he had his bitter arguments with Paolo Cortese, who was nevertheless an erudite and resourceful young man, and the author of *De hominibus doctis*, a criticism of Latinists from Dante to his contemporaries, Poliziano said to him: « You say that after studying Cicero for so long I still do not express myself like Cicero. But I am not Cicero, and it is precisely by studying him that I have learned to be myself ».

It was the age in which the humanist schools and the schoolmasters taught, in addition to polemics, the new sense of life and art which now began to fill their world, and the great mist from the Middle Ages which had shrouded Dante, Petrarch and Boccaccio was now beginning to lift under a brilliant mid-day sun.

Two words, both metaphorical, describe this new reality. They were born in the schools, from which they came out into the world, humming with festive joy like swarms of bees: the first was *Rinascimento*, which expressed a movement of life and thought, especially in the figurative arts; the second was *Umanesimo*, which established the new order of studies as a basis of good living, that is of human living. Both of these words, the schoolmasters explained, reestablished the bases of doctrine and art in a renewed classical tradition. From this it is clear that as a corollary to their concepts of Renaissance and Humanism the schoolmasters would require each writer and his work to be judged on their own merits, objectively, independently and with sensitivity, and that their own observations were merely a guide to this end.

Another important factor affected the educational world of the fifteenth century: school text-books were completely revised. The famous *auctores octo*, whose works had been used with generations of pupils, disappeared. The reform was so rapid as to be virtually revolutionary, and so all-embracing that by the middle of the sixteenth century it was extremely rare and it aroused great curiosity to come across one of those ancient text-books which had required children to learn by heart such texts as « *Chartula nostra tibi portat, Raynalde, salutes ...* » which ended « *Cordis in aure sonent, sic retinere memento* ». This particular passage was reproduced in hundreds of manuscripts.

The medieval texts disappeared quickly from the more enlightened schools, but survived for a time in more backward-looking establishments. The change of books reflected a different outlook on teaching methods, and meant more than a simple substitution of one

ledge, comparing it all with the new age and the new sensibility. The works of the classical writers were used as texts in the Studium, because they were important, not so much from the knowledge they imparted, as from the insight they brought to the schoolmasters and the students of the way in which knowledge is sought for and won. They also showed that science in 1400 could not be the same as science in 500 B.C., and that its results must be the organic, rational conclusion of accurate experiments. Yet there were still in the Florentine Studium some who thought that the purpose of classical studies was to teach the student to write in Latin in the style of Cicero. To these Poliziano retorted: « in Cicero I, however, learn how the perfection of style is a part of his personality, his thoughts and his feelings. Cicero teaches us that the closer we can become to him, and be his true disciples and scholars, the more we shall fulfil ourselves, and the less we shall be his slavish imitators ».

anthology or manual for another. Texts written solely for the purpose of rote-learning, with rhymed formulae and rules to be mechanically applied, were rejected in favour of selections from works of great scientific and literary importance, and passages which brought the student into contact with the great classical writers themselves.

When we realise that some of these new text-books, introduced into the schools with such happy results, were used for the study of Latin style, and that at the same time their content brought young minds into contact with unprejudiced thinking which was revolutionary at the time, it is clear how sweeping a change had taken place.

The humanists took great pains to instil into the student's mind, through criticism and historical research, the sense of a complete civilisation and the elegant use of words through the finest Latin and Greek examples, while at the same time identifying the author, the man, with the theorist, reading behind the epigraph to discover the human being.

Two of the new texts which became very popular in the humanist schools were the *Cornucopia* of Niccolò Perotto and the *Elegantiae* by the ambitious, restless, quarrelsome Lorenzo Valla. In place of the unnatural and artificial jargon of the old-style text-books, these two works presented the real Latin language, pure and deeply rooted in history and at the same time endowed a great people with a voice which had succeeded in giving expression to a complete age of history. There was perhaps more than this: in the new education, it was not Vulgar Latin which the classical replaced, but a barbarous dog-Latin. The Vulgar remained, and was greatly improved by the solid grammatical basis of the classical, and the revelation of a wider historical background.

SCIENCE, ENGINEERING, CRAFTSMEN

The fifteenth-century scientist, in Florence as elsewhere in Europe, received his training by studying the classical authors. Science was thus based, not on individual experiment and evolution, but on something static and incontrovertible. Florence was like Oxford, where masters and scholars were publicly warned that any error or difference of opinion offending against the logic of Aristotle's Organon *would render them liable to a fine of five shillings. It is not surprising, therefore, that science made very little progress and that those who held any unorthodox ideas were considered to be sorcerers and persecuted as such.*

There was, however, considerably more progress in engineering, where the situation was quite different. Engineers were always able to experiment, and they could draw on the services of highly-skilled craftsmen. Yet it was only towards the end of the Renaissance that this progress really began to make itself felt, as the craftsmen showed themselves reluctant to reveal the secrets of their traditional skills, and it was some time before they would consent to the necessary personal supervision of their work by engineers experimenting on new methods and techniques.

The supreme example of the experimenter was, of course, Leonardo da Vinci, whose desire to penetrate the mysteries and reveal the minutest secrets of nature and art led him, by strokes of intuitive genius, to ever-widening fields of knowledge, with unpredictable results.

The student of the history of science may be surprised to find that at the end of the Middle Ages and the beginning of modern Europe there were properly speaking no real « scientists » in the present sense of the word. Yet there is some evidence, albeit sporadic, of considerable development in technology and of inventions in several branches of engineering, which seemed to be well in advance of their time.

The Middle Ages and the Renaissance have been considered by some scholars as a dark age for science and technology, but it is a fact that scientific knowledge and technological potential were greater at this time than in any preceding period. If there is little documentary evidence to support this it is because of a lack of organisation in science and technology compared with other branches of learning.

Very little, in fact, was written on the subjects during the Renaissance. This is due mainly to the prevalence of classical and literary studies in higher education and the cultural outlook of the ruling classes.

A Greek-based humanist culture had been welcomed enthusiastically, and had won the admiration of men of letters everywhere in Western Europe. Those who were able to read the classical texts, having a knowledge of Greek and Latin, or even those who read them only in translation, soon came to be convinced that the easiest way to all knowledge and culture lay in the study of the ancient « masters », rather than in independent enquiry and observation of natural phenomena. It could even be held, and classical texts supported this, that the human faculty of inquiry and criticism was fallible, and that when a conclusion could be reached by pure reason the result was more valid than when deductions were made through the senses.

This, moreover, was a period when the concept of authority was fundamental. It was thus possible to enunciate the principle that knowledge was acquaintance

Design for an armoured car with mounted gun. Leonardo's original sketch and a model. The upper part of the sketch shows his design for a chariot fitted with scythes to cut down enemy troops (Leonardo Museum, Vinci).

with the wisdom of the ancients. The symbolic representative of this knowledge was Aristotle, and the humanist school built its curriculum around a study of his works and those of other classical authors. The basic subject was philosophy, and in the field of science the most important element was mathematics, a science of reasoning rather than of observation and experiment. All that could be known in the natural and physical sciences had been set down by Aristotle, and in mathematics the supreme authority was Euclid with his « Propositions ».

The atmosphere of the higher culture was thus distinctly conservative.

On the other hand, the demands of life have always led men to study the diagnosis and cure of the ills of the body, the methods of protection against the elements and human adversaries, and the ways to improve transport and communication. There were many who devoted their lives to these things, and their inventions were of lasting benefit to humankind. But their labours were not honoured with the title of « science ». They were « techniques », or even « arts »; those who invented things were « artists » and those who worked on them « artisans ».

THE CRAFTSMEN'S « SECRETS »

Craftsmen rarely went to training schools and were often illiterate. They learned their trade young in their master's workshop, where they were treated like his children, and the knowledge and skill they gained stayed there with them, often preserved in the shop as jealously guarded secrets. This system is described in Benvenuto Cellini's autobiography, where he often uses the word « secret » to describe his own trade, and the techniques he acquired which brought him such fame. The great goldsmith, who had given extraordinary proof of his skill in the casting of « Perseus » and the colossal « Neptune », did not wish his discoveries to be known, even when these were not trade secrets. « I had a musket which I made with my own hands, and inside and out there was never such a one to be seen. Also I made myself a most excellent gunpowder in which I discovered the finest secrets such as have never been equalled from that day to this, and of this powder I will say but little, only to reveal one thing which will cause wonder among those who are not expert in this profession: with one

fifth of the quantity needed with other powders, this one would give me sufficient force to propel a projectile two hundred paces » (horizontally, that is).

These artisans, therefore, wrote little or nothing, for the good reason that they did not wish to communicate the secrets of their craft, or simply because they were illiterate.

In certain circles men who today would be honoured with the title of research scientist had in those days come to be considered dangerous persons and were often persecuted. A typical example of this was the alchemist who, in fact, was in many cases engaged on work not very dissimilar to that done today in the chemistry laboratory.

As almost all the « arts » of former times are now considered to be sciences, and although there is still some kind of hierarchy which tends to put researches of a more theoretical and general nature on a higher level than those of a practical and particular kind (the first being called « scientific » and the second « technological ») there has never, in fact, been any satisfactory definition of their differences.

A typical example of medieval procedure in the world of scientific discovery, compared with what is done today, is the development of spectacles. No-one has ever succeeded, in spite of exhaustive research over the centuries, in identifying the inventor, who was certainly an artisan and probably a master glass-worker of the late thirteenth century. Other craftsmen continued the manufacture of spectacle lenses and finally perfected them, adapting them to the user. They discovered that to correct myopia the lenses had to be concave, and for hypermetropia convex. Fundamental discoveries of this nature would bring glory to any University Institute of Ophthalmology and fame to the inventor. These early scientists, however, are completely unknown; nor do we know where these discoveries were made, or even in which *century*. We only know that convex lenses were in use at the end of the thirteenth century and concave in the second half of the fourteenth, when craftsmen were making them and applying them to the correction of myopia.

THE FLORENTINE CRAFTSMEN

We now come to the craftsmen of Florence. If we wish to know the extent of scientific and technical progress in this period we shall find the answer, not in the works of high culture nor in the academies, but in the industrial activity of the times, especially in the military, architectural and artistic fields.

There was in Florence at this time a flourishing trade in wool, silk and glassware, with a tradition of exquisite workmanship. The wools and silks of Florence, together with those of Prato, were exported all over the world, and they enjoyed everywhere a considerable reputation for the finest quality. This was due in no small measure to the enterprise, skill and intelligence of the masters of the respective guilds.

The fine buildings which are one of Florence's finest legacies, and which have at least until the recent and most tragic flooding so successfully resisted the ravages of time, are a tribute to the skill of Florentine architects, not only in designing a type of building which has given its name to a period of architectural history, but in devising building materials and techniques so perfect that even today they arouse the admiration of experts.

Typical of so many unknown master-builders was Filippo Brunelleschi, who achieved the greatest architectural feat of the fifteenth century in the miraculous construction of the large dome of Florence's Cathedral. He used a new and highly original technique, and succeeded in vaulting the dome « without an overall stable framework ». The people of Florence, Vasari tells us, followed with amazement and wonder the growth of this enormous construction which had no scaffolding on the outside, and no visible tie-beams on the inside. Brunelleschi's scheme aimed to neutralise the considerable thrust using « chains of long slabs of stone, well tied with iron rods »: these are the external vaulting ribs which mark off the rib sections and bind together the two structures forming the dome. Brunelleschi invented special machines to lift the very heavy material to heights which varied from 165 to 300 feet. These used the endless screw principle and had a constant force of two-bullock power; they were adapted to differing loads by the use of drums of varied diameters and could lift blocks of masonry weighing several tons.

Exceptionally good work was also being done in the field of military engineering, but here there is very little documentary evidence. Most of the work was secret, and plans were scarcely ever published. There were, for example, developments in the construction of defensive walls, which reached the peak of their efficiency at this time, and Florentine military architects were greatly in demand everywhere.

LEONARDO DA VINCI

A well-known and particularly interesting figure, characteristic of the Renaissance, is Leonardo da Vinci (1452-1519).

He was born in Vinci, some thirty miles from Florence, in a modest peasant's house, a little way out of the town in an area called Anchiano. He received his early training as a « studio boy » under Verrocchio, never attending school regularly, and thus remaining always the typical Florentine Renaissance artisan. He liked to style himself as « an unlettered man ». His extraordinary genius and versatility, his thirst for knowledge, and his understanding of natural phenomena led him to continuous study and observation of everything which came his way. He achieved his greatest fame in painting, but he exerted a powerful influence over an enormously wide field.

The thousands of notes he left behind are a mine of ideas and observations of the greatest interest in mathematics, physics, optics, natural sciences, chemistry, and particularly anatomy and biology. He also made drawings of all kinds of machines.

Studies of Leonardo and his work form a library in themselves: there is, in fact a Leonardo library in the ancient fortress overlooking the town of Vinci, established by the municipality. There are, of course, some who maintain that not all the notes and drawings of Leonardo are by his own hand. It was quite natural that he should base his thinking on the work of his predecessors, but the remarkable thing about him was the extent to which he was able to push forward the frontiers of knowledge so far and in so many fields.

Some of his most remarkable studies bore on mechanically-assisted flight. These ideas were conceived between Florence and Fiesole. Knowing only the feeble motive power of the human body, he based his theories on an ingenious, though too theoretical, use of the forces of air and wind. He projected the parachute and a screw-driven helicopter. His work in hydraulics is further evidence of his inventive genius. Not only did he design canals and irrigation channels, some of them brilliantly conceived, but he invented particular types

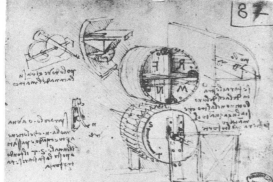

Above: *types of bellows « without leather » as they appear in a design by Leonardo and in a model (Leonardo Museum, Vinci)*. Below: *plastic model of a system of canal locks studied by Leonardo (Leonardo Museum, Vinci)*.

Regiomontanus' astrolabe (History of Science Museum, Florence).

seems certain that the most interesting were those for submarines, certain types of firearm, bridging equipment and armoured vehicles fitted with artillery weapons. His studies on mirrors and lenses are the only ones which have come down to us in the period from the thirteenth to the fifteenth century. The only equipment capable of making spherical lenses of long radius of curvature (to be used for « seeing the big moon ») of which we have the design from this period is that described by Leonardo in his manuscripts.

He wrote a highly original and informative « Treatise on painting ». It was Leonardo who introduced the principle of *sfumato* to achieve the transition from light to darkness through gradations of shadow (for which he had made interesting and original studies of the properties of light). He was never content to paint and merely look at the fruits of his labour. He tried always to penetrate the mystery of a work of art, and always seemed to see, behind and beyond the brush-strokes on the canvas or the wall, figures which he himself had never painted.

It is very likely that Leonardo, together with other fifteenth-century artists, studied anatomy and natural sciences, not so much to advance scientific knowledge as to make their paintings and sculptures more realistic and life-like. A study of the paintings of Pollaiuolo and Verrocchio, for example, show the care with which they had studied human anatomy and physiology, and Sandro Botticelli's pictures reveal an extraordinary knowledge of botany. There is no doubt that Leonardo learned how to study nature in Verrocchio's studio. Then the pupil soon outstripped his master.

Leonardo made interesting notes on the problem of perspective. His researches were evidently intended to perfect his technique in painting, but there is no doubt that they were also connected with his interest in mathematics.

LEON BATTISTA ALBERTI

The problems involved had been more systematically treated, however, by one of the pioneers in the new science of perspective which was being widely recognised in the artistic world: Leon Battista Alberti (1404-1472). We know more about him than we do about most of his contemporaries, because he wrote extensively, not only on perspective but also on architecture as, for

of tools required for their construction. For the Republic of Florence he drew up a scheme for diverting the Arno River west of Pisa. This was an idea long cherished by Machiavelli, but it was never brought to fruition because of lack of finance.

Although, as has been said, our slender knowledge of the history of technology in Renaissance times makes it difficult to establish with certainty the prime inventors of the fifteenth and early sixteenth centuries, it is likely that in military engineering as well, about which we know so little, Leonardo was an acknowledged expert.

It is not easy to see, among the many manuscripts he left behind, which of them contained projects to which it was possible to give immediate realisation, but it example, in « De re aedificatoria », a complete treatise on building science, which completed the ancient and celebrated work on the same subject by the Roman Vitruvius. His « Five Orders of Architecture » is a classic of its kind. His interests were not, however, limited to architecture and building. In his « Mathematical games » he describes an « odometer » for measuring distances and speeds, an « equilibra » or pendulum level, an « Albertian bolide » for measuring the depth of the sea. He observed the breakdown of light without realising its importance, and failed to investigate the phenomenon, contenting himself with a gracious apology: « The sun, shining through a glass of water, had described a rainbow on an altar, and the water boasted that the beautiful effect was his creation, but the glass replied: ' If I were not transparent and shining this would not happen '. The altar, hearing this argument, silently rejoiced that the glory was his ».

The idea of geometrical perspective comes from Leon Battista Alberti and Filippo Brunelleschi. This was based on a single vanishing point and the use of squares and other devices to obtain a mathematical, or rather geometrical, representation of buildings and panoramas in spatial recession. These studies have dominated painting techniques all over the world ever since.

The figure of Leon Battista Alberti is nearer to the modern scientist than to the Renaissance artisan. This is even truer of another famous person, who has been much discussed, especially in connection with the discovery of America by Christopher Columbus: Paolo del Pozzo Toscanelli, who was born in Florence in 1397 and who died in 1482. He worked as an astronomer and an astrologer. As an astronomer he drew up numerous charts of the heavens showing the orbits of several comets, including the one discovered later by Halley and which bears his name today. As an astrologer he was something of a sceptic, and his own life would appear to justify this: he lived to the ripe old age of 85 and could never trace, even with the most accurate observations, any promise of longevity in the constellations present at his birth. In astronomy he was a precursor of Copernicus, Tycho Brahe and Kepler.

He is remembered for the gnomon he built on the Santa Maria del Fiore Church in Florence for astronomical measurements. These were very accurate for the times. He was fascinated by geography and the descriptions of voyages, which were becoming daily more interesting and important. He eventually had a

Decorated solar clock by Bonsignori (History of Science Museum, Florence).

decisive influence on the enterprises of Columbus. In 1474 he wrote a letter to a Portuguese cleric, Canon Fernao Martines, in which he showed, with the aid of a map, that the quickest route to Eastern Asia was not that opened up by the Portuguese round the Cape of Good Hope, but by way of the Atlantic along the latitude of Portugal. Recent studies of Columbus suggest that he knew of this letter, although it is still possible that he came to the same conclusion first.

These astronomical and geographical studies of Toscanelli's indicate that he was something of a scholar, and this is confirmed by the many books he wrote, but he coupled these intellectual activities with others of a very practical nature. He engaged extensively in commerce, and used his expert knowledge to organise a vast import and export trade to the farthest regions of the world.

The interest of the Florentines for these kinds of activity, which had such a practical application as commerce and international trade, contributed in no small measure to the exploration of the world. This is further shown by two other sons of Florence, Amerigo Vespucci (1451-1512) and Giovanni da Verrazzano.

A great deal has been written about Vespucci and his voyages to the New World. There is no longer any doubt that the name « America » was given to the new continent after his successful voyages in 1499 and 1500, although there have been attempts to find a different origin for the word.

Da Verrazzano has recently become well-known for his voyages of discovery along the Eastern coast of North America and Canada in 1523-1524 and again in 1528. He explored the mouth of the Hudson River, where New York now stands, and he has recently been honoured in a great bridge over the narrows in New York Bay at the mouth of the Hudson which has been named after him.

Thus we reach the mid-sixteenth century, when there was something of a crisis in the scientific world. Still apparently bound to the ancient classical masters and to the unquestioned authority of Aristotle, theoretical science was now lagging behind the practical advances in technology, and the artisans, skilled workers in the laboratory and outside it, were no longer content to recognise an authority based on out-of-date knowledge. Peripatetic philosophy was no longer capable of stemming the rising tide of revolt, and there were signs of the coming ideological revolution associated in the seventeenth century with the names of Francis Bacon, René Descartes and especially Galileo. Florence's part in this development was considerable, in that the high quality of her scientific thinkers and the practical skill of her craftsmen raised the standard of experimental work to a truly scientific level, far beyond the reach of the high priests of the old philosophy. Soon scientific work was to be backed by the authority of the schools and the universities, and by all the means of communication and the facilities for training available, to ensure its progress for the benefit of humanity.

WEAPONS AND MEN AT ARMS

Florence's military history in the fifteenth century is not very different from that of any other Italian state. She had an army of mercenaries, led by skilled and courageous adventurers, which fought the long wars of the period with that air of indifference and calculated tyranny associated with the professional soldier of the time. After a long period of peace, however, under the Signoria of Lorenzo de' Medici, Florence found herself in 1494 under a republican government whose first difficult task was to create an efficient military organisation. An ordinary citizen, Domenico Cecchi, a member of the Piagnone *group which supported the policies of Savonarola, proposed the formation of a people's army to fight in the name of Christ and of Florence for the defence of republican liberty, and if his proposals came to nothing, it is because a great number of the people were already fighting for the conquest of Pisa. The idea of an army based on the conscription of both the citizens of Florence and the men from the outlying districts was taken up, however, by Niccolò Machiavelli, and was the basis of his military thinking when he was Secretary of the Army and Ordnance Board. This army was to fail in 1512, when it was scattered by the Spanish militia, but in the brief period of the last glorious Florentine Republic, during the terrible days of the siege, the citizens' army fought valiantly against the might of Spain and the Holy Roman Empire, and closed the chapter of Florentine liberty with a page not unworthy of the political passion of the « Secretary of Florence ».*

Florence's military history in the fourteenth century was not a glorious one. Beaten by Uguccione della Faggiola at Montecatini in 1315, by Castruccio Castracani at Altopascio ten years later (in both these battles the Florentine Guelfs, who supported the papacy, lost to the pro-imperial Ghibellines), and put under the command of the Duke of Athens for failure to bring to an end the Lucca campaign, Florence found herself in a very inferior position, both militarily and politically, compared with Milan under Giangaleazzo Visconti, and had reasons to fear for her very existence. Thus it was a series of reverses and humiliations.

Florence's congenital weakness in the military field must be related to the way in which, at the end of the twelfth century, she had given herself a constitution and a social order which was eventually to govern her existence. The « Ordinances of justice » by which the *magnati*, or noblemen, and the knights had been put into a condition of restricted liberty, and, on the other hand, the increasingly important part played by the bourgeoisie of the guilds in public affairs, had deprived the city of the military cadres which, in the Middle Ages, had formed the backbone of the city's defence.

Fourteenth-century Florence was a city of merchants, artisans and working people, in which even the older noble families had chosen to abandon the pride and idleness of their ancestors and enter the world of commerce and banking. It was also a city in which the military spirit was weakened by faction and party strife. Very soon the local pro-Guelf militia, which had fought the Ghibellines, at Montaperti (1260) and Campaldino (1289), had practically ceased to exist, as the wealthy middle-classes which formed the core of the units were able to pay substitutes to take over their duties in the field, and these substitutes, as the chronicler Matteo Villani testified, were usually of humbler extraction.

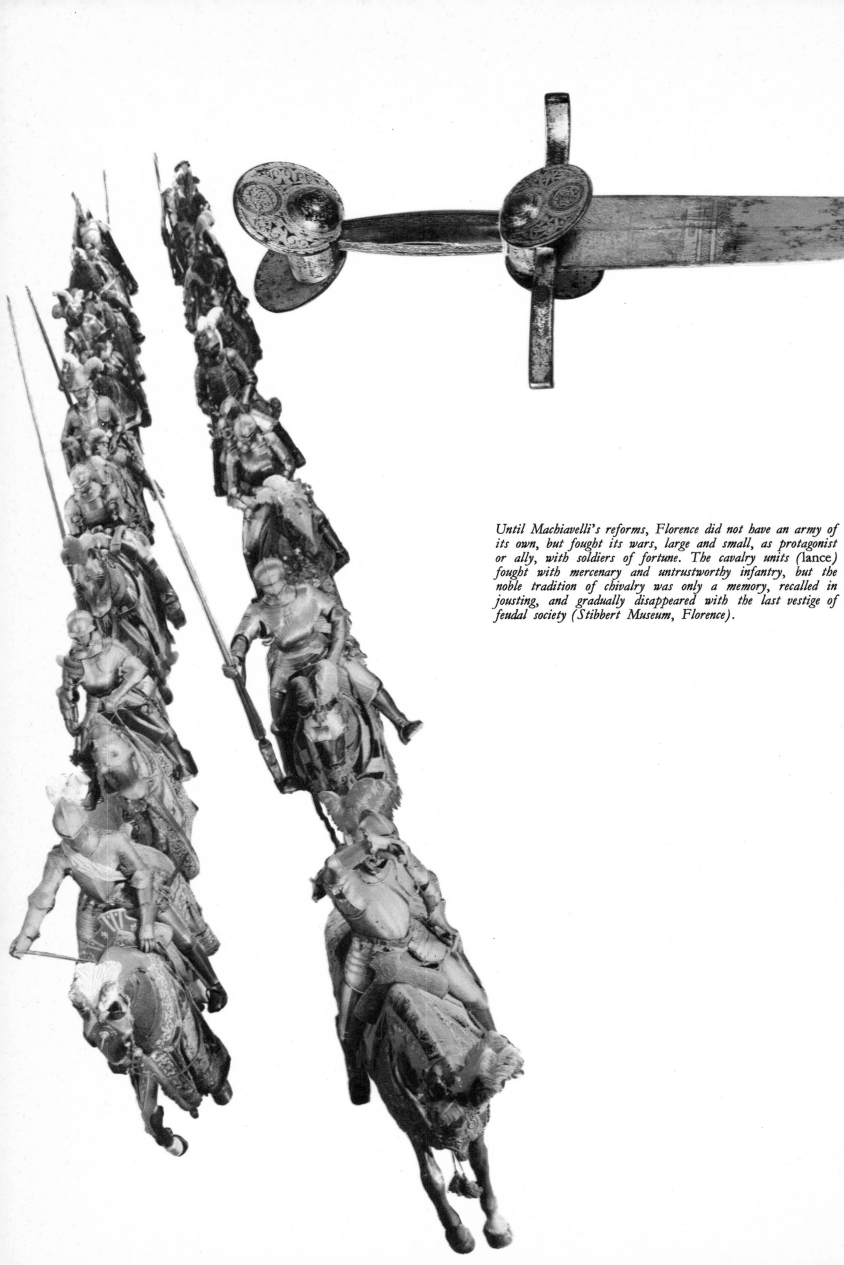

Until Machiavelli's reforms, Florence did not have an army of its own, but fought its wars, large and small, as protagonist or ally, with soldiers of fortune. The cavalry units (lance) fought with mercenary and untrustworthy infantry, but the noble tradition of chivalry was only a memory, recalled in jousting, and gradually disappeared with the last vestige of feudal society (Stibbert Museum, Florence).

THE MERCENARIES

As was the case in other Italian states, the core of Florence's armed strength in the second half of the fifteenth century consisted predominantly of mercenary troops. At one time most of these had been foreign: Englishmen, Scotsmen, Burgundians who had had their first experience in the bloodthirsty battles of the first part of the Hundred Years' War. Then, in the fifteenth century it was the turn of the Italian condottieri, most of whom came from those regions of Central Italy lying under the power of the Holy See. These areas were a mosaic of small townships, free communes and feudal possessions, and the condottieri were often petty lords from the Romagna, barons from old feudal castles or the plains around Rome, or successful adventurers who had usurped the lordship of some district in Umbria or the Marches.

In 1478, after the Pazzi conspiracy, when Florence was faced with attack by the combined armies of the Pope and the King of Naples, the army which she managed to assemble in haste for her defence consisted of mercenaries from Milan, Venice, Mantua and Rome and units under the command of Roberto Malatesta from the Romagna, Constanzo Sforza from Pesaro and Carlo da Montone from Umbria. As has been justly remarked, the Florentine army consisted for the most part of mercenaries from the very states against which it was fighting.

The structure and organisation of Florence's army in the fifteenth century were no different from those of any other forces in the service of other Italian states. Its backbone was heavy cavalry with units, or *lance* of three men: the man in armour, his page and his groom. The man in armour was clad in iron from head to foot; with greaves, cuisses, arm-guards, iron gloves, cuirasses,

Paolo Uccello « The Battle of San Romano » (Uffizi Gallery). A battle was little more than a joust and became a confusion of single combats, missiles fired from slings, shattered lances, and duels fought with sword or pike. Below: mercenary soldiers armed with sword and pike and a magnificent shield from the Royal Armoury, Turin.

gorgets, helmet, vizier, lance and, for close combat, a knife; he was a kind of living battering-ram and the spearhead of attack in the open field.

As we shall see, however, military tactics were gradually being adapted to the necessities of wars of siege and attrition. The cavalryman's armour became lighter and the armed infantryman assumed a more important rôle. The cavalryman was generally armed with a crossbow and the infantryman with crossbow or musket.

The relationship between the Council of Florence and the condottieri in its service was not an easy one.

Heavily clad in armour from head to foot, the mounted knight was a powerful element of attack and often determined the outcome of a battle by his sheer mass and virtual invulnerability.

If there was any delay in their agreed payment, the condottieri would not hesitate either to mutiny or to go over to the enemy. The amount of payment, which was proportional to the number of soldiers the condottieri brought with him, was a constant source of dispute. It was not unknown for the *connestabili* who commanded the various contingents to add to their nominal rolls the names of the dead and the absentees, sometimes even with the complicity of officials of the City Council, who could easily be bribed to turn a blind eye, or some friar or priest who was prepared to issue a certificate attesting that those who failed to appear at the muster held regularly by the Council were either dead or sick.

The cost of maintaining an army was, however, considerable. In his *Storie fiorentine* Machiavelli calculates that the cost of Florence's war against Filippo Maria Visconti was as much as 3,500,000 ducats, and in this Florence had the assistance of Venice. This may be an exaggeration, but it gives some idea of the great financial burden of a war by hired soldiery to a city such as Florence which was not by any means poor. It was especially difficult when the City Council was not prepared for any political bargaining with the condottieri. In contrast to her great rival Milan, which eventually came to be ruled by one of her hired condottieri, Sforza, Florence always showed herself jealous of her *libertas*, and preferred as overlord a banker to a soldier.

If the relations between the State and the condottieri were difficult, those between the townsfolk and the mercenaries were even more so.

As we have indicated, military tactics changed during the fifteenth century towards sieges and wars of attrition. When the bad weather was over, the armies left their winter quarters and began to beat an area of country, prepared to come to a decisive action only when there was a fair chance of victory. The cost of these manoeuvres and counter-manoeuvres, skirmishes and assaults naturally fell on the local inhabitants, whose fields and crops were often ruined and who found themselves forced into heavy labour digging out excavations for a siege or making roads for artillery or food waggons. When army mules were insufficient to drag these loads, the peasants often had to supply bullocks.

There was thus very little sympathy between the mercenaries, who were unfeeling and tyrannical, and the peasants who were patient and peace-loving and who despised the nomad, adventurous life of the soldier of fortune.

The inconveniences of the system of mercenary armies were thus many and serious, yet this was the only way a state could ensure adequate protection for its interests in the political, economic and social conditions then prevailing.

It is not in fact true that the mercenary army caused a deterioration of the arts of war to the point that there were battles, such as that at Anghiari (a Florentine victory over the Visconti in 1440) described by Machiavelli, which were hardly fought at all, so very small were the numbers of dead and wounded. It was rather that the tactics of the day were against open battles in the field, which, it was felt, could never resolve the military situation.

This does not mean that warfare in the fifteenth century was not harsh and cruel. It was not infrequent for the defenders of a garrison which had surrendered after a siege, in contempt of any armistice terms, to be put to the sword to a man or hanged from the battlements. Such ferocity was particularly frequent in the wars fought around Florence and in Tuscany, and showed a bitter factiousness in local affairs which had deep and ancient roots.

The invasion of Italy by Charles VIII of France in 1494 and the appearance in the various theatres of war throughout the peninsula of Swiss pikemen, drawn up in their massive squares, and the powerful French artillery, dealt a mortal blow to current military tactics and practice in Italy. Many were beginning to see the need of creating a force of infantry, like the Swiss, capable of attack and, when supported by artillery, of resolving quickly and decisively the military situation in the field. This, however, begged many questions: the problems of large-scale recruitment, as infantry-based warfare needed large forces, and of armament and tactics.

THE PIONEER CORPS

Venice had partly solved this problem by the creation of *cernite*, or infantry units conscripted by the State, whose numbers reached the respectable figure of 20,000 men. Could not Florence do the same? The idea matured during Savonarola's time, when Venetian institutions stood high in prestige and were well known in Florence.

The idea of military reform was propagated by an ordinary citizen, Domenico Cecchi. He was a fervent admirer of Savonarola, and set out his proposals in a work called *Riforma santa et pretiosa*. The best elements in the city and its surrounding area were to be conscripted, armed with cuirasses and, according to availability, with long lances, muskets, slings and bill-hooks. The conscripts were to exercise periodically in the use of their arms and in military tactics, and they were to receive payment, full in war-time and half in time of peace. Thus Florence would have her own army at last, and the country people would be free once and for all of the burden of mercenary soldiers.

Cecchi's reforms, however, remained a dead letter. Not only did they appear difficult to realise, but to many they seemed politically dangerous. Arming the common people, according to the dominant mercantile and financial oligarchy, meant introducing into the internal structure of the State an element of potential agitation and unrest.

On the other hand, what was the solution to the military problems which were now becoming acute in the new Republic, following the banishment of the Medici? There was a long and difficult war on hand with Pisa, which had rebelled against Florence. There was need for a great artillery park stocked with large bombards firing iron cannon-balls, which would be much more effective than the mortars and culverins used previously. There was need for arms, to be supplied by the famous (and expensive) manufacturers of Brescia. There was need above all for infantry. The 4,000 Swiss and 2,000 Gascons sent in 1500 by the King of France had not been a great success, showing themselves more zealous at collecting their pay than at facing the enemy, and finally they had deserted. In these difficult circum-

stances the Republic, unable to stand any longer the tremendous financial burden of the war, was obliged to resort to hiring *comandati*, or local men on whom enlistment notices were served, and who were paid from 10 to 12 *soldi* a day. They performed auxiliary duties, acting as messengers, diggers and porters in the baggage train. The strongest and most resolute of these men, who formed a kind of pioneer corps, often became combatant soldiers, and by the time of the war against Pisa they formed more than a quarter of the infantry force.

THE LEVY

The recruiting problem thus came to solve itself gradually by conscription rather than by voluntary enlistment. It was definitely settled and legally sanctioned at the end of 1506, when a Militia and an Ordnance Department were set up with a controlling Board known as I Nove (The Nine). Niccolò Machiavelli was appointed Secretary to the Board and he combined these duties with those of Secretary to the Second Chancellery. The choice was not fortuitous. Not only had Machiavelli had a hand in enlisting infantry in the Appenine hill area, Mugello, and drawn up the legal document instituting the militia, but he was in particular the author of two works: *Discorso dell'ordinare lo Stato di Firenze alle armi* and *Discorso sopra l'ordinanza e milizia fiorentina*, which are the Magna Carta of the Florence militia, and lay down the fundamental concepts of army organisation.

Firstly Machiavelli thought that recruitment should be on a fairly large scale, so that extensive mobilisation might be possible in case of need. He proposed three classes of men: the very fit, the valid and the less suitable. In case of war within the State itself, all three classes would be called up for service; for a war in other parts of Italy, only the first class would be mobilised. Conscription was not to apply to the whole State of Florence, however; districts were excluded which contained the larger towns conquered by Florence: Arezzo, Cortona, Borgo San Sepolcro, Pistoia, San Gimignano, and others whose inhabitants were considered not as citizens but as subjects.

It would have been unwise, Machiavelli thought, to recruit in these areas, where there was still considerable resentment at Florentine domination: there would have been a risk of discontent or even of sedition throughout the army.

The most reliable men were to be recruited from the *contado*, that part of the State which formed the oldest and most faithful nucleus and comprised Florence itself and Fiesole and the surrounding district. Outside this region, there were also the men from the mountain areas, such as the Luni, where the inhabitants were also trustworthy and amenable to discipline. In fact, though he did not particularly specify this, Machiavelli relied for recruits to his militia particularly on the men from the Appenine hills and valleys: the Mugello, Casentino, Pesciate and Luni.

The highlander, as he was to write in his *Arte della guerra*, was a « simple, rough fellow », most likely to make a good soldier, « brave and faithful », like the Swiss whose valour and discipline had amazed all Italy.

THE ARMY

How could this improvised soldiery be welded into an army? How could they be brought under military discipline? It was necessary to proceed, not by using either « all entreaties or all force » but « with that authority and reverence which a prince should have for his subjects ». In other words, extremes were to be avoided, as had certainly not been the case with the mercenaries, whose treatment varied from extreme licence to the harshest restriction. To this end it was advantageous for the enlistment of the men in the various units to be done on a territorial basis, so that a soldier would have companions from his own district, and all would be aware that they were fighting and soldiering for a common cause. On the other hand, discipline could best be ensured by appointing officers to command them who came from other parts of Italy, or even abroad, and to prevent any excessive familiarity with their men the officers were transferred every year to other units. It was thus hoped to combine the advantages of a territorial militia with the need for conscription and good military discipline. To strengthen even further the unity of the armed forces, it was also necessary, in Machiavelli's opinion, to « mix in something of religion ». This derived from Savonarola, whose doctrines the Secretary to the Board of Militia was far from accepting as strictly as the *piagnoni*. The army, he wrote in one of his instructions, must consist of « soldiers, not monks ».

The way in which the army of Florence was created eventually followed very closely the ideas of the one who had been its instigator and inspiration.

Firstly all heads of communes and their deputies were ordered to draw up lists of all males over the age of fifteen, dividing them into those liable for military service and those who could be excused as unfit, or because they had family responsibilities. Of these only the 18 to 30 age group would be called up. Certain privileges were then granted, such as being excused from all fines incurred up to the time of call-up and the right to carry arms in public places.

Cavalry was organised in lance *of three men: the cavalryman proper, called* uomo d'arme, *his page, who acted as his personal servant, and his groom, who looked after the horse (detail from a fresco by Piero della Francesca).*

A Renaissance army encampment as painted by Vasari in his « Siege of the Castle of Empoli ». With the changes in army organisation and war strategy, army camps had completely lost by the late Middle Ages the permanent defensive character of the Roman castra *and their fortifications and earthworks which turned them into fortresses when they were not needed for war.*

Enlistment was on a territorial basis. Each commune constituted a troop under a captain, and several communes in the same district made up a battalion under a *connestabile*.

Training took place on feast-days and every month there was a *mostra*, or battalion parade.

Twice a year there was a *mostra generale*, followed by a celebration of mass and a speech by a local magistrate. Each company had its own drum, and exercises were performed to drum-rolls in the Swiss or German manner. There were very severe punishments for anyone who missed a parade, swore, gambled or hired out or sold his arms to pay his gaming debts. Finally there was

a mobile force of fifty infantrymen and thirty crossbowmen under a Spanish « guard commander », whose duty was to exercise a general supervision over all the battalions. Machiavelli insisted, against strong opposition, on giving the command of this unit to the notorious Micheletto, who had earned a sinister reputation as one of the more ruthless agents of Valentino Borgia.

ARMAMENTS

An important new element in Florence's reformed militia was its armament.

Tents were sited to take advantage of the natural resources and defences of the terrain and were of the most varied design. Some were luxurious. In a siege they were often sited near to the enemy walls, and could still be out of range of the cannon, which in those days could not fire more than three hundred yards.

It was laid down that seventy per cent of the conscripted infantrymen should be armed with pikes, on the Swiss model. The remaining thirty per cent were to have halberds, spears, cross-bows and muskets. This radical change of weapons, which had formerly consisted of the sling type, indicated a determination to increase the infantry's power of attack, in line with the new military tactics introduced into Italy by the Swiss. Why should not the Mugello or Casentino highlanders, armed with pikes cut from their mountain fir-trees, also succeed, as they advanced in serried ranks, in forming the spearhead of a victorious attacking force in the open battlefield?

The cavalry too was reorganised. In 1511, also as planned by Machiavelli, the necessary ordinances were passed and a conscript force of cavalry was created. They were armed with crossbows and muskets and, like the infantry, recruited on a territorial basis.

The strength of the cavalry, however, remained far below that of the infantry and did not, in fact, exceed 500 men, whereas the infantry reached 20,000.

Thus Florence had created its own army, and from Rome, Cardinal Soderini, the brother of the Republic's Gonfalonier of Justice, was pleased to note that finally « Tuscany had taken up arms and the nation had demonstrated that it was capable of things other than

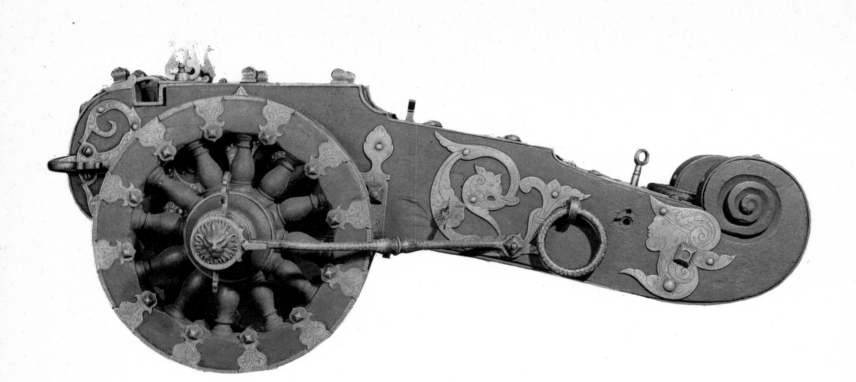

trading, thus rediscovering its former glory (*secundum anticam gloriam*) ». The new conscript army was welcomed by the citizens, who had watched with considerable pleasure the first large-scale parades. It had its first engagement in the final stages of the war with Pisa, in which, though in a subordinate rôle, it acquitted itself honourably.

In what should have been, however, its moment of triumph it failed lamentably. In 1512, when the Spanish forces arrived to restore the Medici to power in Florence, they met the local army at Prato, and the Florentines fled even before any proper battle could begin. Guicciardini, who had never shared the enthusiasm of his friend Machiavelli for the conscript experiment, recorded in his « History of Italy »: « The Spaniards were astonished that there could be in any military men such cowardice and inexperience ». Thus the end of the Republic brought also the end of the conscripted territorial army. The hopes of transforming into Swiss soldiers the brave highlanders of the Mugello, the Romagna and the Casentino were dashed once and for all.

THE SIEGE OF FLORENCE

The Florentine militia had a brief return to glory in the restoration of the Republic and the siege of the city. In the fever of collective enthusiasm for the ideals of Savonarola, the army was reconstituted, and did in fact contribute notably to the heroic defence of the city. The fighting spirit of its soldiers can still be understood today from Bartolomeo Cavalcanti's speech on May 15th 1528, in which patriotic feeling and religious sentiments are happily combined: the defence of Florence was the defence of Christ, who in those very days had been proclaimed King of the City. Cavalcanti, the author of *Retorica*, an anti-Medici tract, took part in the siege and voluntarily went into exile after the murder of Alessandro de' Medici in 1537. This state of mind, a mixture of patriotism and religious mysticism, very closely connected to the particular and exceptional circumstances of the moment, was clearly not destined to last. Mass exaltation soon gave way to discouragement, and Florence was soon to forget its brief hour of glory. It should be remembered, however, that the Florentine army at the time of the siege, recruited as it was primarily from within the city, was very different in quality from Machiavelli's militia, and more like that dreamed of by the disciple of Savonarola, Domenico Cecchi.

The military history of Renaissance Florence is thus not very different from that of the thirteenth-century city. Except for the glorious epilogue of the siege, it is a story of defeat and inefficiency, which seemed to

The role of cannon in a siege was not limited necessarily to breaking down the enemy defences. It was soon realised that they could very efficiently cover an infantry attack. Left: *a model of a gun-carriage (Artillery Museum, Turin)*. Right: *a bombard*.

confirm the ineptitude of the Florentines for the use of arms.

Not that they were any worse than the soldiers of other Italian states. Individually they had often shown a courage verging on temerity and a bravery nearer to ferocity. Was not that John of the Black Bands a Medici ? A man, according to Machiavelli, « audacious, impetuous, of great reputation and a maker of great decisions », who had succeeded in forming a select body of soldiers capable of submitting to an iron discipline. Were not most of the men in these Black Bands from Tuscany ?

The fact is that what Machiavelli had said of all Italian soldiers applied even more to the soldiers of Florence: they were « superior in strength, skill and intelligence » to almost any others, and could be « numbered among the few »; « but when it comes to making up an army, they fail to appear ».

THE ART OF WAR

Good soldiers, therefore, even rashly brave on occasions, but bad armies. What were the reasons for this contradiction? Why had not the Italians, and the Florentines in particular, learned to apply to the arts of war those lessons from classical antiquity which they had found so useful in the revival of letters and the arts ? These were the questions which preoccupied, among others, Niccolò Machiavelli when, after the fall of the Republic led by Soderini and the return of the Medici in 1512, he was reduced to enforced idleness in his villa at Albergaccio.

The fruits of his meditation were published in « The Art of War », which has had a far-reaching effect on modern political and military thinking. The work is a penetrating and radical criticism of the feudal-type army, using the term in its most general sense. Both the older type of cavalry and the soldiers of fortune led by condottieri were, according to Machiavelli, two typical institutions of a form of society which was breaking down, in which the military profession, together with many other fields of related activity, was the preserve of certain social classes and particular individuals to whom the State, so to speak, handed over the task of ensuring its defence against internal enemies. The social structure was disintegrating, personal privilege was rife and the army too was an organism independent of the State and in itself more a collection of private armies

The siege of Florence by Charles V (at the instigation of Pope Clement VII de' Medici) lasted almost a year. Florence raised her own army which fought valiantly to save the Republic, now abandoned by all its allies, and

than a united force, in which the units and their commanders were jealous of each other. This in itself seriously affected the conduct of military operations.

The Roman army, on the other hand, had been quite different, with its huge disciplined legions united under

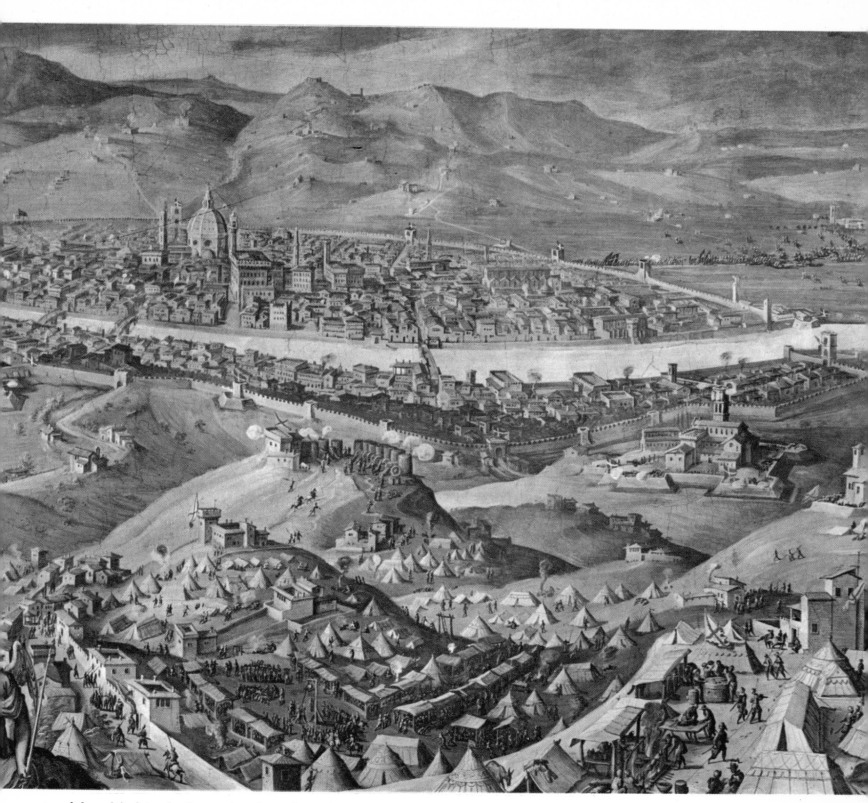

struggled to defend its freedom against forty thousand men. The coalition of Pope and Emperor was victorious, however, and Florence was forced to submit to the rule of the Medici who had twice been driven out of the city. (Vasari: « The Siege of Florence », Palazzo Vecchio).

the command of the *imperator*. Just as the medieval army reflected the disintegration of the body politic, so the Roman army was the expression of a unified coherent social structure, of a *patria* with its distinctly recognisable classes of patricians, knights and plebeians. In the arts of war, therefore, there would seem to be a need for a return to Rome, to a unity based on firm laws, sound customs and good weapons. These had ensured ancient Rome's grandeur and strength.

Machiavelli's thoughts thus came round to a rediscovery of the classical civilisation which was the basis of Renaissance thought and culture. Not, however, a rhetorical classicism in this case, an impotent worship of deeds past. Good weapons, sound laws and customs, and the integration of the military and civilian powers

resulting errors of appreciation, « The Art of War » clearly postulates a modern army for a modern state. It was to be read in the coming modern age and have a profound influence on political and military thinkers such as Du Bellay, Milton, Montesquieu and Rousseau.

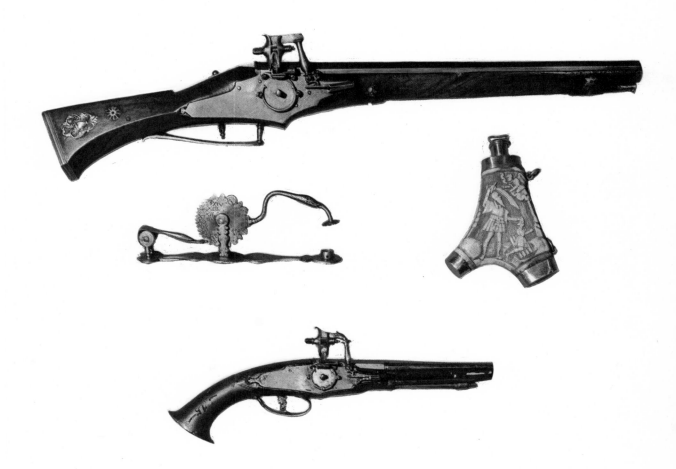

were not only a mark of Roman society, but a necessity of the modern age. There was also a need, as far as the arts of warfare were concerned also, to return to first principles, to gain the strength and the stimulus for further advance. Thus, in spite of its classicism and its

From the bitter experiences in the political and military fields which had led to her decline, Florence, through the person of one of her greatest sons, had elaborated a system of thought which she was able to hand down to future ages.

POLITICAL INSTITUTIONS

The structure of Florentine political institutions also withstood, at least formally, the regime which went under the name of the lordship of the Medici, and ruled for sixty years, from 1434 to 1494. The government of the State remained in the hands of an unrestricted oligarchy, tied in various ways to the Medici family, but substantially supported by the lower classes.

The constitution was virtually suspended for long periods owing to the abusive system of making major political appointments by designation instead, as previously, by the drawing of lots. The gradual concentration of government into increasingly restricted groups was, on the other hand, legalised by the creation of the Council of a Hundred, and finally the Council of Seventy.

The severest blow to the traditional forms of government was inflicted under Lorenzo de' Medici: in 1480 a Court of 240 citizens elected, in addition to the Signori and Colleges already in office, a permanent College of Seventy chosen from the « wisest and most reputable citizens », who virtually controlled the government of the Republic. But Cosimo and Lorenzo had tried to govern Florence formally as private citizens. Then followed the period of the Medicis' banishment from the city and their return, imposed on Florence by foreign arms. The election of Pope Leo X in 1513 gave the Medici regime a further shift in the direction of the Principate.

The constitutional and administrative government of Florence in the late thirteenth and early fourteenth centuries was based on a territorial division of the city into four districts: the Santo Spirito, Santa Croce, Santa Maria Novella and San Giovanni. Each district was subdivided into *gonfaloni* so named from the banners or 'gonfalons' which distinguished them. The population entitled to vote was divided into twenty « guilds ».

The government of the City-State was entrusted to an oligarchy which was much less restricted than is generally realised. It contained heterogeneous social and political groups. The principal executive body was the *Signoria* which consisted of eight Priors, two for each district, three quarters of whom belonged to the major guilds, and a Gonfalonier of Justice, *primus inter pares*, who was a member of one of the seven major guilds and appointed in turn from one of the four districts. The presidency of the *Signoria* was held by one

of these nine members in turn, who was then known as the *proposto*. Priors and gonfaloniers alternated every two months.

The *Signori*, or members of the *Signoria*, were elected by drawing lots, three days before they were due to take up their appointments. This was done in special *borse* (purses), containing the names of citizens judged suitable for office, and these were then appointed to various commissions, whose members were called *squittinatori* and, later, *accoppiatori*. The *Signoria* represented the Republic in its relations with other States, supervised its general administration, appointed appropriate councils, and had the exclusive right to initiate legislation in the form of statutes. In these and other matters, the *Signori* were assisted by twelve *buonomini*, three for each district, and sixteen *gonfalonieri delle compagnie*, one for each *gonfalone*. All these officials also were elected by lottery every three or four months. The three bodies, *signori*, *buonomini* and *gonfalonieri* together formed the *signori* and *collegi*. For the more serious political business, some of the more important citizens were co-opted. These were called the *richiesti*, and often included technical experts and lawyers, called *savi*. The minutes of these meetings were called the *consulte e pratiche*. In theory the supreme constituent and legislative power was vested in the *parlamento*, or the assembly of all the citizens who could be summoned on to the square by the ringing of the bells. This was resorted to only in cases of changes of government, to contest any constitutional reforms which might have been decided by restricted groups.

Approval of draft laws, regulations and the principal administrative acts was generally restricted to the appropriate councils: the Council of the People, consisting of 285 members drawn from the *gonfaloni*, the *capitudini* (heads) of the guilds, and expressly excluding all non-members of guilds, or *scioperati*; the Council of the Commune, with 208 members, including a small representation of the *magnati*, or leading industrialists, bankers and merchants who, until the passing of Giano della Bella's « ordinances of justice », had been excluded from the principal offices of the magistrature. Every bill, to become law, that is a *provvisione* or *riformagione*, had to be approved first by one then by the other of the appropriate two Councils with at least a two-thirds majority. In certain cases the bills had to have a double or treble reading, and be approved successively two or three times. After the last approval by the Council of the Commune the bill became law. In 1412 a third assembly was created for the preliminary discussion of more important bills, especially fiscal measures. This was the Council of Two Hundred, renewable every six months, membership of which was restricted to those elected to the three major offices—priors, *buonomini* and *gonfalonieri di compagnia*.

The constitution, the essential features of which are outlined above, could be suspended by the creation of a *balìa*, or temporary committee with wide, even dictatorial powers. The *balìa* consisted of a large number of citizens, elected by the *parlamento* or by the appropriate councils at a particular time, for the purpose of dealing with difficult internal affairs.

The ordinary administration was entrusted to a large number of officials and College magistratures, composed of *squittinati* and *imborsati*, that is drawn by lottery for each office, or others elected by show of hands or acclamation. These officials were known as *uffici di dentro*, as their duties were confined to the city itself, and they came exclusively from the middle classes, as also did the corresponding *uffici di fuori*, the *capitani*, *vicari* and *podestà*, who functioned in the smaller towns dependent on Florence.

The judiciary power, apart from the special duties reserved for the Signori and the Colleges and other city magistratures, was delegated to three *rettori forestieri*, the *podestà*, the *capitano* and the *esecutore degli ordinamenti di giustizia* (later suppressed). These were elected every six months from among persons having no connection with the city and fulfilling certain conditions (the first two had to be noblemen by birth). They would arrive in Florence with a motley accompaniment of « doctors of law », that is justices of the peace who would preside at district « courts », notaries, and so on. Their duties were not always clearly defined. Generally speaking the *podestà* and his courts would deal with civil matters, the *capitano* with criminal and the *esecutore* with the observance of the ancient statutes which protected the rights of the common people.

In matters of jurisdiction, wide powers were reserved to the various guilds, each one of which was administered by a College of *consoli*. There was a *tribunale della mercatanzia* consisting of an *ufficiale forastero*, who was a doctor of civil law, and six councillors, five from the major and one from the minor guilds. These held their offices for three months (later for four).

AFTER THE FALL OF THE MEDICI

When Lorenzo de' Medici died on April 8th, 1492, the regime was at the height of its power. The Council of Seventy, created twelve years previously, controlled, directly or through its committees, the entire machinery of government, while the *accoppiatori*, key officials since the days of Cosimo, elected the *Signoria* which, according to the statutes of the Republic, should have been appointed by drawing lots. Having had, periodically, their terms of office extended by five years, the Council of Seventy was well on the way to becoming a Medicean Senate, whose members would eventually serve for life. Recruited from the inner circle of the regime, the Council proved an efficient and powerful instrument of government through which the Medici could effectively impose their will on a city which still outwardly preserved most of its ancient republican institutions.

Until 1434 election to public office in the Republic was by drawing lots. There still exist some of the little sacks containing the small rolls of paper on which candidates' names were inscribed. On taking office, the successful candidate took the oath with his right hand on the Gospels. The richly-bound volumes and the sacks are preserved in the Florence Record Office. Left: the text of the Parte Guelfa Constitution of 1420.

But before two and a half years had passed, this regime, which had been gradually perfected over sixty years, was swept away after Lorenzo's son Piero had fled the city on November 9th 1494. His flight amidst a popular uprising was caused ultimately by the *Signoria* turning against him as a result of his disastrous diplomacy, and thus precisely by the failure of the principal control that was meant to guarantee the security of the regime, namely election of the government by show of hands. Having, in loyalty to Florence's ally, the King of Naples, consistently refused to assist King Charles VIII of France in his Neapolitan expedition, Piero had sur-

rendered to him on his entry into Florentine territory and handed over some of the most vital of Florence's fortresses to the French. By opposing Piero, the *Signoria* not only identified itself with the growing opposition among the Florentines to his policy towards France, but also with the criticism among the leading citizens of his arbitrary actions and his autocratic behaviour.

Such criticism, which had begun soon after the death of Lorenzo, showed that the Medicean regime still required a master to handle it successfully. In peacetime, Piero might have learned to govern, sooner or later, but he was incapable of handling the crisis that broke over Florence in the autumn of 1494. The consequences of his mistakes became apparent only after his flight: on the day of the revolution, Pisa, which he had handed over to the French, rose against Florence, and the failure of Florence to reconquer one of the most important of her subject towns darkened all but the last three years of the history of the new Republic.

For Piero's flight was followed by the end of the regime, and no attempt was made to save it under different leadership. The institutions of the Medici regime having been superimposed one by one on the republican constitution, the most natural way of filling the political vacuum caused by the expulsion of Piero was to restore the pre-Medici pattern of government. This, moreover, had been the aim of the last serious attempt (1465-6) to curtail the rising power of the Medici, and it was natural that it should be tried again. Two days after Piero had left Florence, an ordinance of the *Signoria* abolished the principal institutions of the former regime, and these measures were confirmed and extended by a « parlamento » summoned on December 2nd, four days after Charles VIII had left Florence, which he had entered as a conqueror on November 17th. Since it was decided that the *Signoria* and other high magistracies were now once more to be elected by lot, the *parlamento* decreed that an electoral scrutiny be held at the end of the following year. Meanwhile the *Signoria* was to be elected by a newly appointed Commission of twenty *accoppiatori*. After that, the system of government in force before 1434 was to be completely restored.

Such a restoration was, however, not only a matter of constitutional reform: the twenty *accoppiatori*, who for the time being were to exercise much the same control over the elections of the *Signoria* as their Medicean predecessors had done, were deliberately chosen from the *ottimati*, the most important families in Florence.

To put the clock back to 1434 no doubt meant, in the view of most of the *ottimati*, to return to the oligarchical regime that had prevailed after the revolt of the Ciompi in 1378. Piero Capponi, one of the « Twenty », and a scion of one of the great Florentine houses, expressed this attitude in idealistic terms when he said that, in his conviction, « in Florence there can be no government unless, by the consent of the people, not by law, but by tacit concession, twenty-five or thirty men, setting aside all private passion, ambition and avarice, take upon themselves the duties of attending to that poor city ». Men of the type of Piero Capponi might well declare themselves satisfied with the reform of December 2nd. These ideas, however, were not shared by all. Only three weeks later a second, and much more radical, constitutional reform was passed by the councils of the People and Commune, which placed the government and the legislature of Florence on an entirely novel, and more democratic, basis.

The person most responsible for this turn of events was the Prior of the Dominican Monastery of San Marco, Girolamo Savonarola. Since the day when, a native of Ferrara, he had first come to Florence in 1482, he had acquired a growing reputation and popularity amongst the people of the city. His influence took on political significance when his prophecies of impending disaster appeared to have been fulfilled with the French invasion of 1494. After the fall of the Medici, his passionate preachings of peace, which were doubtless responsible for the virtual absence of political persecutions and *vendette* against their followers, could still be considered to fall into the normal scope of clerical guidance. Also Savonarola's adversary, the Franciscan Domenico da Ponzo, preached the « *pace et unione* » of the city. But in his sermons of December 7th and 14th, Savonarola went beyond such teaching of Christian forgiveness,

The centre of political life in Florence was the Palazzo Vecchio, built in 1300 on the site of an older building. Right: the Salone dei Cinquecento (Hall of 500), the largest assembly-room in existence at the time, was built by Cronaca in 1495 to house the meetings of the Grand Council after the second expulsion of the Medici.

An illuminated page of the Codice Squarcialupi *(Laurentian library), showing the Captain of the twelve Ancients taking the oath: « I will defend, maintain and recover the honour and the rights of the people ».*

and began actively to intervene in what was then the burning political question: the nature and functions of the new regime. On the 7th he warned the Florentines that further reforms of the constitution were needed; on the 14th he exhorted them to take active steps to remodel it on the Venetian pattern. His suggestions were evidently followed, as the Florentines created, on December 23rd, their Grand Council.

The new Grand Council might have been modelled on that of Venice, but it differed from it substantially in its social composition. In its subsequent form it contained a much larger popular element, and incurred thereby the increasing disapproval of the ruling classes, eventually causing their total opposition to republican government. The principal reforms of the Grand Council, which invalidated the reform of December 2nd were, firstly, that its members were not elected, as had been the case of the ancient Councils of the People and the Commune which it now replaced, but were normally admitted by hereditary right; secondly, all major offices in the State were to be filled by election in the Council, and not chosen by lot as the statutes had provided. The Council had full legislative authority, but all draft laws had first to be submitted to a select Council of Eighty

(elected every six months by the Grand Council), which was also to debate current questions of importance, particularly in the field of foreign policy. In its hereditary membership, its electoral system, its supreme legislative powers and its delegation of some of its authority to a smaller Council, the Great Council closely resembled its Venetian model. Yet the new constitution differed in substantial aspects from that of Venice. There was no Doge: Savonarola had expressly vetoed this element of the Venetian constitution; the Council of Eighty was not for life like the Venetian Senate, and therefore wielded far less power; and the membership of the Council, although hereditary, was not limited exclusively to the nobility, as in Venice. In fact the new constitution opened the doors of the Council to a vast number of citizens, many of whom occupied only a modest position in Florentine society. This was to permit the admission of all those who, either by their own merits or by those of their fathers, grandfathers or great-grandfathers, had been nominated or had seen their names drawn (*seduti* or *veduti* as it was called) for one of the major bodies such as the *Signoria*, the Sixteen *Gonfalonieri* and the Twelve *Buonuomini*. When the reform was approved, it was not clear just how many citizens could be admitted in this way, but it was thought that the number of *beneficiati*, as the citizens qualified for the council were called, was less than fifteen hundred. It was therefore decided that if this number were exceeded, the Council would be divided into two or perhaps three equal parts, each one sitting for six months. As it turned out the number was over three thousand, and the Council was divided into three. Even in its single sections, its size by far surpassed that of any of the past councils of the Florentine republic.

The personal authority of Savonarola who, after his sudden rise to political leadership in 1494, was considered by everyone to be the architect of the new constitution, had a very great influence on Florentine politics. His power was probably greatest during the months immediately following the revolution of November 1494, before misunderstanding and disapproval had clouded the fulfilment of his prophecies, his constitutional reform and his apparent influence over the King of France, to whom he was sent as ambassador, first immediately after the latter's arrival in Florence, in November 1494, and a second time when the King was returning from his journey to Naples and passed through Tuscany. There was no lack of disapproval at his meddling in politics: « It is one thing to rule over a convent, but it is another thing to govern a city, people would say », while after his second mission to Charles VIII, it was commonly held that « according to the well-informed, Friar Girolamo brought back from the King more losses than gains ».

Important legislative measures such as the limitation of the criminal jurisdiction of the *Signoria* and the *Otto di Guardia* (eight citizens charged with the administration of justice) by the introduction of appeals to the Grand Council, and the solemn prohibition of the popular assemblies or *parlamenti*, whose power to vote by acclamation had been used by the Medici to bolster up their power, were certainly due, in whole or in part, to the impact of Savonarola's preaching and personal influence. Similarly he was almost certainly responsible for the dismissal in June 1495 of the twenty *accoppiatori*, who were suspected of oligarchical tendencies. In foreign policy, his support of the French alliance, concluded when Charles VIII was in Florence on December 25th 1494, had a powerful effect on Florentine relations with France and its enemies.

The importance of Savonarola's influence on the political events of the times must not, however, be exaggerated, as it sometimes was by his friends and foes alike. He did not play a very important part in the expulsion of the Medici; the new constitution, although fashioned on the Venetian model, was firmly rooted in earlier Florentine institutions, and was the result of a variety of political interests and ideals; the abolition of the exclusive powers of the *Signoria* and the *Otto* to condemn citizens for political offences by a two-thirds majority was something which had been demanded thirty years previously, and the French alliance was in essence a return to the Francophile tradition of Florentine diplomacy in the fifteenth century. Even if Savonarola's influence was probably decisive in legislative reform, his counsel was not always followed completely. Thus in December 1494 he had advised a democratic form of consultation in the sixteen *gonfaloni* into which the city was divided, to form the basis for the debate on the constitutional reform. In fact, only the highest magistracies were entrusted with the preparation of the reform scheme and the new constitution was probably less democratic by far than Savonarola had intended. As for criminal jurisdiction, he had suggested that appeals should be made to a small Council of eighty or a hundred members, and not to the Grand Council, and the event was decided in March 1495.

Perhaps Savonarola's greatest political achievement after the fall of the Medici was the prevention of widespread persecutions and private *vendette* against the Mediceans by citizens who had suffered under the old regime, and particularly by those who had been exiled and deprived of political rights. « He alone », said Guicciardini, a member of one of the ruling families, some ten years after Savonarola's death, « checked the spread of strife and violence ». But he could not prevent the revival, together with republican ideals and traditions, of political party strife, the bane of all Florentine governments, which the Medici had been so successful in stamping out. In fact, in spite of their impassioned sermons on unity and peace within the State, Savonarola and his followers contributed in no small measure to the revival of factions with their political influence and their ambitions. The city was thus divided between the *Frateschi*, as Savonarola's followers were called, and their enemies, a division that ran across that between *Bianchi* (Whites) and *Bigi* (Greys) as the republicans and the adherents of the Medici had come to be known. The *Frateschi*, who in 1497 had an energetic leader in the person of Francesco Valori, vied with their adversaries in the bid for political power by way of majorities in the *Signoria* and the Grand Council. These quarrels were aggravated and complicated even further by diplomatic issues. Florence's continuing loyalty to France, which continued even though Charles VIII had failed in his attempt to reconquer Pisa, could be defended on a variety of grounds. However, Savonarola's support of France tended to identify his cause with that of the French alliance and was taken, rightly or wrongly, as the main reason for Florence's firm refusal to join the League of Venice, which the other great Italian powers, the King of Aragon and the King of the Romans had concluded in 1495 against France.

Savonarola's attitude to France and the League of Venice was, at least at first, a more important reason for Pope Alexander VI's turning against him than the sermons denouncing the corruption of the Curia and demanding the reform of the Church. It would seem that it was Savonarola's stand in the diplomatic field which first caused the Pope to act against him, and this action led to Savonarola's excommunication in 1497, doubtless also fomented by his enemies at home. The immense popularity which had been the basis of his political influence, together with his success in reforming Florentine manners and customs, disintegrated overnight when, following the confessions extorted from him under torture after his arrest in April 1498, and later published as propaganda, he was branded as a false prophet and political opportunist. « And I found I could hear the charges being read out », wrote the Florentine pharmacist Luca Landucci in his diary, « whereat I wondered and was greatly amazed. And I felt grief in my heart that a man should be brought so low, having once been so high, for having built his life on one single falsehood ». Such feelings were doubtless shared by many Florentines who, like Landucci, had passionately believed in Savonarola, in his divine mission and in his work of moral and ecclesiastical regeneration, and this may help to explain why there was no public outcry when he was burned at the stake on the Piazza della Signoria on May 23rd 1498.

Savonarola's death had no appreciable effect on the internal constitution, nor, for that matter on the foreign policy of Florence. The Florentines did not join the League of Venice, and remained, for better or for worse, faithful to the French alliance, in the belief that this would eventually enable them to reconquer Pisa. The Great Council continued to function and to accept changes in its constitution, maintaining the same line of conduct as before the death of Savonarola, for almost immediately after it had been established, the new problems it had created had led to fresh reforms.

These problems were mainly a result of its large membership and its complex functions. Already a few weeks after the first of the three sub-divisions of the Council had begun its first Session, it became clear that it was going to be difficult to form a quorum, mainly because of the rule which prevented anyone who had not paid his taxes from attending the Council's meetings until all his debts were paid. The temporary disqualification from office-holding because of tax-arrears was a regular feature of the Florentine constitution, but this was of particular significance when it applied to the Great Council, whose work was seriously hampered when the absence of so many members made it impossible to form a quorum. Because of these difficulties it was decided in the summer of 1495 to abolish the division of the Council into three sections, and to establish the quorum at one thousand members, which was in line with the original concept of the Great Council. This brought the need for a new meeting-place, which had already been decided upon previously, but which was now a matter of urgency. The original hall had proved inadequate even for one third of the Council. Building was speeded up, and on February 25th 1496 the whole Council was able to meet in the new *Sala del Consiglio Grande*. More than one thousand seven hundred members attended, but it soon became evident that difficulties of regular minimum attendances had still not been overcome. These difficulties were to some extent increased by the changes in the Council's constitution. Because of the great number of matters to be dealt with, in particular the election of so many officers, frequent and long meetings were necessary, and these made serious demands on the time of merchants and artisans, and interfered with their business activities. The members found these long sessions much more wearying than those of the three sections which met only once every six months.

Consequently, notwithstanding the heavy fines imposed by the *Signoria*, absences were continually high, whilst the heavy taxes levied for the war with Pisa increased the number of those in arrears and prevented them from attending the meetings. There were only three ways of breaking the deadlock: reducing the quorum, abandoning the tax-paying rule, and reducing the

heavy agenda of the Council. Only the last solution was adopted in the end, because it was felt that the presence of large numbers of members and the principle that all those present should have paid their taxes were cornerstones of the constitution. As a result, a series of laws passed between 1497 and 1499 gradually reduced the numbers of those to be elected to the Council, in favour of election by the drawing of lots. After the last of these reforms, in May 1499, all the highest magistracies, including the *Signoria*, where appointed by candidates being first nominated in the Council, voted upon, and the names of those who obtained more than half the votes cast being put into an urn from which that of the successful candidate was finally drawn. The other offices were now filled either by a combination of election and the drawing of lots, or by lottery alone.

The return to lottery, while primarily necessary for technical reasons, so that the Grand Council should have sufficient members to function effectively, had also important political and social implications. Whilst it appeared to the ordinary people by far the most democratic system, it did not find favour with the leading citizens, who claimed that election to the Great Council should give a premium to social prestige, individual experience and economic wealth. Discontent among the leading citizens with the republican regime led to the creation in 1503 of the office of Gonfalonier for life.

This latter reform, the most important after the creation of the Great Council, must be seen against the background of the military and financial crisis which followed the unsuccessful war with Pisa. Because of the increasing fiscal burden, the Great Council not only repeatedly refused to approve new taxes, but even vetoed, in 1499, the election of new officers to the War Department, known as the *Dieci di Libertà e Pace*, most of whom came from the leading families of Florence. « Neither *Dieci* nor *danari* (monies) do they give for our peers », ran a slogan of the time. As a concession to the poorer classes, the *Signoria* introduced at the end of 1499 a progressive property tax, the *decima scalata*. This in its turn not unnaturally caused discontent among the wealthier citizens, who were already carrying the burden of high taxation and forced loans. In 1501 and 1502 the Pisan war was temporarily overshadowed by the threat from Cesare Borgia, the son of Alexander VI, whose expanding dominions were closing in on Florentine territory. In 1501 he had to be bought off with a *condotta* from attacking Florence itself. The threat

was most dangerous in June 1502, when one of his *condottieri*, Vitellozzo Vitelli, took Arezzo, but the King of France, who up till then had been mainly a political and financial liability for Florence, came to the rescue of the city and forced Vitelli to hand back Arezzo. At the same time the financial crisis was leading to a virtual breakdown of the normal credit machinery. According to the leading citizens, the most serious reasons for Florence's present troubles lay in the predominantly democratic tendencies of the Great Council: only by giving the leading families a more important part in the government of the city, could Florence be saved. Discussions were then started on the creation of a life Senate on the model of the Venetian *Pregadi*. This would have been a most acceptable solution to the leading families, but it was eventually decided instead to give the Gonfalonier of Justice office for life, again on the Venetian pattern, as this was more acceptable to the majority of the Great Council.

Life-office for the Gonfalonier marked a radical departure from the traditional system of government in Florence, under which the term of duty of the *Signoria*, including the Gonfalonier, expired after two months. The new reform gave Florence a new element of stability in foreign and domestic affairs, which it had sorely lacked,

The Imperial charter of 1537 declaring Cosimo de' Medici to be the successor of Alessandro who was invested by Charles V in 1531 « Head of Government and State » and subsequently called « Duke of the Florentine Republic ».

193

and thus revived, albeit in a different spirit and within the framework of an effective republican constitution, one of the principal benefits of the Medici regime. Although the powers of the *Gonfaloniere a vita* were strictly limited both by the authority of the Great Council and by the law, the danger nevertheless remained that these powers might be abused to the detriment of the Council itself. Piero Soderini, the first (and the last) life Gonfalonier, a convinced and ardent republican, never admitted this possibility, but loyally respected the authority of the Great Council. He supported the democratic tendencies of the regime, and disappointed those members of the leading families who had hoped that he might steer the government of Florence in the direction of oligarchy. This was doubtless the main reason for the growing hostility towards him among the upper classes, and for the revival of the Medici faction. The time when Lorenzo had ruled over Florence was beginning to take on the golden hues of the good old days, when peace and order reigned in Italy and Florence before the foreign invasion. After the death of Piero in 1503, his brothers, Cardinal Giovanni and Giuliano, busied themselves in Rome stirring up sympathy for their family. One result of this was the marriage in 1508 between a Medici girl and a member of one of the richest Florentine families, Filippo Strozzi.

Yet at least one member of the ruling families, Francesco Guicciardini, who was Soderini's greatest critic, could not deny that under Soderini there was considerable improvement in Florence's disastrous financial position. The army was strengthened, on Machiavelli's advice, with the creation of a territorial militia. In 1509, Pisa was reconquered, in spite of many strategic errors during the preceding campaign. The one great problem of the republican regime had thus been successfully handled, and the regime had demonstrated that it had sufficient strength and power of resistance to survive dangers from both without and within, and sufficient adaptability to accept change. In spite of its imperfections, the regime could certainly count on the support of a majority of the citizens, who saw in Michelangelo's David, which the *Signoria* had had set up in 1504, a symbol of republican liberty and independence and in Donatello's « Judith and Holofernes » which, once the property of the Medici, stood since 1495 in front of the same palace, a symbol of victory over tyranny. The republican regime fell in September 1512, not because of internal dissatisfaction, but from outside military pressure.

Like Savonarola before him, Soderini considered the French alliance to be the cornerstone of Florentine diplomacy. In fact, notwithstanding the small assistance Florence received from France in the war with Pisa, there were valid reasons for endeavouring to avoid a probable attack from France by putting herself under the protection of the French King, who had been not only the ally of Florence from the very first days of the new republic, but had held control over the Duchy of Milan since 1500. After the battle of Ravenna in April 1512, French dominion in Italy suddenly collapsed. Florence found herself alone — as she had done in 1494 when she had sought the favour of Charles VIII — and facing the military power of Spain and Pope Julius II, who was determined to restore the Medici in Florence and thus secure the loyal collaboration of the city against the French.

Unaware of the extent of the dangers that threatened them, the Florentines were confident that they could withstand a siege of the Spanish army; but the fall of Prato, where the militia proved a complete fiasco, radically changed the situation. In an atmosphere of acute crisis, a group of Mediceans forced the Gonfalonier to resign and to flee the city. Yet the conditions which were subsequently agreed upon with the Spanish viceroy, while postulating the return of the Medici as private citizens, did not demand the suppression of the republican constitution. In fact, the only constitutional reform which was adopted after Soderini's flight was the abolition of the Gonfaloniership for life in favour of an annual office: a reform which it could be hoped would silence the critics of Soderini. But on 16 September, the Medici, who in the meantime had entered the city, resorted to the device which had been so effective in the past, and had a *parlamento* called to the Piazza della Signoria, despite the law prohibiting such assemblies. In the presence of mercenary troops, the *parlamento* decreed the appointment of a council with full powers (*Balìa*), which in its turn abolished the Grand Council. But although it seemed the clock was put back, the Medici regime after 1512 differed substantially from that which fell in 1494. Cosimo and Lorenzo had tried to rule Florence as private citizens: Lorenzo's sons and grandson had returned to the city with the help of a victorious army; and the election in 1513, of Cardinal Giovanni as Pope Leo X gave Medici rule a further shift in the direction of the Principate.

ECONOMIC LIFE

In the account-books of the Florentine merchants and bankers one may read that « Messer King Edward » or « Messer King Philip » or « Messer the Pope » owes so many florins, and often with the note « but we shall be at great pains to recover them ». Sovereigns called the Florentines « dear friends », and their treasurers left their office doors ajar so that these « friends » could enter without having to knock. Wherever there were Florentines present, they were sought out and became involved in the game of high politics: in the North by the Popes to receive payment in kind, in the form of seal-skins and whalebone, of the tithes levied by the Church; by Philip VI of Valois to pay for his annexation of the Dauphiné to France; by Edward III to finance the first campaign of the Hundred Years' War and by monarchs in general to represent their interests in other Courts.

The Florentines had undertaken their great trading and banking adventures in distant places in the expectation of returning rich in experience and money. On their return they satisfied their ambitions by building a great Town Hall, monumental Churches and fine town houses worthy of princes. It is not without significance that these men, after travelling the highways of the world and leaving everywhere the stamp of their genius, their passion and their daring, should have expended such loving care on endowing their city with the perfect beauty of a matchless jewel.

Trade-associations, called *Arti* (Guilds) or *Corporazioni* (Corporations) became widespread at the end of the twelfth century and the beginning of the thirteenth. This was a time when the economy of the Western World was beginning to revive, and they gave considerable impetus to its development. They have so many points in common and are so well known that it might seem idle to dwell on those of one city alone, but there were differences, and as each city has distinct physical characteristics which single it out from the rest, so it is with its institutions. A rapid glance, therefore, at the purpose and functions of the Florentine guilds from the thirteenth century will throw considerable light on the city's individuality.

The first and most important purpose of the guilds was political, and in particular they aimed to bring those inscribed on their rolls into the sphere of public affairs and gradually to enlarge the cadres of the ruling class, as the number of guilds increased. There were the so-called « greater » guilds, of which the first was the Calimala, whose merchants bought unbleached cloth in Champagne, dyed and finished it in Florence, and re-exported it. Then followed others, known as « middle » and « lesser » guilds. This has led people to believe that the regime became progressively more democratic, but this has meaning only when we compare it with the rigidly aristocratic regimes of other republics such as Genoa and Venice. In an absolute sense it is incorrect, because Florence, except for a brief period after the Ciompi uprising, was always governed by an oligarchy of the upper and middle classes.

A few dates will suffice to show when the influence of the guilds began to be felt, and finally had a determining influence on the constitutional history of Florence. 1207: the first associations of craftsmen, formed in opposition to the solidarity of the *consoli*, and strong enough to exert an influence, requested the transfer of the judiciary from the *consoli* to the *Podestà*

The Palazzo dell' Arte della Lana (Wool-traders' guild) as it is today.

(Mayor) and his Councils; the first *Podestà* appointed from outside the city in order to guarantee greater impartiality, then successors from within the city. 1250: a further step forward with the creation of a *Capitano* attached to the *Podestà*, who sanctioned the entry into public life of what the Florentine chroniclers Dino Compagni and Giovanni Villani called the « *primo popolo* ». 1266: the constitution of the « *secondo popolo* » with which the guilds, reviving after the temporary successes of the Ghibellines, the party of the old Consuls and the *Podestà*, reentered political life with banners flying. 1282: the triumph of the « *popolo grasso* » (upper middle class) and the creation of the *Signoria dei Priori*, the supreme judicial authority, consisting of representatives of the greater and the middle (after this also called « greater ») guilds. 1293: the lesser guilds also admitted to the government, thus making a bloc of twenty-one guilds constituted « for the honour, defence, praise and tranquillity of the Lords Prior and the Gonfaloniers of Justice, and of the whole population of Florence ».

The twenty-one guilds were: the Calimala (a guild of cloth-dyers and finishers), the Moneychangers, Justices and Notaries, Doctors and Apothecaries, Wool manufacturers (as distinct from the Calimala, covering every phase of manufacture, from the scouring of the fleece, to the weaving, dyeing and finishing), Silk manufacturers (their guild was dedicated to Santa Maria), Furriers (including those trading in squirrel skins), Butchers, Shoemakers, Smiths, Stonemasons and Woodworkers, Tanners, Vintners, Bakers, Oilmongers, Locksmiths, Flax merchants, Cabinet-makers, Cuirass-makers, Harness-makers, Innkeepers. The Priors, elected by the *Capitudini* (Heads) of the guilds, nominated the State officials, managed finance and international relations, and, with the convocation of the assembly, formulated all the laws, whilst the Gonfaloniers of Justice, of whom there was one to each prioryship, commanded sufficient men-at-arms to see that the Priors' orders were carried out.

THE GUILDS AND THE STATE

If it is realised that, within the sense of the Ordinances of Justice of 1293 mentioned above, no one who was not « a good Guelph and registered with a guild » could hold public office, it becomes clear that from then onwards the twenty-one guilds are in fact the State. It is

Wool-traders' coat of arms (terracotta attributed to Luca della Robbia).

important to insist on the implications of the law of 1293, which marked a turning-point in social history, by giving work, both manual and intellectual, full civil rights and raising it to a dignity unknown to the Greeks and the Romans. Although honest toil had been rehabilitated by the coming of Christianity, arduous labour had come to be regarded as a means of redemption of original sin.

Nor should it be thought that membership in a guild was a mere formality without meaning. Piero Soderini was a member of the Wool-manufacturers' guild and Niccolò Machiavelli was enrolled with the Vintners, and neither of them had ever engaged in the respective trades. The most famous example of this is Dante, who was registered with the Physicians and Apothecaries, and he certainly never boiled a single handful of herbs to make a potion, or ever performed a blood-letting as a surgeon. In fact, as there were no guilds for writers or politicians, the enrolment of Dante and others into some trade means that they were accepted as workers. This

The Florence State Record Office also contains the Statute of the Guilds. Top right: *preamble to the wool-traders' statute.*

must have come hard to Dante, who prided himself on his Cacciaguida ancestry, and scorned the industrious peasant of Aguglione, only to find that a trade or profession was a *sine qua non* for entry into the *Signoria*. 1378: access to government was extended to include all workers, even the lowest, formerly excluded from associating, but now organised under their own gonfaloniers. The Ciompi uprising ended the evolution of the republican constitution. The return of the middle-class oligarchy prepared the way for the aristocracy, under whose government the energies of a wonderful civilisation based on work gradually withered away.

THE GUILDS IN THE ECONOMY

In addition to their political activities, the guilds performed economic functions which were, after all, their *raison d'être*. These were common to all the guilds, and had the following objectives: to create for their members a monopoly in their trade; to enforce regularity in processes of manufacture and methods of sale so that production costs and selling prices remained uniform; to forbid any kind of competition, including advertising; to regulate supply to demand and not to stimulate demand artificially, and to protect the consumer from fraud.

It might be thought that if all these objectives were secured, the growth of the economy might have been arrested instead of stimulated. This was not the case, however, and business reached great heights of prosperity. It might also be thought that all business concerns might have been depressed to the same level. Again, this did not happen, and there were small, medium-sized, large and very large concerns, so closely linked that a failure of the larger ones set up a chain-reaction amongst all the others.

The fact that the ultimate result of guild activity was so different from what we might expect from reading their Statutes may possibly be explained by considering those business concerns which took the initiative of conducting their affairs outside the city, where they could escape the trammels of co-operative control. Their success was due to a mixture of initiative, courage, intelligence and open-mindedness. Although they continued to come to Florence, which they considered the centre of their trade, they could clearly not be prevented by the guilds from establishing themselves in widely-differing markets, including those abroad. Faced with this situation, the guilds could only accept it and eventually favoured it by encouraging the more prosperous concerns and discouraging the others. « In January », to summarise a subsection of the earliest statute of the Calimala guild to have survived (1301), « there shall be elected six merchants from among those who do business in France (i.e. in Champagne), who may take measures against smaller merchants unable to achieve good sales, to establish the quality and the quantity of cloth which they may import, not wishing to entrust it to open market; the decision of four out of the six shall be final and the *consoli* are charged to see that it is observed ». Thus the « superfluous » (i.e. the smaller) firms could be put out of business and the market concentrated on a few.

The measures taken against internal competition cannot be said to have been respected either. To recall a few of these measures, merchants could not seek to gain the consideration of officers of the guild with gifts, loans or other such bribes, nor make gifts to third parties to procure clientele; they could not attract passers-by into their shops with too ostentatious a display of their wares, nor call them in, nor tempt them with samples. Cloth-merchants could not deal directly with tailors. But if we turn the pages of the account-books and the brokers' records, we see how many infringements of the rules the guild had to punish, that is if it managed to discover them. To certain digressions, although punishable by statute, the guild seems either to have turned a blind eye, or even suggested ways of getting round the prohibition. This seems to have been the case particularly with the interest charged on loans, which the Church had branded as « usury », whatever its amount. The guild, though paying lip-service to the Church by threatening punishment for usury, suggested immediately that the word « interest » should not be entered in the books; instead the moneys paid out should be shown as an unsolicited gift to the borrower by the lender.

It was then laid down that at the beginning of every year the merchants should forgive « usury », so that the Church, which usually intervened at the request of an aggrieved party who denounced his creditor, should not have to set its tribunals in motion. In the first statute of the Calimala guild we may read that every year the consuls were expected to pardon, or to cause to be pardoned, all usury between members of that guild; in the second statute, dating from 1315, it was added that any merchant who had refused could not hold office in the guild, and if he continued to refuse he would be sentenced to further punishment. There is no need to emphasise that this system of pardon favoured the bigger merchants and the more prosperous concerns, and that the smaller firms were scarcely likely to be the ones making the loans.

There seems no doubt either that the wealthier tradesmen did in fact often escape fines by currying the favour of the officials, and, in any case, they could make a shrewd calculation of what they stood to gain by breaking the law and what they would lose by paying a fine, and it was usually to their advantage to transgress.

Those who did not get away with it, however, were the small tradesmen. The records of « criminal proceedings » in the Florence State Archives show that a number of small shopkeepers, especially grocers, were sent to prison because they were unable to pay their fines.

COMPETITION ABROAD

The very detailed regulations mentioned above, together with the strict control of all the manufacturing processes had, however, another result, which turned out to be very important in the development of the economy of Florence: they favoured the establishment of business abroad.

Limiting our examples again to the textile trade, a basic industry of the times, one vital factor in a competitive market was quality. Florentine cloth was perfect: not only was the manufacture closely scrutinised at every stage, but every piece was examined by an expert before being sent for sale. The officials of the Calimala guild responsible for this final testing were called « Ufficiali delle macchie (stains) e magagne (flaws) », and if the defects were seen to be above a certain tolerance (and the faults were marked on the cloth itself) the piece was immediately destroyed. Another essential factor in the fight against foreign competition was price. The guild could also see that this was competitive, as it controlled the workers' wages and forbade them to form associations which might have led to an improvement in their very bad working conditions. With excellent quality and advantageous prices, it is easy to see how the cloth-merchants were able to buy raw wool from England, pay duty on it and considerable transport costs to bring it to Florence, scour, weave, dye and finish it, then export it back at a profit to England, where in fact, it was preferred to native cloth.

Another objective of the guilds was to match production with demand. Manufacturers clearly had to concern themselves with unsold stocks at a time when most of the population could scarcely make both ends meet. The few who could spend at all freely did not make frequent purchases, mainly because the products

Original loom preserved in Florence in the Guild of Silk Workers, a craftsmen's association which continues the ancient Florentine traditions.

(cloth, furniture and so on) were of such high quality that they scarcely ever wore out. The few very rich, who might have bought frequently to keep up with changing fashions, were often prevented from doing so by the current sumptuary laws.

It should be quite clearly understood that there was no mention in the statutes of the guilds of permission to limit production. This was done, however, indirectly, by providing for a number of fixed holidays and by restricting work to the hours of daylight.

If to these fixed holidays are added the other non-working days, the Sundays and the great religious festivals in honour of a number of saints, the total time lost to industry was more than four months in the year. This does not seem to prove, as has sometimes been maintained, either the workers' tendency to idleness or the great attraction of the Church, which might rather see them at mass than at the bench or the loom.

As for the limitation of work to the hours of daylight, which meant that comparatively little work was done in winter, this has sometimes been put down to the fear of fires. In fact, since the houses and shops were mainly of wood and illumination was by oil-lamp or candle, fires were not infrequent, and sometimes whole streets were destroyed.

There may be some truth in these suppositions (except for the idleness of the Florentines, who were, in fact, very hard-working) but one could maintain that underlying all these measures was the desire to limit excessive production.

The principle of relating demand to supply must in general have inspired the political economy of the age. This may be illustrated by comparing Florence with Venice, though here we have two differently-based economies: that of the Republic of San Marco, a maritime city, almost entirely, and for centuries exclusively, dependent on trade, and that of Florence, the inland city, dependent on manufacturing, trading and banking.

The rulers of Venice were interested not so much in increasing the traffic through their city as in the balance between exports and imports. This is borne out in contemporary documents and explicit legislative provisions. In fact, the use of money, or gold and silver ingots for the purchase of goods, generally of a high price, in the Levant, had to be kept to a minimum, and the maximum use had to be made of barter. When, for some reason or another, the balance of trade was upset,

the capital invested in trade was called in by the state and reinvested in manufacturing. This happened particularly in the second half of the fourteenth century.

PROTECTING THE CONSUMER

The final objective of the guilds was the protection of the consumer, who might be deceived by inaccurate reports of the quality of merchandise or by unjustified high prices. The purchaser was encouraged to buy his goods with the assistance of a « sensale » (broker), a public official trained to distinguish the various qualities of products. If the product asked for by the client was not available in a particular shop, the sensale quickly accompanied him to another. Shops and workshops concerned with the same trade were for this reason situated along the same street. In addition, and this would have been impossible for anyone who was not himself a high-class merchant, the sensale could read the tacca (tally), a thin strip of parchment sewn on to the piece showing the various prices: the price paid to the foreign manufacturer, with his name and the « visas » of the guild consoli on detachment abroad; the costs of transport, which could not exceed certain prescribed limits, and the duties paid, including those required to bring the merchandise into Florence. It was then comparatively simple for the sensale to calculate if the price asked was reasonable or if the mark-up was too high. Finally he had to record the negotiations so that the guild could claim its due percentage.

The textile guilds succeeded one another in order of importance: first came the Calimala, which began to decline with the failure of the Champagne market, then the Wool-manufacturers' guild, which gradually weakened as the raw-material markets shrank, due to the spread of manufacturing in countries which had been primarily exporters of wool, a process speeded up by protective tariffs; then the Silk-manufacturers' guild, which prospered with the increased pomp and ostentation at Court and in the houses of the great families.

The political power of the guilds declined under the Signoria, and their economic position also weakened under the Principate, when the direction of the political economy and of politics in general was concentrated in the hands of the Prince himself.

The chronicler Giovanni Villani, referring to the four-year period 1336 to 1339, an age of gold, writes that the Commune of Florence, having but little income, had to resort to excise duties, forced loans and other forms of taxation from merchants and citizens. The interest on the loans was to be paid out of the duties and taxes.

The duties, called *gabelle*, which were levied on consumer goods and on business turn-over, brought in annually some three hundred thousand gold florins « which », according to Villani, « would be a great amount to any realm; King Robert has not so much income, nor has the King of Sicily, nor the King of Aragon ». The loans could be voluntary or forced; the latter usually bore no interest, if they were « general », that is imposed on all citizens, whereas they were usually with interest if they affected merely certain groups of the wealthier citizens. Voluntary loans always bore interest which, according to the state of the money market, could be anything from 5 per cent upwards.

In 1342, six years after the start of the two campaigns against Mastino della Scala, the Commune owed 800,000 gold florins, which it was quite unable to repay from the income from the *gabelle*. This had recently doubled, and further increases would have been out of the question.

In 1347 all debts, « reduced » to 504,000 florins, were consolidated into the *Monte*, an accumulation of bonds no longer repayable, but reissued at a reduced standard interest of 5 per cent and transferable (which had not been the case previously) by change of registration on the books of the *Monte*. The interest rate of 5 per cent, though apparently modest, was in effect exorbitant, according to Villani, because immediately after the conversion the bonds fell to 30 per cent of their nominal value. Those who were constrained to sell lost two thirds of their capital and received no further interest, whereas those who were able to buy at 30 per cent of the nominal value were getting a return of 15 per cent. As a result of this speculation the *Monte* bonds, picked up by those who had most ready money, tended increasingly to be concentrated in fewer hands.

This was not all, however. In setting up the *Monte* to relieve the pressure on the State finances, an undertaking had been given not to have recourse to any further loans. This turned out to be impossible, just as

The money-changer (detail from a painting by Jacopo di Cione and Andrea Orcagna, commissioned from the latter by the Guild of Money-changers in 1367). The money was kept in the little box, but only enough for the day's transactions.

it was impossible to keep interest rates down to 5 per cent after the 1347 affair. From June 1362 to August 1364, during the campaign against Pisa, no fewer than fourteen loans were taken, each one varying between 500 and 100,000 florins, and it was impossible to find anyone to underwrite them at a rate of interest less than that current in other investments. Thus, not only were other *Monti* set up (called the *Monte Nuovo*, the *Nuovissimo*, the *Monticino*, and so on), but certain expedients had to be found to get round the 5 per cent limit without formally violating the fundamental rule of the first *Monte*. There were the « *Monte* one-two » and the « *Monte* one-three » which, according to Villani, operated as follows: the individual paid 100 florins into the State funds and the cashier entered up 200 or 300 against his name at the standard rate of 5 per cent interest.

When the lesser guilds came to power after the Ciompi uprising of 1378, the keystone of their financial policy was the reduction of the State debt, « returning to the intentions of those who founded the *Monte* ». But, apart from the short duration of their government, force of circumstances would have made this impossible to realise, even if they had held power for much longer.

It had, in fact, become impossible to base financial policy on indirect taxation, and the time had come to listen to the voice of the people, now demanding with increasing persistence a system of taxation based on each individual's capacity to contribute.

Direct taxation had existed in Florence in the thirteenth century, and Villani talks about taxes and duties levied according to « a personal standing », a system which could lead to the most bare-faced favouritism.

We know, however, what the people wanted. In a discussion in the Councils on the « reform » of 1285, Borgo Rinaldi had proposed an assessment for taxation purposes of all possessions on the basis of a 5 per cent valuation for houses in the city, 6.66 per cent for country property, and 10 per cent for expensive furnishings, the latter being considered a particularly lucrative source of revenue. Rinaldi, though continuing to talk of « personal standing », really had in mind a register of land and property. Naturally his proposal was rejected by the representatives of the mercantile classes who formed a majority in the Councils.

How long could the merchants have held this position, however, if in the next wars they were going to need the support of the lesser guilds, and the guilds had made a condition of this support a more equitable distribution of the tax burden?

In fact, on the eve of the battle of Altopascio, won on September 23rd 1325 by Castruccio Castracani, *signore* of Lucca, the oligarchy attempted to reconcile the

of the city guilds. Extreme right and left coats of arms of the Money-changers' Guild: gold coins on a red background (Uffizi).

people with a « *provvisione* » (resolution) stating that « in consideration of the iniquity and inequality evident in Florence in the imposition and the exaction of taxes, a new assessment register shall be drawn up by which each one shall be required to pay according to his capabilities ». It was only a promise, which no one had the intention of keeping: in fact when it came to defending the city, now threatened at its very walls, they preferred to hand over the entire government temporarily to a representative of their friend the King of Naples.

CHARLES OF CALABRIA AND THE DUKE OF ATHENS

But the representative himself, Charles of Calabria, upset these calculations. As soon as he took command in Florence, where it was intended he should stay only until victory was achieved, he declared his intention of ruling the city for life. To achieve his purpose he sought the favour of the people by causing his government to put into effect, as their first act, the above *provvisione*. He drew up a census of private possessions from written sworn statements, he classified them into groups for taxation purposes and, remembering that the highest profits were obtained from the investment of

money in the manufacturing and trading concerns and in the manipulation of loans, he was lenient with town- and country-property owners whom he assessed at 0.83 per cent and 1.25 per cent, but financiers with capital available for loans were taxed at 1.66 per cent, and the income from private industry was taxed on a sliding scale. These measures produced, in two tax periods, 120,000 gold florins.

This was a bitter blow to the leading merchants who had called in the Angevin prince, and no sooner did they take up the reins of government again (Charles left in December 1328) than they burned the tax registers and indemnified the hardest hit.

Some, however, had anticipated Charles's move and had tried to protect themselves in advance. There is evidence of this in the account books of the Peruzzi. These show the amount of the working capital every time the company was reconstituted. In 1312 it stood at 118,000 florins, but on November 1st 1324 it had fallen to 60,000, in spite of large profits and high dividends throughout the period. Evidently as soon as it became likely that the government of Florence would be handed over to the Angevin prince late in 1324, the company decided to hide a proportion of its capital from the tax authorities. This evasion, however, had unforeseen consequences: clients of the company, both in Italy and overseas, became alarmed, and many of the stockholders withdrew their deposits.

There was another attempt to establish a tax register by yet another Angevin prince, Gualtieri di Brienne, Duke of Athens. Called in to govern the city during the war against Lucca which began in 1336, he too proclaimed himself perpetual ruler in September 1342. He was driven out on August 3rd 1343 and the documents he had collected for his register were burnt.

THE CATASTO

Time was pressing, however, and the Ciompi uprising of 1378 must have opened the eyes of the old oligarchy when it regained power. Yet we have to go forward to 1427 before we see any substantial change in the Florentine tax system. This year saw the introduction of the *catasto*, a complete survey of movable and immovable property, of business profits, professional incomes, money-changers' profits, liquid assets, civil and commercial credits and interest received from government loans. From the total of these « assets » was subtracted the value of the house occupied and the workshop used for business, plus 200 florins per head to cover « the necessities of life » and the remainder, called *sostanza* (property) or *sovrabbondante* (surplus) was taxed at $1\frac{1}{2}$ per cent.

This was doubtless a victory for the generations of men who, for two centuries, had been pursuing the ideal of equal sacrifice in taxation. It was an act of social justice and a guarantee of external peace, « because it pained them » (i.e. the rich), wrote Machiavelli, « not to be able to stir up war without harm to themselves, having to contribute to the expense like everyone else ». Wars continued, nevertheless, even if the rich man's burden increased to such an extent that, as Jacopo Pitti remarked, « those who before had paid twenty now paid three hundred ». This was a victory for the people, and there was good reason for the support the new tax-laws received from Giovanni di Bicci of the Medici family. He was preparing, on that family's behalf, the development from the Republic to the Principate, and was anxious for popular support.

Some sixteen years later, in 1443, Cosimo il Vecchio introduced a supplementary tax on a sliding scale, ranging from 4 per cent on incomes of from 1 to 50 florins to 33 per cent on incomes above 1500 florins.

This tax came to be called, ironically enough, *graziosa* (lenient) because it favoured the underprivileged.

The *decima scalata*, a land-tax levied on a sliding scale, for which there was a precedent in the draft legislation of the popular government of 1378, was also a result of a military campaign: Florence had to defend herself against the threat of Filippo Maria Visconti, *signore* of Milan, whose aggressive ambitions were being encouraged by Rinaldo degli Albizzi, the rival of the Medici. The money brought in by this tax certainly contributed to the victory at Anghiari over the Milanese in 1440, but those who had been forced to pay out were less interested in the liberty of Florence than in the emptiness of their purses. Comparing the Medici to two unpopular figures of the past, people said (according to Cavalcanti) that « Cosimo takes our persons when he takes our possessions, just as the other *signori* Carlo and Gualtieri did ».

After the war was over, the discontent over taxation came to a head, not in a popular uprising, naturally, as the ordinary people would scarcely have been affected, but in legal measures. In 1444, when appointments to public office were being renewed by secret ballot, from the scrutiny of the voting-papers, called *fiordaliso* (fleur-de-lys, beautiful to look at but smelling unpleasantly), it turned out that all those elected belonged to the anti-Medici faction. Cosimo's reaction was immediate: he annulled the elections, prosecuted those most closely involved and nominated to finance posts ten *accoppiatori* from among his most devoted followers.

In 1447, on the occasion of the nth struggle for the succession to the Duchy of Milan, this time between the *condottiere* Francesco Sforza, supported by the Medici, and Alfonso of Aragon, King of Naples, these gentlemen imposed a further tax which became known as the *decina dispiacente*, from the ten (*decina*) who imposed it, and because the absolute power they were given and the heavy burden the tax imposed were displeasing (*dispiacente*) in the extreme. In fact, until now, if the taxable *sovrabbondante* was small, the tax-payer could often settle with the tax-official for a smaller figure, and the law allowed for this; those who could show that the whole of their small income was entirely earned could « pay at will », that is without becoming liable to prosecution if they failed to pay on the due date. All these concessions were now revoked, and Cosimo's tax policy, designed to discourage, and even to destroy, his opponents, became even clearer:

The money market (detail from painting by Jarves, Keeper of the Chests).

no longer heeding either *sicurtà* (safety) or *composizione* (moderation) he could strike at anyone he wished, even the smallest.

When the discontent really became widespread in 1449, the situation in 1444 was repeated with the renewal of public appointments after the five-year period of office had elapsed. This time Cosimo, who foresaw the results of the voting, but now did not dare to quash the ordinances of the Republic which established the liberty of scrutiny, preferred to manipulate the elections in advance by getting the principal families, especially those less favourable to him, to recognise the position he had achieved.

This recognition was ratified in a « sworn pact » the terms of which might be summed up as follows:

« (*a*) every good citizen must care for liberty, and for liberty to exist there must be a correct administration of justice, so that the cause of all discord, both public and private, may be removed; (*b*) at this moment we recognise that this justice, and therefore our liberty, is being affected for the good of the State of Florence, and we therefore affirm that under the present regime we live politically and morally as we should; (*c*) we join together, under the bond of our oath, with the firm intention of maintaining this premise during our lifetime, and ensuring for the lifetime of our children a regime exactly similar to the present, which shall do right by all, in civil and in criminal justice, which shall distribute offices according to merit, and the burdens, that is to say the taxes, according to the ability

Statutes of the Parte Guelfa and of the Money-changers' guild (State Record Office, Florence).

of each to pay ». The conclusion, though not expressed, was « since we are of the opinion that the present regime represents the *optimum*, in the elections for the governing body, we shall choose persons who undertake to ensure the continuity of this regime. In other words, with effect from now we guarantee that as far as it lies within our power there shall be no repetition of the *pronunciamento* of 1444 against Cosimo », (then follow the signatures of the representatives of 64 of the leading families in the city).

Thus Cosimo was invested with the power he asked for, and he opened the way for his family successors up to Lorenzo the Magnificent. The old oligarchy capitulated: they had not yielded an inch over the just distribution of taxes demanded so passionately by the people, and now they really had given in to their master.

We have thus traced the path from indirect taxes, for centuries the basis of the finances of the Commune, to direct taxation, the mainstay of the *Signoria*; from the early valuation registers to the *catasto*: a path that leads us to believe that History, however remote, can always illuminate the present and direct our steps for today and tomorrow.

THE GOLD FLORIN

Charlemagne's monetary reforms, which produced a currency based on silver instead of the Roman gold *soldo*, had been adequate for an economy which was extremely poor in both the quantity and the quality of its goods and services. Not only was silver the basis of the new system, but only very small coins were put into circulation. These were the *denari* (pence), of which 240 were cut from a *libbra* (pound) of silver; twelve of these *denari* made up a *soldo* and twenty *soldi* a *lira*, a purely imaginary coin used for accounting purposes only.

This was no longer adequate for the situation which had arisen after the reopening of the Mediterranean by the Crusaders, and the formation of international trading centres such as the Champagne fairs, which dealt in rich merchandise from the East. A length of oriental silk or a necklace would have cost sackfuls of *denari*. Moreover, trade negotiations were complicated by the uncertainty of the value of money, as the right to strike coins, invested in a number of persons in different towns, produced a variety in quality and weight, favoured debasement and encouraged falsification, both official and private.

Thus between the end of the twelfth and the early years of the thirteenth centuries, the principal Italian cities took to striking the *grosso*, a coin of the value and weight of twelve *denari*, which brought into being the *soldo* as money. In the second half of the thirteenth century they then began to strike gold coins, first the Florentine *fiorino*, the Genoese *genovino*, the Milanese *ambrogino*, and finally, in 1284, the Venetian ducat. Thus in effect the *lira* became a coin, concentrated in a small quantity of more precious metal (3.536 grammes of gold in the florin) equivalent to a pound of silver. Anyone who took the mint 240 *denari* could have them exchanged for a florin, and vice-versa. Otherwise, to keep the *lira* equivalent to the florin, the value of gold with respect to silver would have had to be kept the same as it was on the Western markets in 1252. The value of silver rose, however, as the demand for it increased when it came to be used in luxury articles as well as in coins. The weight of silver in the *denari* thus came to be reduced as supplies fell, and it was mixed with a baser metal. The 20 *soldi* of 1252 were worth 33 in 1283, 37 in 1301, 51 in 1302, 58 in 1315, 61 in 1318, and so on.

There were two consequences. The first was the complication which ensued in the merchants' accounts, as their books continued to refer to the *lira*. This was cleared up in 1371 with the creation of a « money of account » (that is, not actually minted): the *lira a*

fiorini, officially equal to 29 *soldi*, a value which remained unchanged. The second consequence was that florins and other denominations finally became the coinage of two different classes: the florin, with its fixed purchasing power, was used by the great merchants and the upper bourgeoisie in general; the smaller coinage, the purchasing power of which was constantly decreasing, was used by the lower classes. Thus the monetary system, as well as the system of taxation and the organisation of the guilds, again reflected the difference between the social classes.

To remedy the situation it would have been necessary to make the payment of goods and wages on a sliding scale tied to the value of silver, but the Statutes of the Guilds, confirmed by the Commune, opposed all increases in wages. The government, faced with the impossibility of halting the depreciation of the smaller currency, should clearly not have attempted to contain the fall of the florin. Yet this is what the oligarchy demanded, for fear they should have to pay their workers more, and lest a rise in the price of silver beyond a certain point should bring down the price of gold.

The brief government of the Ciompi, however, was against the depreciation of the smaller currency, but was incapable of any measure beyond the suspension of minting, a fruitless procedure, as the depreciation continued by force of circumstances. What has been said about currency depreciation and the unwillingness to pay higher wages emphasises the success of Florentine goods in competition abroad: their quality was high and their prices were low because of the low cost of manpower.

The benefits which the Florentine merchants obtained from their florin-based currency went further than advantages on the world markets. Their currency was acceptable everywhere, and all other currencies were related to it, so that it became a standard, like sterling and the dollar in our day. There were two reasons for this success: first the undertaking given when minting was begun (and scrupulously adhered to) that the florin would not be changed in either weight or quality, and second the artistic perfection of its design. On the obverse it showed Saint John, the patron saint of the city, and on the reverse the stylised lily, the city's emblem. The beauty of its design might account for its widespread use. It turned out to be much more popular than the *genovino*, the

ambrogino or the *ducato*, although these currencies too had a fixed value, and, if imitation is the sincerest form of flattery, there were forty-eight attempts to copy the florin, beginning with the Curia. Another coinage which became popular through the perfection of its minting was Maria Theresa's Austrian *thaler*.

The rise in the fortunes of the florin coincided with the decline of Siena. The tide began to turn decisively in favour of the former when Florence began minting the gold florin, whilst Siena, out of pride and fidelity to the coinage which had brought such prestige to the city, still hung on to silver. Even before the merchant family of the Bonsignori from Siena went bankrupt in 1304, Florentines were bankers to the Pope, who introduced them as « dearest friends » to princes from all over the world, thus setting them on the road to high adventure.

The high purchasing power of the gold florin has several times been mentioned. A question repeatedly asked of the historian is: « What would the florin be worth today ? ». It is impossible to say. We know what we can buy with 3.356 grammes of 24-carat gold, but, remembering the massive imports of gold from America after Columbus, and the ever greater and more rapid circulation of money, we cannot possibly say what this amount of gold would have bought in the period from the thirteenth to the sixteenth centuries.

As a guide, however, and so that the reader may judge the value of the figures quoted in the preceding pages, the cost to the Commune in 1338 for « food and drink to the Priors and their families » (in all, including trumpeters and arms-bearers, several tens of persons, many of whom were not content with a modest dinner and supper, but wanted young capon, pigeon, quail

Two pages of the « Fiorinaio », the large manuscript in which the Officials of the Mint recorded their deliberations concerning the various issues and the stamping of new coins, with the slight differences in the dies which distinguished one series from another. The « Fiorinaio » is preserved in the State Record Office.

and trout and the like) amounted to some 3,600 *fiorini*, or 1,160 gold florins a year, that is some three florins a day.

Further information concerning the minting of the florin and its many denominations, *largo, stretto, di suggello* (« broad », « narrow » and « sealed » respectively, the latter because they came from the mint in closed bags so that they would not be worn down by use or subject to fraudulent « scraping ») may be obtained by consulting in the Florence State Archives the huge manuscript known as the « Fiorinaio ». This was where officials of the mint recorded from time to time the *provvisioni* (resolutions) by which the issues were authorised and established. The design remained substantially the same, except for slight variations when the punches were changed. They also entered the different hallmarks used by the various coiners. This has meant that surviving pieces can be dated with some accuracy by numismatists.

THE MERCHANT COMPANIES

To enable them to conduct their business on an international scale, Florentine merchants had to take certain measures which necessitated a certain type of association, the *compagnia*. Firstly, the several members of the same family united their forces, sharing the profits and the losses in proportion to the sums they had put into the *Corpo di compagnia*. Then, as these forces were insufficient to meet the demands of the growing business, the nearest relatives were brought in, then friends, and finally strangers. The original name of the company remained unchanged, even if the holdings of the latter, at a figure around 5 per cent interest, finally came to exceed those of all the partners.

The legal structure of the company was suggested by the initial constitution: men of the same blood who ate at the same table in the family mansion, sensitive to the *honor familiaris*, pledged themselves to third parties with all their patrimony and answered for each other. This was the beginning of joint unlimited responsibility, which was to be characteristic of future general, unlimited partnerships.

On the business side, the companies, or at least the largest ones, devoted themselves to industry, trade or banking, according to the objective for which they were formed: to make their undertaking more profit-

The florin: recto the Florence Lily, verso St. John the Baptist, the patron saint of the city (Bargello Museum).

able, avoiding the cost of intermediaries. With this end in view, the industrialist was his own salesman and distributor and could raise bank loans to further either branch of his activities. The guiding principle behind the guild, by which it had the exclusive right to permit its members to exercise a particular trade or profession, was deliberately violated when it became possible for a person to enrol in one or more trade association. This was not irrational on the part of the great merchants, but proof of common sense in spreading their business activities, just as it was common sense to spread their risks by investing their money in real estate, in country property and in government securities.

Manufacturing, commercial and banking businesses required an organisation based on branches in the most important marketing centres, and on a large personnel functioning in various grades from the general administrator to the chief accountant and his assistants, the notaries (the nucleus of the present-day legal department) to the messenger boys. It also required a system of accounting which would enable the management to follow the course of business throughout the concern. For example, in the early years of the fourteenth century the Bardi company had branches in Ancona, Aquila, Bari, Barletta, Castello di Castro (Cagliari), Genoa, Naples, Orvieto, Palermo, Pisa, Rome, Venice and, abroad, Avignon, Barcelona, Bruges, Cyprus, Constantinople, Jerusalem, London, Majorca, Marseilles, Nice, Paris, Rhodes, Seville and Tunis. Between 1310 and 1345 it had a personnel of about 400 engaged in administrative, executive and clerical work. The bookkeeping, although not done on the double-entry system until the second half of the fourteenth century (when it came into general use, based on the manual of Luca Pacioli, who did not, however, invent it, but merely described it) was extremely complicated, but suitable for the purpose intended.

THE BARDI AND THE PERUZZI

Another characteristic which was common to all these big companies was that each had a relatively short life which ended up in bankruptcy owing to excess of credit and operational risk, especially abroad.

As for credit, a mere rumour of financial embarrassment, which a little calm consideration might have shown to be unfounded, was enough to set shareholders demanding an immediate return of their investment. The working capital, as we have stated previously, was far from enough to cover the large sums involved, and moneys owed by third parties were difficult to recover quickly. Thus in the middle of the fourteenth century, after a series of failures, the Bardi, Peruzzi and Acciaiuoli companies went bankrupt. These companies had been so powerful that Villani had called them the « pillars of Christianity ». As for operational risks, the position was as follows: to function in the various centres, the merchants needed the protection of the local *signori* and the right of permanent residence (and not temporary as the laws required of foreigners), customs facilities and protection from native merchants and the local population, who held that the Florentines should be permitted to operate only at their own risk. Matthew Paris, the English historian, wrote that the Lombards (a term which included all merchants from Italy) never brought with them a single ducat, but only a piece of paper in one hand and a pen in the other, and fleeced the people to whom they lent money.

There was, however, the other side of the picture: in exchange for the favours they granted, the monarchs asked for loans, especially for the conduct of war, and repaid only after long delay, if, indeed, they repaid at all. This was the case with Edward III (1327-77), to quote the most glaring example, and the Bardi and Peruzzi companies, from which he asked for a loan for the first campaign against France in what was to become known as the Hundred Years' War. Against the grant and direct collection of all the State revenues, they were to provide all the expenses of collecting an army, transporting it across the Channel and providing it with arms, munitions and food, whilst within the Kingdom they were also to pay the civil service. It might justifiably be said that a handful of Florentine merchants were the real sovereigns of England and the King a penniless beggar. After setting sail for France, he remembered that it was his wedding anniversary and sent back a representative of the Peruzzi to buy (out of the funds of the company) a pearl necklace and present it to the Queen.

It must not be supposed, however, that the Florentine merchants took this risk, which in any case they could scarcely have avoided, and merely prayed to God for an English victory. Knowing, on the other hand, that success might favour the King of France, they came to terms with him also and promised him loans through their branch in Paris. The rival monarchs were not, of course, intended to know of the double game, but Philip discovered it and immediately sequestrated the companies' entire assets. The reasons for the eventual bankruptcy of these two giants of business is therefore rather more complicated than it would at first sight seem from reading Villani, who puts the entire blame on Edward III for defaulting on his debts.

These debts amounted to a million and a half gold florins. Fanciful calculations have been made over the years as to how much, in capital and compound interest through the intervening centuries, the British Crown owes the heirs of these ancient merchants, if any, and if not, the Italian State. The calculations would be pointless, however, for many reasons, one of which is that there has never been the required periodic recognition of the debt and the obligation has therefore lapsed with the passing of time. Researches at the Public Record office in London have revealed a document dated 1391 which shows that the question was settled during the reign of Richard II (1377-1399), when both parties (the Florentines owed money to the Crown as well) declared themselves satisfied and undertook to enter no further claims against each other in the future. There is one further curious factor: as it was then believed that the debtor who died before satisfying his creditors would remain in Purgatory until his heirs had honoured his debts, and as the

solemn act by which Edward III had promised to « reinstate my beloved merchants » had been underwritten by his young son, and a number of nobles and prelates, Gualtiero dei Bardi, representing the interests of the Florentines, liberated the souls of them all, recalling them each by name, and enabling God to bear them off to Paradise, provided, that is, that they had no other sins than their insolvency.

THE MEDICI COMPANIES

Having dealt at some length with the largest of the companies set up in Florence and operating in Italy and abroad up to the middle of the fourteenth century, there is no need to linger over the many that preceded them, all of which had the same type of constitution, functioned in the same way and had the same fate. It is better to take a leap forward in time and consider the Medici companies of the branch of Giovanni di Averardo, or Bicci, that is of Cosimo the Elder, Piero and Lorenzo the Magnificent. This will allow of comparisons with the past and a consideration of how the company developed during the fifteenth century.

Whereas previously capital was subscribed only to the head office of the company and branches were merely administrative units, dependent on the head-

quarters in Florence, now the central organisation and the branch-offices were legally separate units, although headquarters still had certain overall administrative control, and kept the current holdings. The Medici, who founded the first business in the city, were partners in this and in all the others which had gradually come into being since, and they owned more than half the shares. As an example, the contract drawn up for the Bruges company on March 23rd 1456 shows that of the registered capital of 3,000 Flemish *grossi*, the Medici owned 1,900, Galeazzo Pigli 600 and Agnolo Tani 500. This gave certain advantages to the partners. Previously they had all stood equal and it had been their duty, acting in collaboration, to appoint and dismiss the staff, delegate powers to their agents to enter into binding contracts on their behalf, draw up a balance-sheet at any moment before or after the date laid down in the company's rules and proceed to the liquidation of the company. All this was now the prerogative of the Medici family members (called *maiores*, whereas other partners were called *minores*). Formerly, branches were run by paid agents; now they were under a partner known as a *governatore*, who was paid by having his expenses reimbursed and his dividend increased.

The chief accountant had laid down accounting procedure, directed and controlled the bookkeeping and provided the data for the balance-sheet, which was then drawn up by the manager of the company and

his associates. Now he had the title of « Director of the Bank of Florence », and as the counsellor and right arm of the head of the company and its senior partners he had very wide powers. After agreement with the « Chief » he drew up the orders for the *governatori* and the company's travellers, examined the reports sent by letter or brought in personally by agents and checked their balance-sheets. These high-placed officials of the Medici companies sometimes had their place in history for reasons other than their business activities. Francesco Sassetti, for example, was immortalised by Ghirlandaio in Santa Trinita Church, and Francesco di Jacopo Nori lost his life in 1478 in the riot following the killing of Giuliano de' Medici, brother of Lorenzo the Magnificent, in Santa Maria del Fiore.

As to the financing of these companies, the working capital continued to come mainly from outside investors, though the risk here was not as great now that depositors were required to give six months' or, in some cases, a year's notice of withdrawal. This protected the company against a sudden concerted run on the bank. Compared with these outside interests in the company, the share capital of the original partners was quite small, and sometimes merely underwritten and not subscribed. Nor could the company rely on the liquid assets of the partners, who often invested outside the company, and in any case the partners'

Registers used by merchants and entrepreneurs for accounting and trading transactions: cash-books and large notebooks full of jottings and columns of figures (State Record Office, Florence).

shares earned a higher interest than the others. The Medici, in fact, far from investing their own wealth in their companies and injecting them with new life-blood, took out all they could in demands for loans from all their banks, both the central and the branches, which they then invested in other businesses. After Piero de' Medici had been driven out of the city in 1494 his liabilities were found to exceed his assets, including his own share capital, by more than 1,000 gold florins, and Cardinal Giovanni, the future Pope Leo X, had an overdraft of 7,500 florins.

It should be added, finally, that the Medici, whilst continuing to be bankers to the Papacy, could not draw, even temporarily, on the tithes they collected for the Church, as these were scarcely ever sufficient to cover the advances demanded by the Apostolic Camera, which found itself increasingly short of ready cash as the Papacy became more and more involved with politics. These advances put the Church in debt to the Medicis in 1473 to the tune of 69,918 florins, used in the struggle against the Hussites in Bohemia and to help Mattia Corvino against the Turks.

THE RANGE OF THE MEDICI ACTIVITIES

Passing from the legal and administrative structure of the Medici companies to their trading activities, they operated over a wide area with branches in Avignon, Bruges, London, Milan, Rome, Venice and Geneva, the latter being transferred eventually to Lyons where there were increasingly important markets. Like the thirteenth- and fourteenth-century companies, they had representatives, either individual or company, in all the most important trading centres.

Again like the older companies, their activities were multiple: manufacturing, trading and banking. They had textile factories in Florence which produced high quality woollen and silk materials; these were exported to the English and French Courts, to the House of Burgundy in Flanders, and the Papal Curia in Rome. The company dealt with a wide range of imports and exports: in addition to finished cloth for England, the Netherlands and the Levant, it had interests in other articles such as foodstuffs including spices, oil and fruit, dyestuffs, especially alum, and silver.

Two of its undertakings, one maritime and the other mining, are of particular interest.

The Medicis' maritime interests started with the building of three galleons in the Pisan shipyards of Philip the Good for a crusade which was never begun. These were adapted for merchant traffic both to the Levant and to the West, and large profits were expected. They were registered under the Burgundian flag to escape the regulations and the dues of the Florentine authorities, the *Consoli del Mare*. It was not long, however, before things began to go badly. Almost immediately one ship was lost in a storm, and in 1470 the other two were seized by Charles the Bold of Burgundy and incorporated in his fleet to fight Louis XI of France. They were eventually ransomed, but almost immediately afterwards one of them was captured in 1473 by a Hansa pirate. It was carrying the famous triptych « The Last Judgment », which the Medici agent Agnolo Tani had commissioned from Memling and was having shipped back to Florence; it is now in the Marienkirche in Danzig. The other galleon sank the following year in a storm.

The Medici had better luck in their mining activities, at least in the beginning. These started with the discovery of a large alum deposit on Church land. After the loss of Focea in Venetia, this was of such importance that the discoverer, Giovanni da Castro, announced it to Pope Pius II in terms of great enthusiasm: « Holy Father, today I bring you victory over the Turk. Every year the Turks extort from the Christians more than 300,000 ducats, because Ischia produces but little and the alum mines of Lipari have been worked out since the times of the Romans. Today I have found seven mountains so rich in alum that they could furnish seven worlds. You will be able to supply alum enough to dye the cloth of the whole of Europe and thus snatch away the profit from the infidel. The raw materials, wood and water to boil the rocks, are in abundant supply, and there is a port nearby, Civitavecchia. From this moment you may start to prepare your crusade against the Turk. The Tolfa alum mines will finance it ».

When it came to the exploitation of the deposits, the Medici stepped in, as they always did where there was a chance of large profits. They were well aware of the importance of alum, and it was Lorenzo's interests in its alum mines which had brought about the sack of the town of Volterra.

To obtain the results they had hoped for, the Medici had to see that alum prices did not fall through

A fifteenth-century shop with counter and, on the shelf, the cash-book and accounting documents. Detail from a predella by Paolo Uccello (Gallery, Ducal Palace, Urbino).

competition or excessive production. The Church took charge of the first of these dangers by threatening with excommunication and sequestration of their cargoes, on the high seas or in the port of embarkation, all Christian merchants who bought alum from the infidel. The second danger was taken care of by the Medici who took complete control of the extraction and the selling, bringing the whole concern within their trading and banking network. The Rome branch provided share capital for the « Tolfa Company »

217

set up with the Pope; the branches at Bruges, London and Florence undertook the marketing of the product against purchases of wool or for cash. The Pope kept control over the stocks in the Civita-vecchia warehouses and took a fixed sum per *cantaro* (about 150 lbs) together with two thirds of the extra profits.

Finally, it was necessary to have the co-operation of State rulers in putting into effect Rome's edicts on the purchase of alum, and preventing the entry into their territory not only of Turkish alum, but also any other alum which did not come from Tolfa. This is where the troubles started. Edward IV of England (1461-1483) refused, realising the danger of a monopoly in alum to the growing woollen cloth industry in his kingdom. Charles the Bold, more closely connected to the Medici, agreed at first, but then had to give way to public opinion. In Venice agreement had to be reached with the biggest local wholesaler, who won the concession of the exclusive sale of 6,000 *cantari* a year in the city, in Lombardy, Romagna, Southern Germany and Austria. The rulers of Southern Italy extracted an agreement for a twenty-five year cartel fixing the selling-price, limiting the quantity mined and dividing out the market. If to all these difficulties were added those of increased contraband, it is clear that the prices, which the Medici had hoped to manipulate, would eventually end up by conforming to those of the general market.

However, these trading activities came to an end when the power of the Medici was broken by the Pazzi conspiracy of 1478, and the possessions of the Signori of Florence were sequestrated by Pope Sixtus IV.

THE MEDICIS' BANKING ACTIVITIES

The third of the Medicis' mercantile activities, banking, was the most extensive. This was in keeping with the custom of the times whereby, since the end of the fourteenth century, business men had tended to pay less attention to commercial transactions which, moreover, as a consequence of political events, were becoming more and more restricted to the Western world.

After the end of the Mongols and the coming of the Ming dynasty, an increasing xenophobia was closing down the trade routes opened up by Marco

Two details showing certain aspects of trading: the merchant's departure (a miniature in the Riccardiana Library) and, below, a detail from the « Procession of the Magi » (Benozzo Gozzoli).

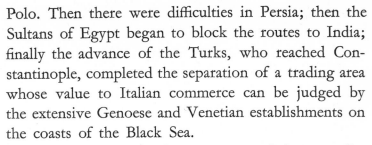

Polo. Then there were difficulties in Persia; then the Sultans of Egypt began to block the routes to India; finally the advance of the Turks, who reached Constantinople, completed the separation of a trading area whose value to Italian commerce can be judged by the extensive Genoese and Venetian establishments on the coasts of the Black Sea.

This combination of circumstances led to a redistribution of capital in two directions: firstly into the traditional industries, though here less money was put into textiles and more into mining, because of recent technical progress, and into metallurgy, in response to the increased demand in the military field; secondly in loans to sovereigns, not in themselves an innovation, but now reaching gigantic proportions consequent upon growing nationalism and intensive political activity. These loans were eventually to bring down the whole fabric of the Medici business.

Before analysing the causes of the fall of the Medici, two things must be made clear: firstly, the financial empire of the Medici did not collapse at one go, but crumbled slowly as a result of successive failures; secondly, those responsible were well aware of the dangers of financial relationships with the sovereigns of the states in which they were operating, and were in the long run the victims of circumstances which no one could control.

Bankruptcy was warded off by the political power of the Medici who, in case of need, drew even on the State funds. Lorenzo, for instance, seized the *Monte delle Doti*, a charitable fund to provide dowries for impoverished young girls, and used it to fend off a crisis in the family business.

That it was well-known that the fortunes of the business could prosper only in mercantile activities is proved beyond a shadow of doubt by the contract of 1455 setting up the Bruges branch. This was to be in a city which had the largest market for the export of the finest Flemish tapestries and the import of Florentine textiles, and especially dyestuffs. The document lays it down that the *governatore* was not to issue letters of credit in favour of princes spiritual or temporal or their officers, but only to accredited merchants, and then only after the most rigorous examination of their credentials.

It was not possible, however, to operate in this market without the favour of the sovereign, and by 1471 we find that the branch was being allowed to lend up to 6,000 Flemish *grossi* to Charles the Bold. After 1473 there was no limit, and once the gates were opened there was no holding back the flood. At his death in 1477 the Duke of Burgundy owed the bank 9,500 *libbre di grossi* (114,000 gold florins), and immediately afterwards Maximilian of Austria had a loan of 3,000 more, for which he pawned the fleur de lys, a famous crown jewel, and conceded to the bank the revenue of the *tonlieu*, or customs. Needless to say, the debt to the branch was liquidated, and merely by

way of a business transaction, after the collapse of the Medici bank the following year.

The same kind of thing happened to the English branch. Once set on the road to industrialisation, England exported less raw wool and more manufactured cloth. Yet English wool, which was of high quality, was indispensable to Florentine craftsmen. Hence the need for the Medici to keep a branch in England in order to satisfy their workmen. But could they refuse loans to the King if he asked for them?

Unloading ships (detail from a painting by Ambrogio Lorenzetti).

If Edward III had needed the help of Florentine merchants for his wars in Scotland and France, would not Edward IV also ask for assistance against the Lancastrians in the Wars of the Roses? He had already dipped into the Medici coffers for his first victory in 1461, and in 1464, on the death of Cosimo, the London branch was complaining of a difficult situation. Edward was driven out in 1470, but neither before this, nor on his return, was he able to honour his debts; in the meantime many of those who owed money to the Medici (and they were to be found on both sides) had been killed and their goods and property sequestrated.

Then there was the conspiracy of 1478, in which the Pazzi family and others, with the support of Pope Sixtus IV, plotted to kill Lorenzo the Magnificent and his brother Giuliano in the Cathedral at High Mass on Easter Sunday. Lorenzo escaped wounded, but his brother was killed. Most of the conspirators were captured and put to death. After this Lorenzo had to support himself by the strongest friendship he could find abroad. He chose Louis XI of France, who called him « cousin », overlooking his common birth. Louis now held the stronger hand, and again asked Lorenzo, this time successfully, for those loans which had been refused formerly. This was virtually the Bardi and Peruzzi situation all over again, but whereas they had tried to steer a course between Edward III and Philip VI of Valois, Lorenzo was playing the game on three fronts, Flanders, France and England. It is hardly surprising that he was beaten and that the London branch had to be closed.

THE END OF THE MEDICI BANK

To the consuming anxiety of their role as money-lenders to royalty, which gnawed at the foundations of the Medici companies, was added yet another worry, that of the progressive disinterest of the family members in their business undertakings.

Generally speaking Cosimo the Elder had taken an intense personal interest in the management of the companies and had exercised a restraining hand on his collaborators of all ranks. But can we imagine Lorenzo sitting in his small study in the Palazzo Riccardi from morning till evening dealing with business correspondence, when we know that his interests lay in decipher-

ing precious manuscripts, conversing with humanists and dealing with major questions of politics?

Thus gradually the reins were relaxed on the necks of the *governatori*, and an attempt was made, though with little success, to create a new appointment, that of *ministro*, a man of trust to whom it would be enough to say a couple of words on the more serious problems of the business, and he would look after everything. Cosimo chose a certain Francesco Inghirami, a man as active in the Medici interests as he was diligent. Lorenzo continued with the services of Francesco Sassetti, formerly appointed by Piero, but once he started to work for Il Magnifico he allowed himself to be beguiled by his love of letters, by his passion for collecting works of art and manuscripts and by the company of philosophers and artists.

Thus it is not surprising that in the last years of the Medici business, there was a certain amount of administrative disorder and arbitrary judgments by local branch managers.

There had been evidence of this even at the end of Cosimo's life. Agnolo Tani almost brought about the ruin of the Bruges branch by involving the company in an unlucky scheme with a group of Lombard money-lenders. The Lyons branch was almost brought to bankruptcy by the dishonesty of Lionello De Rossi. Flemish affairs took on a grave turn after the relaxation of the maximum amounts for loans to sovereigns, a relaxation applied after pressure by the *governatore*-partner Tommaso Portinari who boasted of his per-

sonal friendship with Charles the Bold, for whom he had acted as a witness at the signing of the Franco-Burgundian alliance in his own house and had been sent as ambassador to the Duke of Milan.

After the closing of the Venice branch in 1470 (the reasons for this are not known) and the winding-up of the Bruges and London branches in 1478, the company was left with its Lyons branch abroad, and, at home, those in Rome and Milan, together with the Central Bank in Florence. The company never really recovered after the Pazzi conspiracy in 1478, but the end did not come until 1494, two years after the death of Lorenzo, when Piero was driven out of Florence and all the possessions of the Medici were sequestrated. Thus even the « Bank » of the descendents of Giovanni di Averardo did not escape the destiny of all the companies which had succeeded one another since the thirteenth century and had the same characteristics: a sudden rise to prosperity and an equally sudden fall. Truth to tell, these companies took greater risks than they should have done, and the moment was bound to come when they would be shown up for what they were: colossi with feet of clay.

THE ACCOMANDITA

Whilst the legal form of the company, the origin of the unlimited partnership, was evolving as above in the fifteenth century, Florentine merchants began to acquire the capital necessary for their undertakings by another method also, better known in Venice and Genoa, for example, under the name of *commenda* or *colleganza*, which gave a form of company known as *in accomandita*, or with limited partnership.

According to a well-known theory, a company is a characteristic form of association in an inland city, whilst a *commenda*, a kind of agency, is commoner in coastal towns. As trading was done initially over the seas, the idea of unlimited responsibility had not been welcomed owing to the great risk of the loss of the vessel and all its cargo by shipwreck, fire or piracy. Similarly any form of permanent association tended to be avoided when the company was formed to last merely during the ships' voyage, and generally consisted of persons without any bonds of family or friendship who were content merely to know personally those to whom they entrusted their money and their goods.

Bearing in mind this theory, which was substantially true, and noting that the Florentine law instituting the *accomandita* dates from 1408, it has been suggested that there is a close relationship between this and the purchase of Pisa in 1406. Once Florence had an outlet to the sea, her merchants set up the type of company already in use in coastal towns. It may be supposed, however, that the law did not precede, but followed, the event, and put a tidy legal form to what had already been common practice. This would appear to be supported by the preamble to the law, in which the merchants demanded of the *Signoria* « licence to trade such

223

as is enjoyed by all other manner of men », and not only on the restricted basis of the *commenda* regulations, which « otherwise they might be constrained to violate ». In effect, therefore, if they speak of violation, since the Statutes did not forbid, but merely ignored, the *commenda*, this violation must have been going on for some time.

On the other hand, the importance to the Florentine economy of this outlet to the sea must certainly not be exaggerated: some have even gone so far as to speak of Florence as a maritime power rivalling declining Venice. There was, of course, great enthusiasm among the Florentines, and on April 20th 1422, when the first « light armed galley » set sail for Alexandria, great processions wound their way « through the whole countryside », and among those taking part were schoolchildren and artisans who had locked up their workshops. The principal merchants of Florence had also done their utmost to compete with Venice, even to the extent of seeking the friendship of the Turk. They opposed Pius II's appeal for a crusade of Christian States, and in 1453, when Mahomet II took Constantinople, they sent their congratulations and a request for customs facilities. In 1461, during the struggle between Venice and the Mohammedans they supplied the Sultan with information of the Venetian leaders' plans, obtained via their diplomatic representative in Venice.

Hopes were high and dealings were fair and openhanded, but success was limited. Sixteen years passed after 1406 before the first ship was ready; it was 1428 before a small fleet had been formed and this was little used by the merchants who, although attracted by the concession of subsidies, showed themselves unwilling to enter into contracts. This led to an attempt in 1441 to use the galleys on behalf of the Commune, but this tentative State monopoly in navigation had to be abandoned in 1445 when it became apparent that foreign merchandise was not exactly pouring into Florence, and that what did arrive had increased in price by 10 per cent. Finally in 1480 the departures of the Commune's galleys were suspended for four years and the construction of additional ships was stopped. This set the seal of failure on Florence's maritime policy. In the meantime, the office with the pompous title of « *Consolato del mare* », with seats in both Pisa and Florence, created to see that ships were laid down in the yards in sufficient quantities to have one launched every six months and to let out the contracts, gradually saw its functions reduced until the contracts were handed over to the Guelf Captains and the office itself became a court for trying mercantile cases.

Rather than explain Florentine law on the *accomandita* in 1408 as a direct consequence of the city's gaining an outlet to the sea, it might perhaps be considered that the colossal failures of the mid-fourteenth century prove that total catastrophe does not depend on *fortuna maris*. Shrewd merchants, whose daring was giving way to prudence, must have drawn the right conclusion and limited their own responsibility to the capital they had subscribed. Once this practice became widespread, it required the support and discipline of the law, which in time became refined into some resemblance of what it is today. Nor is it likely that the development of the limited partnership during the fifteenth and sixteenth centuries was directly connected with the increasing maritime trade.

These consequences may be seen as deriving from facts which evolved very gradually: on the one hand changes in the structure of the « company » and on the other the gradual acceptance, without geographical limits, of the *accomandita*, or limitation of partnership. In the long run the two types of organisation had to be combined, not by fusion, which would have destroyed their nature juridically, but using one form or another according to the exigencies of the economic situation. It was thus possible to have the most varied combination of company structures. As one person could belong to several companies there was likely to be less competition and more solidarity between them, and it even became possible to divide the labour between them. It was thus easier to link businesses organised as companies with those organised as limited partnerships.

THE FIGURE OF THE MERCHANT

From what has been said ab   ...lds. finances, money, merchant and banking   realising that the merchant was ri nomic and political life in Flo formed the idea that he was a ma pursuit of profit had stifled all s spirit. He might think that the to improve himself, but only for his work; that he cared for

224

in order to direct the external policy of the Commune into channels which would guarantee protection for his trade, wherever he practised it, and to see that internal policy was not hampered by too much intervention from the lower classes, on whom could be cast the burden of the greater share of taxation and the consequences of the devaluation of the smaller coinage; that he was religious, but would not hesitate to contravene Church precepts if these stood in the way of his profits. Such a picture, however, would not represent the true figure of the Florentine merchant.

As for culture, it is true that the merchant was more interested in vocational training both in the State schools and the workshop, the laboratory or the sales organisation. But he did not neglect the more general schooling which was permeated by humanism.

Giovanni Villani, referring to the years 1336 to 1339, said that there were between eight and ten thousand boys and girls learning to read in Florence at this time, between one thousand and one thousand two hundred were learning arithmetic and algebra, and four large schools were teaching grammar and logic to between five and six hundred.

It was this latter type of school which aimed to produce citizens capable of holding public office with dignity and understanding: from those who sat in the many and crowded Councils, where all questions of both internal and international politics were discussed, as the *consulte*, or minutes of the debates, show, and to take part in these debates required considerable maturity of thought and eloquence of speech; to those who functioned as *savi*, as they were called at the time, or experts who delved into the most difficult, controversial and strictly technical questions; to those who, known as *calculatores* or *rationerii* (a kind of comptroller) formed part of the *sindacati*, or control commission, regulating the work of the *magistrati uscenti* (outgoing) whose numbers, already large from the multiplicity of their functions, was increased by the short time they held office; to those, finally, who went as *oratori* (diplomatic representatives) to other cities, to princes of State or Church, to foreign monarchs or religious leaders who might, in their turn, nominate them their treasurers and ambassadors.

As a final proof of the merchant's culture it is significant that the commercial papers and correspondence, the personal memoirs and the manuals of mercantile practice of the time furnished the compilers of

The « machine for coining money » after a design by Leonardo da Vinci (Leonardo Museum, Vinci).

the dictionary of Italian published by the Academia della Crusca (founded 1583) with much valuable material, and historians have constantly used merchants' diaries and reports as valuable source material, recognising that « Florence's historical archives were started by her merchants ».

Are names wanted? There are many. To begin with one well-known in the field of literature, Giovanni Boccaccio looked after the Bardi company's business interests in Naples, and Franco Sacchetti showed in his « *Sermoni* » that he was an expert in mercantile matters. Passing on to well-known historians, there were Dino Compagni, Giovanni Villani, Marchionne di Coppo Stefani. Compagni founded and directed a company which after his death ran into difficulties in the years of the first great bankruptcies beginning in 1334. Villani was a partner in the Peruzzi firm until 1324 when he went over to the Bonaccorsi, of which his brother Matteo had been a partner, and he was succeeded at the Peruzzi by the third brother, Filippo, who

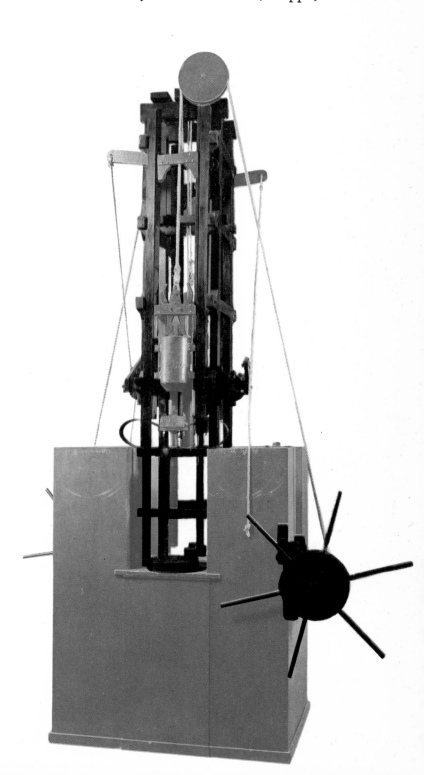

225

then managed the firm's branch at Avignon. Stefani was a partner of the Acciaiuoli. Among the writers engaged in the mercantile business Francesco di Balduccio Pegolotti was an agent for the Bardi and Giovanni di Antonio da Uzzano wrote extensively on his experiences in trade and commerce, thus providing a most valuable source for the economic history of the period. Less well-known, but like Uzzano, available in print today, are Guido dell'Antella (memoirs), Luca di Totto da Panzano (extracts of reports), Giovanni Morelli (reports), Luca Landucci, apothecary, (Florentine diary), Bartolomeo di Michele del Corazza, wine-seller (Florentine diary), Bartolomeo Masi, tinker (memoirs), Domenico Lenzi, corn-merchant (diary). And there are others.

Surviving business correspondence of those days reveals one thing: that, though money was made in the olden days just as it is today, it was made with a greater sense of dignity.

LOVE OF COUNTRY

From culture, the sense of spiritual values, we pass to love of country. The reader may perhaps smile sceptically remembering the party strife which virtually destroyed Florence at this time and the quarrelling and jealousy between groups of families, individual families and even between members of the same family.

This scepticism might be justified if we were to regard history in the same way as Werner Sombart, the German economist and social reformer (1863-1941): consider the past only with modern eyes and do not try to see it, or to relive it, with the eyes and feelings of the period. In fact, all these struggles were not sterile; they were rather the expression of an exceptional vitality which ultimately became something positive. Inter-city rivalry such as that between Genoa and Venice, for example, led to the founding of two empires.

It is true that the mercantile oligarchy unloaded as much of the tax burden as it could by passing fiscal ordinances favourable to itself. Yet in cases of real need it never hung back, but opened the coffers of its businesses and the purses of its individuals. In 1336, for example, some of the larger firms which formed a consortium amongst themselves, undertook « to furnish moneys for the war in Lombardy against Mastino della Scala until the said war shall be terminated », and immediately raised a good third of the hundreds of thousands of florins which the campaign cost. During this war a certain Ridolfo Bardi and a certain Simone Peruzzi, directors respectively of the firms of the same name, and other prominent citizens such as Simone della Tosa and Acciaiuolo Acciaiuoli did not hesitate to abandon their businesses and take up their seats permanently in the Palazzo Vecchio. Nor did they limit their help to money. When the bells pealed out summoning the soldiery to form up under the banner of the Commune, the merchants took up their places in the fighting line.

The bare outlines of these stories of sacrifice are suggested in one folio of the Peruzzi's account books. Here we may read that Arnaldo di Arnaldo, a director of the company, paid with his life: « 100 florins in cash, when the army went to L'Incisa on the occasion of the coming of the Emperor, 35 flo. paid to the porters who brought him back to Florence and to the doctors who treated him, 86 and a half for his burial, he having died on September 23rd 1312, 7 flo. 21 s. for his widow's veils ». Shortly before this Peruzzi, representing the Commune, had been host in his own *palazzo* to Robert of Anjou and discussed with him the treaty against the Emperor. He did not limit himself to affirming, as a statesman, that « Florence does not intend to submit to any lord » but, as a soldier, he paid, in person.

It has been said, and more than once, that Florence won her wars only with her gold. The truth is quite different: the pride of Henry VII was blunted not only by the Florentines' gold, but also on the breast-plates of the citizenry whom that gold had turned into soldiers.

There was a love of country which perhaps affords a glimpse of what Italy was to become. This was evident abroad, where, surrounded by the hostility of the natives, Italian merchants formed strong associations, with members drawn from all over the peninsula.

Thus in 1278 the Florentines joined forces even with merchants from enemy republics to entreat the King of France to allow the return to Nîmes of all the *mercatores* driven out of that city. In 1288 they formed part of the « University of Italian Merchants who frequent the fairs at Champagne in the kingdom of France », and in 1295 they joined the *oratori* (diplomatic representatives) of many other Communes to conclude a treaty of protection with the Dukes of Burgundy.

Authorisation dated XXVI August to the « Gentlemen of the Mint and the Consuls of the two Guilds to make provision for money » (from a page of the « Fiorinaio », State Record Office, Florence).

Patriotism or business interests? Business no doubt played a great part; but it was everyone's business and above all every Italian's business. They were concerned with everything that went on at home, in the country which they aimed to make beautiful, out of love and not out of interest: this is the beauty Italians can boast of today and which all humanity can boast of as its common patrimony.

FAITH

In reviewing spiritual values, let us now consider religious faith. Here too it might be thought bold to assert that the merchant's faith was firmly rooted, when he amassed such wealth by acting in many cases in direct opposition to the Church's teaching on economic affairs.

Once again, however, we must mentally transport ourselves into the period we are studying, and try to experience it as if we were living in those times. We would thus come to realise that the Church was coming face to face with a profoundly different society which was relaxing, explicitly or tacitly, the rigid provisions of a past age, as these were no longer felt to correspond to a real need.

This applies particularly to the canon *de usuris*, which has already been touched on in the discussion on the merchant companies. In the centuries of deep general economic depression, the only loans known were those asked for by the poor man who had absolutely no means of support, or who was unable to pay his lay or ecclesiastical masters what they asked of him, however little that might be, as a subject or a Christian. The pretext of adding a certain sum to the loan when it was repaid would have been considered a sacrilege, and charity demanded that the loan should be settled as a gift. But what was to happen later on, when a revival of economic activity brought a demand for the investment of money in manufacturing, trading, banking which produced more money? Would it have been fair to impose a sacrifice on the charitable lender? If the Church had tried to stem the economic revival, which became inevitable after the Crusades, would she not have risked isolating herself from the business world? Hence the need to make some concessions, remembering that by virtue of the economic revival even the poorest might have a chance, by finding work, of improving their lot.

There could only be one choice, and this was made by Saint Thomas Aquinas when he admitted in his *Summa* the principle of the *Damnum emergens*, or the right to receive recompense for making a loan when it could be proved that this constituted a sacrifice. Even the Apostolic Camera took to contracting loans at interest, and many religious bodies, in particular the richer monasteries and the religious orders of chivalry such as the Knights of Jerusalem required interest to be paid on the loans they made.

Thus the concept of what usury was was not clear, if only from the fact that the very subjective valuation of the sacrifice, and therefore of the recompense, left the whole matter wide open to dispute. Without defining a legal rate, it was admitted by tacit consensus that there was a minimum interest on loans which should correspond to that paid by companies to their shareholders and by the Commune itself to the holders of State bonds. In spite of this, many cases were brought before the ecclesiastical courts, and these caused the judges to ask of the theological experts what they understood by usury.

In such a situation the fear of committing sin remained. Alessandra Macinghi Strozzi (first half of the fifteenth century) asked her confessor if buying and selling *Monte* shares would send her to Hell. The merchants sought to reconcile themselves with their creator by making gifts of alms during their life-time, and by leaving money to convents and monasteries after their death, in addition to charging their heirs to repay the interest received on loans to anyone who might complain that he had been victimised.

Was this hypocrisy on their part? Was expediency rather suggested, moreover, by the Church itself, and having nothing to do with faith in the existence of a God severe to judge but also swift to pardon? And sometimes the uneasiness during the merchant's life was such as to provoke real crises of conscience; repentance on the deathbed could then be absolutely sincere.

Scaglia Tifi, a Florentine merchant of the late thirteenth century and treasurer of the Princes of Burgundy, confessed in Notre Dame that he had appropriated money belonging to his masters and used it for his own business. He was not, incidentally, dismissed, as his employers apparently found him indispensable, but as the years passed his remorse drove him to leave the world of business and retire to a monastery where he died, like Saint Francis, on the floor of the Church surrounded by friars praying for his soul. He too left a will which might help us to revise our idea of the typical merchant. He had quite clearly retained his business instincts as, having set aside a sum in perpetuity for an annual Mass to be said on his behalf and determined the payment for the choristers, he stipulated that if any were hoarse or feeble of voice the sum in question was to go to another with a voice strong enough « verily to reach God ». Yet he also truly loved his fellow-men, for in another passage he stipulated that « annually and in perpetuity, before winter cometh the *maestro* of the Church of the Holy Spirit shall buy twenty-five pounds worth of heavy serge cloth, or other material of similar quality, for the making of articles of clothing for the most poor and destitute of the Parish of the Holy Spirit, specifying the name and the quality of the warm material which shall be given in my name ».

This is a thought which shows such humane feeling that, by itself, it might perhaps have earned him the forgiveness of the merciful Judge.

The same God whose punishment was feared by merchants because of their behaviour in business, was nevertheless deeply worshipped. The wonderful churches with which they embellished the city were the expression of their religious fervour for their Creator, whom they called upon in every act of their lives, whose name they placed at the head of their account books to invoke his protection and for whom, in these same books, they opened an account to enable the poor, his elect, to share in the profits of the business.

The Guilds, in their turn, so representative of the merchant classes, each undertook, at the end of their Statutes, the patronage of one or more Churches. This meant that they provided all the expenses of the services, from the vestments to the priest's honorarium and the candles, and disposed of the private votive offerings brought in solemn procession to the altar; they established the prohibition of and the punishments for swearing; they made it a duty for Christians to visit the sick at their bedside and for all members of the guild to contribute to funeral expenses, those of the poorest being met collectively, after which their dependents were provided for, their sons receiving free training for their trade and their daughters a small dowry.

To sum up, the merchant of the golden age of the Florentine economy, the thirteenth and fourteenth centuries, was a complex person, a prey to complex passions which eventually involved him in real drama. If he did believe fervently in what he was doing, and in his work, which he regarded as a mission, he became irretrievably involved in the tormenting conditions which this implied, and virtue and sin were pushed to heroic proportions.

INDIFFERENCE TO TRADING

Then, though it was true that nothing happened suddenly, everything began to change.

Let us begin with the merchant's passion for business. The objective reasons for the loss of interest in trading, hitherto the chief source of the accumulation of vast capital, have been referred to in the section on mercantile companies. It was but a short step from an indifference to trade to despising the practice of it; at the same time there was an increased regard for landed property.

It is not that property-owning was underestimated in the past, and there is many a trace left in the Florentine countryside of the thirteenth and fourteenth-century manor house and labourer's cottage. Property was looked upon, however, by the merchant purely as a shareholders' security and proof of his reliability (it was the shareholders' deposits which provided the companies' working capital) and income from these properties was shown on the balance-sheets as an asset when the company was beginning to lose money.

Now, however, and more so as the sixteenth century advances, the purposes of property-owning will be quite different. The property becomes the sumptuous country villa, a fit setting for the noble lord and his company of courtiers to entertain friends and amuse themselves with hunting. What a mortification it would be for those who climbed the stairs of the Palazzo Riccardi and the Palazzo Pitti to have to admit that

Francesco Sassetti, the merchant (portrait by Ghirlandaio in a fresco in the Santa Trinita church).

they were engaged in trade! It were better to show a little of that culture, the prerogative of the humanists which made of them privileged courtiers, and for this it was not even necessary to be rich.

Evidence of this is given by Giuliano dei Ricci (1543-1606), who very unwillingly ran a goldbeater's business. His real ambition was to hold public office and even more to be a man of letters like his grandfather Niccolò Machiavelli. He did achieve public office, though in posts without distinction, and he was helped by his marriage to the niece of the powerful Piero Vettori. He neglected his business, which then went badly, and he ended up by being a failure in the literary world as well.

Giuliano's scorn of trading shows through the words he wrote in 1573 at the age of thirty when he complained that his father's ill-fortune, pusillanimity and poverty were the reasons for his having to go into business against his inclinations.

Many examples could be given of descendants of mercantile families turning away in distaste from the business activities of their fathers and grandfathers. Niccolò Martelli declared, on leaving for abroad in 1543, that he « wished to refresh himself from the troubles of vile trading by writing verses » (and he wrote many, most of them very bad, dedicating them to his hosts). Luigi Pulci, who was caught up in the failure of the Bank of Luca in 1456, retired to his villa at Palagio di Cavallina in the Mugello (now the Castel Pulci).

When merchants did devote themselves to business, there were changes in the way they conducted their affairs. The pursuit of wealth continued to be the spur, but the risks and personal inconvenience were reduced to a minimum. We have now reached the figure of the sedentary merchant. Whereas at one time the captains of industry had always been on the move, now (and the example of the Medici is far from being the only one) they began to stay in their studies and send someone else to do the travelling for them. This loss of personal interest led to diminishing returns. It could even lead to the « Chief » playing only a subordinate rôle and being unable to control his employees' expenditure. For example, Francesco di Marco Datini da Prato (1335-1410), who had laid the basis of his fortune in Avignon, where fifteen years previously he had started as a messenger-boy in a Florentine firm, returned home and never left it again except once when he went to Bologna to escape an epidemic. He falsified the balance-sheets to the harm of one of his partners, a most faithful servant of the company, to the tune of 1,000 gold florins, which the courts ordered him to restore to the mother, the heiress of his victim.

Some of these sedentary merchants were, however, quite active in other directions, being drawn in many cases by a passion for discovery. This was the case of Amerigo Vespucci, who has passed into history for reasons other than having been for ten years the « man of trust » of the merchant-banker Lorenzo di Pier Francesco Medici. Others, on the contrary, had passions of another kind, such as Bonaccorso Pitti who did, in fact, trade in money and goods, but who moved on when he could find no more victims to fleece (including princes) with his skill at dicing. For this reason he has become the prototype of the gambler.

Let us continue our comparison of the early and late Renaissance merchants with a consideration of their behaviour towards the State. The years of the *Signoria* saw little of that fierce civic pride, as the State was no longer the common weal, but belonged to the *Signore* who imposed his own policies with soldiers of fortune.

Yet, even before the end of the Republic the merchant was sometimes far from patriotic. Datini, whom we mentioned above, had been in Avignon at the time of the Papal schism. Florence had been under an interdict for declaring war on Gregory XI, and Datini ought either to have returned home or taken refuge elsewhere to avoid imprisonment and the sequestration of his goods. He chose to remain at his post, however, and supplied arms, equipment and money to the Pope for the struggle against his fellow-citizens.

In conclusion, it would be wrong to assume that until the mid-fourteenth century all great merchants were like Arnoldo Peruzzi or in the second half of the century like Datini. Yet the general picture as we have given it for Florence is confirmed as typical of the period in other parts of the peninsula also, particularly in Venice.

There is, moreover, abundant evidence in the *Trattato della Famiglia* (« On Family Life ») of Leon Battista Alberti, a descendant of one of the greatest Florentine families of the type of the Bardi, the Peruzzi and the Acciaiuoli, to suggest that the first generous bourgeoisie born under the Commune, and which under the Commune had made its fortune, gave way to another bourgeoisie whose behaviour is modelled upon and informed by Alberti's dicta, especially his warnings of prudence. « Invest your capital so as to compensate your risks, but above all invest it in land, which is the safest, and in many and well-distributed possessions, so that you may eat and drink always what is yours, warm yourselves with your own wood and when you go to your country villa you need only take a little salt, as all the rest is there. Stay away from public life, a fountain only of enmity and suffering and a distraction from profitable work. Always cry misery so that the tax-collector shall not overburden you ». There were two opposite conceptions of life here, between the thirteenth and fourteenth centuries on the one hand, and the fifteenth and sixteenth on the other. Hence they were two quite different worlds.

COUNTRY LIFE

What for several centuries had been a constant factor in Tuscan history, and Florentine history in particular, the distinction between town and country, began to fade in the fifteenth century until it virtually disappeared. It is not that in the preceding period of the Middle Ages town and country had a completely separate existence. We know, in fact, that the crisis of feudalism and the rise of the typically urban concept of the Communes brought the peasant within the sphere of influence of the town. As the feudal landowners became urbanised, so to speak, urban communities began to look outwards to the countryside and gradually achieved some kind of integration with their rural counterparts. Florence, too, went through this phase, so that it is impossible to think of the city without its surrounding countryside. Yet it is undoubtedly true that until almost the end of the fourteenth century town and country life were substantially different. It was only in the fifteenth century that a network of close and intimate relationships began to develop between the town and country life to the extent that contemporary minds no longer accepted the traditional distinctions between the two. The implications of this new outlook in the fifteenth century were far-reaching, and the close bonds between town and country are significant of a phase of the highest culture.

Already in the second half of the fourteenth century a new phenomenon, soon to bring with it many changes, had arisen: this was the increasing interest of the town-dweller in land, a new type of contact with the countryside and a fresh image of the land as fulfilling a purpose entirely different from that of the long centuries past. When the increasing attraction of the city began to be felt by the feudal lords, compelling them to dwell within its walls, then a new relationship arose between one class of citizens and the countryside, as the feudal lords never severed their bonds with their lands, but rather did they extend their domains by the profits they made from their urban activities. Interest in the land became contagious and spread to the true town-dwellers who began to buy land with their recently-acquired wealth, taking advantage of the agricultural crisis which was destroying the class of small peasant-farmers who hitherto had owned the land together with the feudal lords. Fifteenth-century documents clearly indicate the gradual spread of the town-dwellers' interests (particularly those of the important families) in the land, from the areas adjoining the city, such as the val di Mugnone, the val d'Ema, the piana del Galluzzo, the piana di Careggi, the Diacceto slopes, to the furthest districts such as the val di Pesa, the Chianti, the upper Valdarno towards Figline and the lower towards Signa, the Mugello.

Messer Niccolò degli Antinori desired his villa to be built just over the Arno, and sought an unknown « maestro » to transform his ancient palace into « a cool house with a loggia for eating outside, with but few drawing-rooms for the reception of friends, and few bedrooms, for the family is a small one, and everything at ground-level, as I do not wish to climb stairs. And above ... the store-rooms and the granaries, because the yield of this land is abundant ». This was a property, we repeat, very close to the city, scarcely more than a mile from the outer wall. Similarly, Messer Bernardo

View of Florentine hills and fields (from a fresco by Gozzoli in the Medici-Riccardi palace). Lanes flanked by tall hedges lead from the town to the rich man's villa or the more modest country residence.

de' Rucellai did not have far to go either to get to his villa Lo Specchio at Quaracchi, where his keen eye could encompass his meadow with its box-wood hedge, his hundred-yard vine-trellis, his pond richly stocked with fish and the long avenue running down to the Arno. It was no great distance from Quaracchi to Careggi, where Cosimo de' Medici had his villa. Here Florence's first citizen divided his time between friendly chatter and learned dispute, and supervising the work in the fields such as the pruning of the olives and vines, the grafting of fruit-trees and the care of the vegetable-garden.

There were other similar villas such as Belcanto di Fiesole, and Il Poggio at Caiano. In his delightful villa-castle at Cafaggiolo, Lorenzo the Magnificent, though still mindful of his civic responsibilities, was able to relax with country pursuits, such as cultivating the land and hunting with his falcon Morello, his dog Bontempo and his bitch Turcha. He was thus able to furnish the villa's larder both for himself and for the feasting of his literary friends and his equally numerous acquaintances from the Mugello countryside.

Without in any way contradicting the image of the country as an escape from the town, quite often country

A Medici hunting-lodge.

life turned out to be a continuation, in a more relaxed atmosphere, of the life of study, letters and discussion which went on within the walls of the city. A good example of the typical way of life in a country villa is given by the humanist Giovanni da Prato in his *Il Paradiso degli Alberti*. The villa is in a pleasant country area near Florence and houses a group of learned friends who discuss, meditate and write *novelle* amidst its well-cultivated gardens where domestic animals gambol and play on the lawns ...

It was not only persons of wealth or leading merchant families who turned to the countryside to build their own villas and added a new dimension to their lives. The more modest citizens, simple artisans or small traders, also caught the spirit. Many a minor chronicle and document in the State Record Office tells the same story of the Florentines setting out for their country houses: Cristoforo di Giorgio, the doctor, who took the via del Pian de' Giullari on his way to his small property called « La Costa »; Ser Biagio Corazzaio leaving for his country house « L'Ulivuzzo », Nando the stone-mason for his up in La Pollaiola, Cristofano di Banco on his way to the Monte alle Croci, and also Jacopo Bartoli, needle-maker, to Borgognissanti, Matteo the tanner and Benedetto de' Macci the gold-beater. Men of the people or *signori*, all who dressed in russet colours, like Piero di Bonaccorso, were proud of their country houses or « villas » which they looked upon as their *casa da signore*. This was also a place of refuge if city business did not do too well, as was the case with Luca Landucci, who remained obstinately in his villa at Dicomano, or when one became tired of the unending buffoonery of one's town friends, as happened to Manetto il Grasso, the cabinet-maker, who ran away to his house at Le Corti to work off his annoyance at the pranks of his merry friends.

There was developing a continuous interchange and a mutual enrichment between town and country, so that by the end of the fifteenth century it is impossible to think of them separately, and they influenced Florentine public life together, even in the field of politics. When Florence faced the difficult days of the foreign invasions from the late fifteenth century onwards, the countryside shared the troubles and anxieties of the tormented city right up to the decisive and dramatically significant moment of the siege of 1529-30. This is admirably illustrated in Vasari's fresco in the Palazzo Vecchio, an artistic representation of the siege of great historical accuracy, which had to show the « scorched earth » all around the city and the desolate picture of war spreading out over the Florentine countryside as far as the eye can see.

VILLAS AND COUNTRY HOUSES

The extension of Florentine life into the surrounding countryside is a definite fact which can be quite clearly documented from architectural sources. The building of the « master's villa », and the way in which this

The Medici villa known as « Il Trebbio » as painted on a lunette by Giusto Utens. The several buildings formed a unit and the picture clearly shows the peasants' houses, the cattle-sheds, the church and the castello. The fenced area around the latter contained the orchard and the market-garden (Medici Museum, Florence).

came to be incorporated into the existing scheme of farmhouses, furnish the most notable evidence of the sudden transformation of the rural scene under the initiative of the town.

It is certainly true that in his *Trattato dell'architettura* Leon Battista Alberti describes the farmers' houses as quite distinct from the lord's villa, the former built for a necessary purpose, the latter for pleasure and personal satisfaction. Yet Alberti's distinction, although springing from factors of a moral and psychological order, was nevertheless concerned more with the houses as buildings. What they had in common was greater

than this difference (and today we see more clearly the intimate relationships which exist between all types of buildings), namely their primary and fundamental purpose as a factor in the cultivation of the land.

There are, moreover, other fifteenth-century documents showing the interpenetration of town and country life, such as the figurative ones, of which a good example is the series of frescoes by Benozzo Gozzoli in the Medici Chapel. These show clearly the type of house which was then being built in the country as a result of urban influence. « As we are dealing with a landscape which, though certainly authentic, is nevertheless idealised », comments Gori Montanelli, « we should note as indicative of the mentality of the townsman towards architecture and country life the fact that virtually none of the houses in this landscape could be considered as workers' houses, whereas we see mostly walled-in properties, old castle-type villas, new houses of some standing, with loggias and enclosed courtyards and occasionally the ruins of a tower ».

This means that to late fifteenth-century Florence and the surrounding areas of Tuscany there was no rigid distinction between the functions in the countryside of the upper classes and those of the peasants. In other words the fundamental similarity between the architecture of the villa and that of the town house shows that contact with the land was begun and carried forward in an egalitarian spirit of co-operation both by the townsman, who had recently arrived, and the countryman, for whom it was a traditional way of life.

Moreover this close relationship between the villa and the town-house, in spite of their different characteristics as indicated by Leon Battista Alberti, points to an eventual convergence of style. This will be particularly noticeable when the wealthy townsman begins to choose his country retreat for the pleasure he takes in the environment, the landscape, the ideal and the real value of the land. A significant document in this connection is Niccolò Machiavelli's letter (the fifty-third)

to Francesco Guicciardini on the subject of a property or small holding which Guicciardini intended to purchase through the good offices of Machiavelli. There were two for sale, called Finochieto and Columbaja, and Machiavelli gives a vivid description of both of them, as seen through the eyes of an intelligent townsman capable of sizing up the appearance and the value of country houses. He judges each according to its position and the value, actual and potential, of the land; he then sums up and describes the house as the nerve-centre of the estate, with its advantages and its limitations, and considers it from the point of view of future development and eventual yield. With an expenditure of a hundred ducats, he points out « ... you could provide a small meadow, plant vines around the hillock overlooking the house, dig eight or ten trenches in land lying between the house and the first house on the outlying estate, in which, if I were you, I would plant fruit- and fig-trees; I would make a fountain of fine water to run through your fields and at the foot of your connected rows of vines, which is the finest thing to be seen ... ».

In the middle of the estate stood the house. From Machiavelli's accurate description these were evidently « classical » country houses with an inner courtyard, loggia and first-floor living rooms, and the courtyard was flanked by the kitchen, the cattle-sheds and the

vat-room. It was a country-house designed for a townsman to live in « not dishonourably ». This clearly meant that the owner's desires and demands were at one with those of the place, the house and its rustic environment.

The urban spirit and the country way of life now unite to give one coherent picture whose elements are no longer clearly divisible. We have now reached the highest peak of the Renaissance. Machiavelli's letter to Guicciardini is in fact dated August 3rd 1525.

AGRICULTURE AND COUNTRY LIFE

The wealth of detail in Machiavelli's letters is a reflection of the vast and varied nature of country life. There are not many first-hand accounts of rural life in Renaissance Florence, but such indications as we do possess are sources of the greatest interest.

There are, for example, the letters written by Madonna Isabella Guicciardini to her husband away on public duty in Arezzo. These give a periodic report of the administration of their estate, and present a realistic and most accurate account of contemporary farming: the country house, the farmlands, the work to be done according to the seasons, the repairs to walls and the aqueduct, the care of the market-garden, the gathering of the olives, the retting of the flax ...

The background of alternating good and bad weather, with its corresponding human hopes and anxieties, brings us into closer contact with the country life of the times. The peasant's existence has, of course, always been determined by the vicissitudes of the seasons and the alternating fundamental processes of sowing, reaping the corn and harvesting the grapes. The fifteenth-century *novella* writers pay more attention to the market-garden adjoining the country house than to the cultivation of the fields, the meadows and the woods. Maso, a peasant at L'Impruneta, Griccio, a tenant-farmer on the Varlungo estate, Bellincione who has fields over by Careggi, are all men who give particular attention to their market-gardens. These are always walled-in for protection against thieves and trespassers, and offer a great variety of things for the daily table: basic vegetables, sweet-smelling herbs, cooking-herbs, garlic, onions and the tasty sage, tubers, turnips, spinach and cabbage (potatoes and tomatoes were still unknown). The garden was always well and carefully irrigated.

Only a part of the day was devoted to the market-garden: there were also the chicken-run and the sheep-fold, but these required little attention and could usually be looked after by a boy.

Outside the house and the market-garden it was quite different. The woods and their undergrowth were not directly cultivated and provided dry twigs in abundance for fires and timber for constructional purposes. The culture of the fields, however, was a somewhat complex problem. Here again the *novella* writers give us some idea of the work involved. We see the Tuscan peasant leave his walled house in a still largely primitive environment of woods and pasture. When ploughing he is accompanied by his oxen, but at sowing and harvest-time he works with other members of the household, and the beasts remain in the cattle-sheds. There are contemporary miniatures showing the peasant leaning heavily on his plough as it bites deep into the earth. Other peasants are wielding typical rustic implements: the hoe, the spade, the shovel, the bill-hook and the pruning-hook. The plough is driven over strips of land usually short and narrow and divided off from each other by shallow ditches, olive-trees, vines or fruit-trees. Various types of seed were sown: millet and wheat among the cereals, whilst for animal grazing it would appear that lucern was already in use. Near to the house stood stacks of straw, indispensable for animal litter, and hayricks, with a characteristic system of ventilation, in which animal fodder was stored.

The rudimentary form of work done in the fields by these fifteenth- and sixteenth-century Tuscan farmers was determined by the type of crop they cultivated: wheat, olive and vine. After the reaping came the threshing, done by hand with two sticks tied together by a piece of rope; this was called a *coreggiato* and it still has this traditional Tuscan name. Then the wheat had to be milled to make flour, but it was rare for a farmhouse to have the necessary mechanical equipment for this, although there was usually an olive-press consisting of a large mill-stone turned on a spindle over a tub which collected the precious oil. The quality of the stone was important, and it would appear that the best kind was found in a quarry at Montici near Florence.

There were special places for the storing of grain, flour and oil on the ground floor, as described by Machiavelli in his letter to Guicciardini. These store-places were the centre of all the productive activities of the farm, including, of course, the wine-making. Wine was an essential part of Tuscan and Florentine agriculture, although large-scale regularised production did not come until later when the rural economy had further developed. Late fifteenth-century miniatures show us barefooted peasants against a background of trellises laden with black grapes, with an occasional light-coloured bunch standing out here and there. Red wine, in fact, is typical of Tuscany and was made by the peasant crushing the grapes himself in the vat, or with the aid of a screw press which extracted everything down to the dregs.

The villas and farmhouses were built around an inner courtyard on to which opened the various rooms and buildings needed for the running of the farm: the granary, the vat-room, the wine-cellars, the equipment-store and work-shops for the many maintenance and construction jobs which were required to be done. The farm-worker of Renaissance times had to be something of a blacksmith, farrier, stone-mason, rope-maker, and occasionally even a cooper, although it was customary in the fifteenth century, and it still is today, to employ itinerant coopers who spent from ten to twelve days on each farm.

The need to cope with the many necessities of farming made the Tuscan country house something of an autonomous unit with simple and straightforward life and customs, with plain speech and plain food, simple habits and simple dress. The food was fairly plentiful, but had little variety. In the most spacious room of the house, on the ground floor, at once a kitchen and a general meeting-place, under the huge cowl of the chimney-piece (of which some admirable examples have survived) the food for the whole day was cooked on a wood fire. This was usually *polenta* (a kind of pudding) of millet flour, or, more rarely, wheaten or chestnut flour. Bread had just begun to appear on the peasants' table as a regular food. The rest of the meal consisted of oil, wine, vinegar and products of the vegetable garden. Meat was rare, and such as there was came from the farmyard fowls, pigs and sheep. Some of Boccaccio's *novelle* remind us of the importance of the pig and its products to the country table. Sometimes there was meat won by hunting, but not venison or wild boar: it was usually birds caught by net or snare.

Rustic clothing was as simple as the food. Some contemporary miniatures show the poverty of the

Miniatures from a calendar, clearly illustrating rural customs in fifteenth-century Italy.

They portray, with poetic simplicity, moments from the peasants' working day.

The provision of wood, the rotation of the crops, country life in the alternating four seasons.

cloth. The peasant's clothes were often cast-offs from the *signore*, bought from second-hand dealers, who plied a brisk trade, or roughly woven at home. The simple *saltamindosso* covered both back and front. Heavier garments were the lambskin jacket, or the rough *pinzocco*, often called, and with reason, the *coprimiseria*, a symbol of the harsh life in close contact with nature.

In the last analysis, the outcome of Tuscan agriculture in the period from the fifteenth century onwards was the creation of landscape. Apart from Benozzo Gozzoli's frescoes, apart from descriptions in Machiavelli's letters, we have the impression of an ordered and coherent process towards a studied landscape: a happy alternation of rising and level ground, some left to its natural element of stone, or thickened up with the free growth of woods in the middle distance, some arranged by the hand of man into a variety of crops, meadows and trees. The fields, that miraculous feature of the Tuscan countryside, are not wide-open stretches of land stretching out to the distant horizon, but are clearly confined by their lines of trees (who can forget how lines of cypress trees have been used to mark a boundary?) and offer a harmonious pattern of ploughed land and pasture. The splendid reality of today is already taking shape in the agriculture of the fifteenth century. The only product which has disappeared with the passing of time, and which had considerable importance in the fifteenth century, is the gladiolus. There was a very extensive trade in this plant and its derivatives.

We who are used to talking in terms of landscape should not forget that from the fifteenth century onwards, and almost certainly even before, a great part of the landscape around Florence was given over to the cultivation of flowers. The city's very emblem, the lily, is really the iris, the characteristic flower of the district.

THE MÉTAYAGE SYSTEM

This static view of Florentine agriculture and country life in general would not be complete without reference to the golden rule of traditional Tuscan husbandry, the *mezzadria* (métayage), under which the farmer paid for the rent of his land by handing over half of his produce to the landowner.

The word itself implies a sense of parity and a spirit of intimate cooperation between town and coun-

Villa Edelman, a typical Florentine country house. The benches on either side of the door were symbols of traditional hospitality. The ground-floor rooms were protected by stout iron grilles.

238

try, *signore* and peasant, villa and farm. The *mezzadria* is the most eloquent proof of this partnership in living, in which we recognise the values of the high civilization of Florence and Tuscany.

We can trace the gradual development of this close relation between town and country life throughout a long period of Tuscan history, which reached its height in the fifteenth century and is still with us today, so many centuries afterwards.

The Tuscan system of *mezzadria* was born out of the centuries of crisis in the feudal agricultural economy, when personal bonds of servitude gave way to contractual obligations between landowner and tenant farmer, a gradual growth of liberty which eventually led to a balance between town and country life and changed the face of the landscape.

In Tuscany, and the surrounding districts of Florence in particular, the métayage system reached its most complex form in terms of legal and human requirements. The arid language of the contracts and the more colourful writings of the men of letters, both in prose and poetry of the period, both present, in the ultimate analysis, the same picture. The contractual obligations undertaken scarcely ever involved the land only, that is a concession on the one hand for payment with half the produce on the other, but took into account also the whole complex of a family and a house, with an established property endowed with all the necessary facilities for work, including the equipment and the animals, particularly the oxen, the unrivalled working companion of the Tuscan peasant. « A family », says Imberciadori, « needs more than land: it needs regular work, sufficient food, security of possession, a permanent house on the land, and around it the market-garden, the vine and the olive-grove; within the house-buildings the sheds for the cattle and nearby the grazing land; and next to the stall for the oxen, the accommodation for all the small animals which bring profit and a means of saving to the farm ».

This is setting up a real business, and how industrious and efficient it is! There were clearly other forms of land settlement and other categories of farm-workers, such as the peasants who became landowners, the tenant-farmers and the casual labourers, but the most characteristic was the métayage system. The land is worked, and cultivation increases as the townsman

The Medici villa at Cafaggiolo, a summer residence during their rule of Florence.

takes a greater interest in farming. Urban society finds satisfaction in the physical proximity and the structural similarity between the villas and the farmhouses. When we cast our minds back to the countryside in fifteenth-century Tuscany, we see it as an active, living organism, not static and conservative, but a source of social development and great economic progress. Around 1430 it is significant that almost half the farm properties in the State of Florence were working the métayage system, and there were between ten and fifteen thousand.

COUNTRY CUSTOMS AND BELIEFS

A city like Florence cannot properly be understood or appreciated, as we have said, without considering the vital contribution of « its » own countryside. Here

the city drew some of its strength and renewed its energies, and, we like to think, found the true measure of its own moral and political qualities.

It will be realised that basically it was the work in the fields, with its alternating weariness and forced idleness, which determined the pattern of country life. Here tradition plays the greatest part and shapes that wisdom, simple and yet very diverse, typical of people close to the earth and to work on the land, over which the sky broods eternally with its threats and its gifts, and which is subjected to the remorseless round of the seasons. Tradition is made up of superstitions and prejudice, but also of virtue. There is an authentic religious sense, Christian, but with naturalistic elements, in the peasant life of these times. The worship of God, of Christ crucified and risen from the dead, of the Virgin Mary, is lived and felt in an almost mythical

A castle-type villa (detail from the « Procession of the Magi » by Benozzo Gozzoli in the Medici-Riccardi palace).

form, perhaps with roots in the dim Italic past. Festivals and processions wend their way through the countryside, reliving in country fashion the ancient Christian mysteries.

The farmers in the Mugello, in places such as the Valdarno and the Val di Pesa, equate Easter with the coming of spring, the festival of Saint John, with harvest-time, whilst the date of the Assumption means the time of the year when the grapes are ripe and the state of the olive-crop can be judged by the appearance of the fruit against the more or less dense foliage, and Advent marks the end of sowing.

The little shrines which can still be seen in the Tuscan countryside at the crossing of cart-tracks or along the lanes, bear witness to the peasants' devotion to the Saints whom they invoked to protect them from the fatigues of their labour and from poor harvests.

Hence the cult of Saint Anthony the abbot, the protector of animals and their stalls, and the blessing of the fields, the houses and the animals.

It is interesting to note that country people at this time had some knowledge, albeit rudimentary, of the stars, their constellations, and the phases of the planets and the moon. It is also easy to understand why this was so. The names they gave to the constellations were often only approximate and often familiar ones, which shows that they habitually placed great trust in them. The figure of the astrologer was often to be seen in Borgo San Lorenzo, at the Ponte alla Sieve, at the Lastra a Signa and in market places everywhere.

In certain popular ballads, which doubtless reflect country customs, there is an echo of the popular conception that good and bad weather alternate according to the phases of the moon. The *novelle* of the time also illustrate the utilitarian relationship between the peasant and God and the Saints in Paradise. The peasant speaks with his God as if he were talking to his master: with respect, but plainly, coming to an agreement and imposing conditions. If the harvest is good, the village church shall have two sacks of flour and two newly-weaned lambs. But if Providence does not grant a good harvest, the offer will be reduced to a handful of leaves and a few empty sacks. The peasant in question is an unknown man from the outskirts of Florence, in the little valley of Molin del Piano. He commends himself to the Madonna (probably the Madonna of the Rock, whose cult dates back at least to the end of the fifteenth century) and promises to make a pilgrimage to the caves of the Founder Saints of the Monte Senario hermitage.

It was thus a popular piety, partly still attached to legend, which took in not only the heroic gallery of the Saints and Martyrs, but included also figures of pagan antiquity seen through the mists of fable: Aeneas, Caesar, Charlemagne, the « big baron » Ugo of Tuscany. Boccaccio had written about the origins of Fiesole in his fable *Ninfale Fiesolano*; many of the themes of this poem are of popular, and probably of country origin.

The conservative spirit of the Florentine country-side in the fifteenth and sixteenth centuries was not averse to flights of fancy, a caustic wit and an unbridled imagination. The *novelle* of the time again abound in fresh and colourful anecdotes: the peasant Rosso prefers to sleep in the cattle-shed rather than in bed because he is more afraid of the thieves who might steal his herds than of anyone coming to take away his ugly old wife; the other peasant from the Mugello, Ventura, gives his pigs and goats endearing names, so that calling them back to the sty in the evening sounds like calling a roll for young girls, and yet another, a certain Giusto da Serravalle, takes stock of the few bits of clothing he possesses and consoles himself with the thought that the land and the grass offer « the most comfortable covering ».

The « big boots and the shrewd mind » of these country folk are shown in the verse *novella* called « La Storia di Campriano contadino » which tells of the tricks played by the poor but cunning Campriano on the rich but credulous merchants. Contrasted with the stupid local merchant we have the shrewd peasant, and this would go down well with the audiences of country-folk before whom the story was recited and sung, not only at the fairs and in the market-places, but also in the farmhouses, to while away the long evenings.

There was also a keen awareness of the vitality of country life among some of the great writers of the fifteenth century, from Vespasiano da Bisticci to Pulci and from Sant'Antonino to Lorenzo the Magnificent. Lorenzo's Nencia da Barberino is an unforgettable countrywoman, typical of so many Tuscan peasants of the time, strong, healthy and independent, a representative of a sturdy, wholesome world.

FESTIVALS AND ENTERTAINMENTS

In her games, her entertainments, her theatre, Florence showed a humble yet highly conscious, almost religious awareness that she was a city trying out her civilisation, watching herself, as she progressed, over the whole range of her activities. Her popular May Day festival contained an extraordinary element of singing and dancing which was a compound of Florentine lyric poetry, music and mime. Her most representative poet was Poliziano, and there is nothing more tender, or more ardent in the cultural heritage of Lorenzo than his « Welcome May and the proud flying banner, for then it is that man should turn his thoughts to love ... ».

The great subjects of games and theatrical dancing, and the eternal themes of every civilisation, war, hunting and love, all found their counterpart in illustrious literary texts. So also did the themes of the theatre, both religious and secular. The religious theatre took shape in Florence in the fourteenth and fifteenth centuries, in direct opposition to the Umbrian dramatic « lauda », performed in its own dialect; the secular theatre, the new entertainment, owed much to Florence, and it might well be said that without the experience of Florence in the study of the classical forms and in the translations of Greek tragedies and comedies, the theatre in the modern world could well have had quite a different development.

Florence celebrated the first day of May, the *Calendimaggio* with a ritual of flowers. The *maggi*, or flowering branches, were carried in procession like candles, to celebrate the rebirth of nature and then, twisted into the shape of a crown, were hung on the doors of young maidens to greet them on their awakening. « For one garland that I saw, every flower will make me sigh » said Dante. This gave rise to sport of the opposite kind, however. « The men of those days used to put on masks to disguise themselves as women and go singing and dancing at the Calendimaggio, pretending to be matrons and young maids », recalled Anton Francesco Grazzini. Here we have on the one hand women and young girls celebrating with flowers and dancing the coming of spring, and on the other, men in grotesque carnival costume parodying them in satirical gestures. This interpenetration of carnival and comedy, together with the new way of setting words to music elaborated by the Camerata dei Bardi (musicians and men of letters who met at the house of Giovanni Bardi, Count of Vernio) was the origin in Florence of a new form of entertainment: opera.

Prosodic chanting, the round dance, the procession from place to place and the circle of dancers led by a chorus master and delicately linked only by the contact of the little fingers, now still, now repeating the *ritornello*, were all elements, in Greece and elsewhere, of the earliest form of ritual. The processions were the mode of progression from the place of assembly to the temple, the dancing was the performance of the rite around the altar, where space was limited.

In Florence, however, singing accompanied by dancing, the form of entertainment involving words, music and movement which had the longest continuous history, was very much concerned with realities and had a strong popular element.

THE CARNIVAL

In the fifteenth century the carnival and the wearing of masks had completely lost their ancient associations with the devil and even the symbolical-mystical attributes they had in the Middle Ages. The carnival was the joyous relief from daily cares and the mask an escape from one's personality. The mask, the fictitious representation of another person, then became, through repetitions of the same type, the grotesque caricature of certain personalities or groups of people. The oldest carnival figure in Florence is the man of the woods, that symbol of open-air liberty and the simplest of human beings, yet rich in wisdom and earthy common-sense. The carnival was the time and place chosen to honour him. The city streets were the theatre for the performances of his attendant figures. The people responded immediately to his witty gibes, which were often directed at the best-known personalities of the time. Under the Medici, when it was influenced by their culture, the carnival respected, and to a certain extent revealed, the inner life of certain social groups by the freedom of speech which it allowed in the songs. The costumes linked together whole groups of friends, and particularly of craftsmen's guilds. They were so elaborate and of such high quality that painters, including Leonardo, Vasari and others, were pleased to design the decorations for the carts and the costumes of the participants, the latter often being modelled on the sumptuous clothes of the principal citizens.

The carnival was a compromise between pagan festivities and Christian entertainment before Lent. The pagan element was evident not only in the choice of mythological subjects, but in the spirit of enjoyment and the interpretation of life. The moral allegorical figures had no spiritual significance to the Christian, but represented the spirit, the taste and the moral outlook of the ancients and also of the new humanism. The costumes were fantastic, even for historical characters: vivid in colour, ostentatious, adorned with plumes, veils, gold braid, imitation jewels and imitation precious stones. But the nobles and the wealthy citizens, and Lorenzo de' Medici in particular, dressed up in cloth and veils of priceless quality, brought specially from the East. Their jewels were real, their plumes came from exotic birds, and they used the rarest furs which they wore either as exotic capes or laid on the floor of their carts, to be trampled underfoot.

A festival of St. John painted on the front of a wedding-chest (Bargello Museum). The horsemen bearing the banners of the nobility, the merchant companies and the guilds, proceed towards the Baptistery on a carpet of flowering branches. The young girls and the widows on

JOUSTS, TOURNEYS AND PAGEANTS

Lorenzo dressed most elegantly also for the jousts. Chroniclers have recorded particularly the joust held in February 1468 in Piazza Santa Croce, in which he took part and won the first engagement, « although », as he himself said, « the fighting was not very strenuous ». One chronicler who was present throughout this joust and followed it closely, had an opportunity to see Lorenzo's clothes. He described them enthusiastically and at great length, with details of their cost: one pearl cost 5,000 ducats, a hat 2,000 and so on.

A certain vintner, Bartolomeo del Corazza, kept a chronicle of events and described the tournaments held in Florence at this time. There was a « mighty contest » in 1410 in honour of Filippo Scolari, a Hungarian statesman of Florentine origin (?-1426), known also as Pippo Spano, and another one four years later in Piazza Santa Croce was held in the presence of the most select ladies of the town, who sat on a flower-decked platform covered with silk canopies and oriental carpets. The splendour of this spectacle was eclipsed

either side pray to St. John: « Thou who hast something for all, keep something for me also: thus I might know tomorrow who I shall have as a husband ». Below: youths playing civettino, a common pastime in the streets and squares of Florence. Defending one's self from a slap in the face and being constantly on the move in a restricted space made the players so hot that often they were left at the end wearing only jerkin and breeches.

Carnival processions through the streets of Florence included masked figures and allegorical chariots, each vying with the other in richness of dress and display. The chariot of « Fame » surrounded by famous men: Homer, Plato, Pythagoras, Aristotle, Virgil, Dante.

by that held in 1418 to celebrate the victory over Pisa. But again, all these fade before the magnificence of the tourney put on in 1435 by the Medici in celebration of their expulsion of Rinaldo degli Albizzi whose family had ruled Florence for many generations.

The joust, the tourney and the pageant were medieval entertainments which feudalism had invested with commitments of honour, summed up in a code of chivalry with rigid rules, proclaimed at every tournament by the heralds, against stabbing, fighting outside the ranks, aiming at the horse, wounding a knight after he had raised his vizier, fighting two or more to one. These rules of chivalry were still being observed in the fifteenth century, and the penalty for breaking them was the loss of one's spurs. As in the Middle Ages, the knight still wore his lady's favours and fought, and sometimes died, in her honour. The fighting was with lances, swords and clubs, and to acquire agility, skill and bravery the young men trained regularly in exercises of chivalry with such picturesque names as « dangerous barrier », « shadowy cross-paths »,

« field of thorn », « inaccessible forest », « passage of arms ». They were violent and cruel exercises, but deaths and killings in the jousts were rare in Florence; the fighting was chivalrous and they were sporting contests. Serious killing was reserved for revolutions, party strife and political quarrels.

In addition to feats of arms proper, the Florentines also had other similar entertainments such as the « Struggle of the Powers », the « Assault of the Castles », the « Horse Races », and the « Hunting of Wild Animals ». These were not held on one particular day only, but on several solemn occasions, and all were repeated together at the Feast of Saint John the Baptist. Other Tuscan cities celebrated their patron saints with similar games, and the Florentines would go to watch, or often to take part. There was the « Bridge Game » at Pisa, the « Palio » horse-race at Siena and the « Saracen's Joust » at Arezzo. The latter was also held in Florence, and was a popular, rather than an aristocratic contest. It took place several times a year, either in the Piazza Santa Croce, the Piazza Santa Maria Novella, Via Larga,

The Triumph of Love (from a tympanum by an anonymous fifteenth-century artist). On a golden chariot Cupid, with his eyes bandaged, feeds with fire the love of young girls. « In their pretty angelic costumes, they looked like a thousand heavens ». The tympanum is in the Restorer's room in the Uffizi.

Via Tornabuoni, Via del Maglio or on the Prato. The players, divided into Keepers and Attackers, respectively inside and outside the palisade, enjoyed themselves hugely, provided great entertainment and dealt each other violent blows. The contest almost always ended up (as it has also become a tradition in the Palio at Siena) in rioting between the various districts of the town.

The game became real warfare sometimes, as in 1499 when the two sides engaged in a battle of stones took to arms and one man was killed. This stone-throwing game, which was very common everywhere, was the plebeian continuation of the tournaments fought with blunted arms, and was one of those fights entered into partly as a joke and partly also to run a very real risk of death. When fought at a distance most of these minor scuffles were harmless, and worth watching when by tradition they were held in the same place, like the Bridge Game at Pisa, but some were dangerous and cruel when fought at close quarters and men paid off old scores against their enemies. This also underlines a feature of Florentine entertain-

ments: it was very easy to move from fiction to reality, as men were fleet of foot, lively in imagination and quick to anger. These war-like games also showed a predominantly popular element, the readiness to resort to force, to mass together and to miscalculate the risk, as opposed to the knightly canon of the individual equally balanced between defence and attack, well protected by his armour and the lightning speed of his charger.

THE FESTIVAL OF SAINT JOHN

The height of the city's celebrations was the festival of Saint John, the patron saint, and the activities connected with this, in both church and countryside, show the link between the Christian and the pagan rites. The festival of Saint John, with its night of bonfires, was for all the lands of Christendom the summer equivalent of the winter nativity festival, to celebrate the shortest, as opposed to the longest night. The

Corsa dei Barberi, a race between Barbary horses let loose in the streets, provided much excitement and an opportunity for the display of high spirits.

There was also dancing, a great festivity in which all the inhabitants took part, even when this was held, not in the city squares, but in the gardens of the rich men's houses. The fourteenth-century saying about « keeping open garden » did in fact continue to be observed. There was an open invitation to all the people of Florence to attend at a given hour of the night, when the ladies, young and old, retired, and left the young men of the wealthy families to disport themselves with greater freedom and dance with the wenches of the town.

The greatest festival for dancing was May Day, then came the festival of Saint John, then the Guild festivals, then the festivals connected with the various districts of the city. There were round dances such as the *carola* and the *salterello* and a typical Tuscan dance known as the *trescone*, performed by couples; the *ridda*, in which everyone danced round in a circle with a girl in the middle. There were other dances performed by couples or by three people, such as the *peregrina*, with steps and figures known as the *chirintana, lioncello, bel riguardo, speranza, danza del re* and *bassadanza reale*.

The girls invited the men to dance, and not the other way round. The dancing went on all day and all night, and it is likely that most people wore more than one costume. The wealthy young men and their elegant ladies would often go through several, and with each change of dress they would wear a different hair-style and different jewellery.

One great festival of dancing which passed into history was that held in 1459 in honour of Pope Pius II, then the guest of Florence. His name was Enea Silvio Piccolomini, and he was a poet and humanist. Together with his suite of cardinals he took great pleasure in watching the dancing in the Mercato Nuovo. The spectacle was witnessed by a certain Giovanni Cambi, and he has left us a colourful and accurate description. Present also, and taking part in the dancing and the entertainment, was the Milanese prince Galeazzo Maria Sforza who looked most elegant with curled hair and wearing gloves.

To the sound of fife and trumpet the ladies of Florence appeared in their sumptuous dresses, decked with jewels, on the Piazza del Mercato, which was decorated with all the flowers an April garden could offer. The scene has been described by two poets who have remained anonymous; they composed skilled verses on the refreshments, the light luncheon and the dinner at which the whole of Florence drank and ate. There were flasks of Trebbiano wine by the hundreds, and when the dancing began again after the feasting, pages, valets and young maidens distributed sweets and sugared almonds under the loggia of the Mercato Nuovo. The sweets were shaped like snakes and lions: the snake of Milan and the heraldic lion of Florence.

THE GAME OF FOOTBALL

The same antagonism found in the scuffles and fighting occurred also in a game indulged in by the men of Florence with particular enthusiasm: the *giuoco del calcio* (football). Derived from the ancient ball game of *spheromachia*, known to the Greeks and Romans,

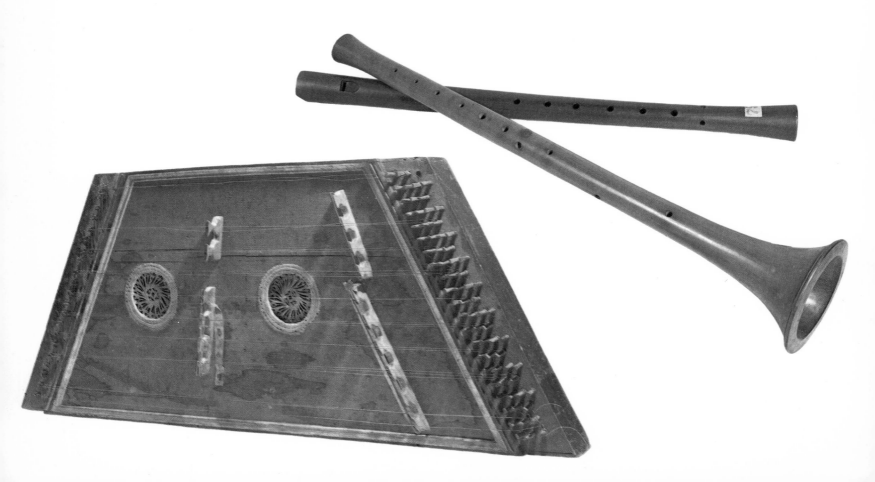

Costumes designed by Giorgio Vasari for a great Medici feast. Heroes of antiquity, muses, Greek gods and goddesses crowded on the « clouds », that is the chariots, where amidst « celestial cotton wool » mythology rediscovered its ancient vitality, recreated lovingly by the Florentine humanists.

football was very popular at carnival time, from January to March.

The game was advertised several days beforehand and the names of the players were published. The latter, by way of publicity, would parade about the streets during the daytime and take part, masked, in the dancing and singing at night. The game was usually played in a public square, so that the noble ladies could watch from the windows of the surrounding houses and the people from the steps of the many stands. The two sides had a total of fifty-four players « not servants, not plebeian, not dishonourable persons, but respected soldiers, gentlemen, signori and princes », all richly

dressed in silk of two colours. They came on preceded by twelve trumpeters, two drummers, two pipers and four men carrying footballs. They were followed by eight trainers and managers with halberdiers and a band to wind up the proceedings.

The procession paraded round the arena, then turned to the stands where the nobles and leading citizens were watching and paid homage to them. The colours of the teams were then entrusted to the referees and the players took up their positions.

The game began when the ball, called a *pallone a vento* (inflated) was kicked off or thrown in. The players were called *datori*, corresponding roughly to half-

Left to right: *a psaltery, two flutes and a lute (Cherubini Conservatoire, Florence).*

backs, *innanzi* or forwards, to whom the *datori* fed the ball, and *sconciatori*, backs or defenders. Although it cannot be seriously maintained that present-day association football derived from this Florentine game of the fifteenth century, it can usefully be referred to in modern terms.

The job of the backs was to outwit the opposing forwards; the half-backs fed the ball to the forwards who, using both hands and feet, tried to get the ball into the opposite goal, which was a tent. If a goal was scored, the supporters of the winning side gave vent to the noisiest enthusiasm, and often to uncontrollable excesses. The side which lost had to carry its banner dipped, but it often happened that in a excess of fanaticism, the banners were torn.

Historians record that Lorenzo the Magnificent, Giulio de' Medici, Clement VII and Alessandro de' Medici were all enthusiastic footballers. They also mention, amongst the most famous games, that played in 1529 in the Piazza Santa Croce whilst Florence was under siege by the Prince of Orange. Varchi tells how the Florentines, so as to be better heard by the enemy, went on to the roof of the church with trumpets and drums. At this mockery the besieging army replied with cannon-fire, but fortunately their aim was bad and they missed.

THE THEATRE

A new theatrical language took shape in Florence in the late fourteenth and early fifteenth centuries. This enabled drama to develop in a different direction from that imposed by the Umbrian *lauda drammatica*. The poets concerned were: Jacopone, who, if he did not actually compose *laude drammatiche*, was an important precursor; the Maestro delle Laudi degli Evangeli, from Perugia; and, within the fifteenth-century Florentine school, Feo Belcari, the author of poems on sacred subjects rather than of sacred plays, and Lorenzo the Magnificent.

The *lauda drammatica*, in its earliest and simplest form, is a scenic intermezzo used in the interval of a meeting of a religious confraternity, and is closely connected with the liturgy and the cycle of the year. Its function is confessedly didactic, it aims at dramatic synthesis, violently, but magnanimously, foreshortens the holy events and shortens the distances and draws aside the veils between the devout believer and Christ.

The Florentine religious play, however, accepts the sense of escape and in place of the rigorous Christ-centred morality and theology of the Umbrian *lauda* it offers the adventures of the lives of the Saints, a cycle which, from its very origins, can be said to be ambivalent in that the lives touched on both reality, with its moral example, and the miraculous. The different metres used in the two types of play clearly illustrate their differences. The *lauda* has alternate verses of eleven — and seven — syllable lines which requires a variety of musical accompaniment. The Florentine verse is in the narrative eight-syllable line throughout, the metre of the epic and the ballad sung by strolling minstrels, an ample, complex, verbal line with a correspondingly simple musical accompaniment in a fixed rhythm.

These religious plays commanded considerable attention from the public. There were many new plays and new productions which testified to the vitality of this early theatre. Throughout Italy at this time religious and secular plays alternated in the churches, in the squares in front of the churches, in the universities, in Latin, and at court, in Italian. There were classical comedies and allegorical extravaganzas: both of these types attracted the enthusiastic attention of Ercole d'Este, a great politician from an area culturally very close to Tuscany. In Florence the theatre enjoyed great prestige amongst the people and owed its success to the fact that it could appeal to a wide popular audience. Lorenzo the Magnificent himself was often to be seen watching the play, just one citizen, albeit more imposing, among the rest. The theatre focussed the religious feelings of a wide variety of Florentines. Jacopone's *Laudi* showed the influence of Savonarola in the 1492 edition, but the religion of the theatre was easy-going and bourgeois.

There are many examples of this kind of religious feeling and its origins go back at least to Sant'Antonino who, in the midst of controversy, succeeded in striking a balance between asceticism and culture. It also sprang more readily from scholastic doctrine than from the teachings of the religious confraternities and has its parallel in the Latin plays of the University students.

THE ACTORS AND THE COMPANIES

The name *Compagnia* was more commonly used than *Confraternita* to denote groups of actors who played fixed parts, not only of angels, saints and biblical characters, but of men and types from city life: the wayfarer, the dyer, the mendicant, the corn-merchant, the washerwoman, the innkeeper, the gravedigger. They could step forward out of the crowd of extras, as if from an ancient chorus, and comment on the « event », even with a single remark, phrase or exclamation. This was a characteristic of the Renaissance theatre: man as the interpreter and protagonist of his own part in life, with his vices, his passions, his hopes and his piety. Thus a type of play developed about a human situation, represented by human characters and not only saints with their penitence, their martyrdom and their miracles. The passions were human, joy and grief, though not entirely without their mystical element. Such was the « Play of Uliva » and of « Stella » and of « Rossana », but of all these the texts have been lost.

The companies which gave the performances were attended by civic pomp, including the carrying of their banner in procession. They bore the name of the church or oratory to which they belonged: San Francesco, San Jacopo, San Raffaele and so on, but they carried another name on their coat of arms. This was paraded like another banner through the streets and squares, a manifestation of a very necessary esprit de corps, and showed that they were popularly

known as the Compagnia del Freccione, the Compagnia del Nicchio, the Compagnia della Scala, or the Compagnia dell'Aquila or degli Acquilini. The players were not men, serious and confident in their strength; they were youths, boys and girls, who might make mistakes but who could be fondly forgiven. Their parents, relatives and acquaintances turned up in their large numbers to watch the tender, pious play. What the wardrobes of the church, convent or oratory lacked was provided by the wealthy citizens, and there was plenty of spectacle which, when it got out of proportion, often produced amusing and moving results. Help was readily given by the artists, even the great artists, painters and sculptors, who were always ready for a little fun, be it modelling snowmen or building up even more ephemeral pieces of scenery.

The eight-syllable lines were recited to the accompaniment of a violin, but the artistic value of the poetry and the music left something to be desired, as the accomplishments of both the artisan actors and the wealthier dilettantes were rather restricted. The un-

One of the Signoris' favourite amusements in summer was hunting. The beat was organised with dogs and the game flushed out, chased and killed with lances or arrows.

certainty of the performance was noticeable from the vagueness of the texts. No exits or entrances were given; all the actors were on the stage at once, those presumed to have left merely sat down (in a strictly dramatical concept no person is ever really absent from the stage, and these early actors seem to have stumbled across a fundamental truth of the theatre) and those speaking their parts stood up. The movements, like the sing-song rhythm of the verses, were required not to be obvious, but subordinated to an overall calm and orderliness which prevailed even in the scenes of violence and martyrdom. Such violence as there was was conveyed by mime, using gestures to convey what in the fifteenth-century secular plays had been told in prose. The variety of gesture and mime required was infinite, as there was no curtain, no division into acts, and all scene changes were done in view of the audience.

FLORENCE AND THE NEW THEATRE

Florence played a great part in the establishment of the new theatre, not perhaps as great as that of Ferrara, but whereas Ferrara was noteworthy from the extent of the plays produced there under Ercole I and his daughter Isabella Gonzaga by poets such as Guarino, Collenuccio and Ludovico Ariosto, Florence was principally concerned with the study of classical forms and the translation of Greek tragedies, to bring an understanding of the dithyrambic theatre and of the masterpieces of comedy of all ages. This was a decisive factor in the development of world theatre, and it came about in Florence by a combination of academic intellectualism and a strong popular tradition in acting.

As for theatrical entertainment proper in the years between the death of Lorenzo and the siege, Florence cannot be said to be in the forefront, but merely to be following well-established paths: creating a religious theatre out of the religious verse and music entertainment, and a secular theatre out of the carnival singing, mime and dancing. This brought together the work of Trissino and Giovanni Rucellai, and some cooperation with Ferrara in the person of Ludovico Ariosto, the most active and gifted writer engaged in the adaptation of the classics. Florence thus became a centre of great activity in the theatre, the results

of which were reflected in Ferrara, Vicenza and Venice, then over the whole of Europe. The complex nature of Florentine democracy, especially in the stormy years of the decline of civic liberties, produced a great variety of theatrical forms. In a word, whereas in Ferrara the theatre showed a coherent evolution through respected and recognised forms, initiated by the political power, approved by public taste and based on the customs of the people, Florence in these crucial years was more concerned with experimentation.

In the fifteenth century Florence became the city *par excellence* of comedy, and just as the artists invented the jest of Grosso the cabinet-maker, and as the comedy of Plautus lived again in the *novella* of Geta and Birria (although Machiavelli used it for a parody against the humanists), so the students revived and reinvented the style of the ancient comedies, The strolling-player and the members of a theatrical company, whom ancient custom had permitted to appear in watering-places, baths and inns, were given the freedom of the city in Florence and in the Middle Ages were brought into the *Studium*. Here Latin plays were given in the original and here new Latin texts were composed, a kind of classical farce which later led to farces in the vernacular; the spirit of the wandering scholar lives again in the new era, in the restless times of the late Renaissance.

All this is admirably illustrated in Niccolò Machiavelli's masterpiece *La Mandragola*.

Against the wider background of the wider theatre, and taking into account the part played by Florence in its development, Machiavelli stands in direct contrast to Ariosto. As an act of faith, as a confirmation of a mode of civic life which reaffirms the concept of love, Ariosto's masterpiece *Lena* stands in direct opposition to *La Mandragola*, as also does another comedy, this time from Tuscany and the Medici times: Bernardo Dovizi's *Calandria*. According to the definition of Benedetto Croce, the philosopher and critic (1866-1952), this is the comedy of the desire of love; its theme is adventurous and its impact explosive. Based in part on the *Celestina*, it is a burlesque of the tragic theme of Romeo and Juliet.

Dovizi, who was also Bernardo da Bibbiena, a cardinal and a man of action, wrote frankly comic theatre; it has its occasional silliness, but this is forgivable and his plays offer better entertainment than the bitter satires of Machiavelli, the man of letters.

PAINTERS, SCULPTORS AND ARCHITECTS

Renaissance Florence reached a new vision in art: in architecture a preciseness through the conquest of space by the science of perspective, in sculpture and painting a definition of man's physical and moral attributes in a proportionate environment. The stimulus of the Renaissance was classical antiquity, which had already penetrated the truth of certain aspects of art to which the Renaissance aspired, but the new art had a moral content, matured throught centuries of Christian civilisation. Florence gave a coherent expression to the art of this period, although she sheltered a rich variety of men of genius and, in her interpretation of the ancients, preserved an independence which was not found elsewhere. Moreover in her buildings and monuments of the Gothic period, Florence had already achieved an architecture of solid masses, and in the sculpture of Arnolfo and the painting of Giotto an intense plasticity. Certain precedents remained fundamental to Florentine Renaissance art. Her architecture may have become more compact and human, but it nevertheless spoke in terms of masses, it was « murata » (constructional) architecture, as they said in the fifteenth century. In the other two arts, form is predominantly plastic, and in this Florence differed considerably from other centres which nevertheless played an important part in the figurative arts during this great period of the Renaissance.

THE ART WORKSHOPS

During the fifteenth century there was a great change in the social conditions of the Florentine artists, in their training and in the very concept of art.

The *paragone delle arti,* or the comparability of the arts, occurred as a theme in all treatises from the fifteenth century to beyond the middle of the sixteenth. It may appear to the modern reader unaware of its implications merely an elegant subject for academic discussion, but in those days it was a very vital question. It meant nothing less than a radical change in the position hitherto accorded to painting, sculpture and architecture amongst the « mechanical », that is, manual arts (as can still be seen in the distribution of the bas-reliefs in Giotto's bell-tower), by bringing them into the ranks of the « liberal » arts, equal in stature to poetry and music. Only later, in the sixteenth century, do we find artists discussing the superiority of painting,

sculpture or architecture among themselves, and gradually the discussion moves into the academies; but the academies were just forming, and by then the ancient workshops were dead. In the fifteenth century the comparability of the arts turned on raising painting to the dignity of poetry and music.

The genius of Filippo Brunelleschi, who formulated the laws of linear perspective, brought about a revolution in art, the importance of which can still be measured today. William Mills Ivins found the sources of his work on the rationalisation of perception in the ideas on perspective emerging at this time and considered this one of the most important influences of the Renaissance. This was where art and science met, and was the starting point of great future developments in the natural sciences and mechanical engineering. The « perspective » wich was born and nurtured in the workshops of Florence, from Brunelleschi's to Leonardo's, is the first link in the chain leading to Kepler and Desargues and to the descriptive geometry of Monge and Poncelet.

The paths of rays of light received by the eye and their angles of incidence and reflection had been dealt with repeatedly in medieval treatises on optics. These had, however, been discussed and commented upon within the doctrinal and scholastic framework of physical and metaphysical theories. When these ideas were taken up by artists, when variations in size and distance were seen to be directly related to the visual angles of the objects and this knowledge was used in pictorial representation, then a new revolutionary movement had begun, based on practice and experience. The corpus of knowledge within the Florentine workshop suddenly increased: the new principles of perspective allowed a pictorial representation of reality and led to research into and a rationalisation of the whole visible world.

It will be realised that the old work-methods of the artisans, on which the workshops had functioned up to now, immediately became outdated. As knowledge grew, from what Leonardo called so well the *discorso mentale*, the old « mechanical », that is, manual, interpretation of painting was rejected by these men who, it is true, might be unlettered, but were well aware of the originality and importance of their work.

They could well have replied with Leonardo to those men of letters and philosophers who took it upon themselves to « criticise their work, alleging that it offended against the authority of certain men of high esteem »: « a much greater and worthier thing do I allege experience to be ... as she ever guided any man who wrote well, and I take her to be my guide in all that I do ». The new era was beginning, and beginning here in the art workshops.

That this could happen is due to the great vitality of the Florentine workshops over a long period of time. They were well organised and had become an integral part of the city's daily life. In the previous century, Giotto had been a powerful and influential figure, and it is well known that in his time, and generally throughout the fourteenth century, the painter had to enrol in the « guild of doctors, apothecaries and haberdashers » in order to be able to exercise his profession. « Painter » meant also sculptor and craftsman engaged in related trades. The fourteenth-century statutes of the guild contain a wealth of information concerning the standard of work required and the way the workshop should be managed, together with instructions on how to record the assets, the income and the details of the workers employed. The statute of 1349 lays down explicitly that « the

Two versions of « The sacrifice of Isaac », the subject of the competition of 1401 for the second door of the Baptistery. Left: Brunelleschi's, right: Ghiberti's, which won. The judges preferred Ghiberti's traditional solution, a balance between the gothic and the classical, to the more daring innovations of Brunelleschi. Ghiberti and the apprentices in his busy workshop were occupied for twenty-seven years (from 1425 to 1452) on the third door of the Baptistery (facing page). Divided into spacious panels, it portrays episodes from the Old Testament chosen by the humanist Leonardo Bruni. In his use of perspective Ghiberti showed that he had now absorbed the spirit of humanist culture.

notary of the said guild shall be obliged to keep every year a book in which shall be recorded all the craftsmen shown on the returns of the workshop », and anyone who does not appear in the book is debarred from « receiving any profit or undertaking any work in the said shop ».

In addition to enrolling by compulsion in the guild of doctors and apothecaries, the painters (and, again, this must include sculptors) often formed *Compagnie* (associations) amongst themselves. Most of our information on this comes from the art historian Ugo Procacci, who supplies a wealth of detail. « These associations of artists », (i. e. painters and sculptors) he says, « appear in certain respects similar to, but in other respects very different from the famous commercial associations which have earned such importance and renown in Florence, and which are to a large extent the economic power behind the city. The commercial associations, or companies, presuppose the association of several persons who contribute considerable capital. The painters, on the other hand, have no need, for the exercise of their calling, of anything beyond the workshop other than a small amount of equipment and materials of little value ».

There were many reasons why the artists felt that they ought to join together: firstly for reasons of work, to combine their forces so that the lesser-known might gain experience and eke out their living from the commissions given to the more famous of their number, and the latter might have the assistance of several skilled workers; secondly for reasons of mutual assistance, in a time when there were no social benefits, so that when he was off sick the *compagno* could continue to draw a share of the profits; lastly for financial reasons, so that not only the profits were shared, but also the losses from the failure of debtors. The profits were divided between the members according to a fixed percentage, but usually equally. This sharing-out of profits and losses, which might at first sight seem strange in the cases where one artist was clearly much more important than the others, is explained by the fact that the workshop was concerned not only with paintings as understood today, such as pictures, altarpieces and the like, in which the more important painters naturally had the greatest share, but also with a large variety of craftwork such as blankets, cloth hangings, shields, lances, axes, helmets,

bards, flags and pennants which, when taken together, formed the principal revenue.

It often happened, however, that debtors could not be pressed, especially as much of this work was for the soldiery (helmets, shields, lances, bards and so on) who were continually on the move. Occasionally the debtor was an important person. « To the account of the Duke of Urbino 60 florins; I hope for 30, but fear I may get none » states Giuliano di Jacopo resignedly in a declaration dated 1458. It also happened, by a curious analogy with modern times, that the insolvent debtor was the Commune of Florence. In his income-tax return for January 1431 Calvano di Cristoforo declares: « And in addition we have on our hands 44 lengths of cloth ordered by the members of the last *balìa* » (a temporary committee nominated in times of emergency) « in honour of two of their number who died, that is to say Dino di messer Guccio and Andrea del Palagio, and we have not had even advice of intention to honour the amount due, nor are we ever likely to ».

These and many other details have come down to us with a wealth of particulars from the declaration of income which from 1427 every Florentine citizen was compelled by law to make, so that a more equitable distribution of taxes could be achieved. Each return had to show the composition of the family, the number of dependents, each person's occupation and income and the names of his creditors and debtors. Each workshop had to give the names of the artists who had formed an association, of the craftsmen, apprentices and boys, the nature of any contracts, the rent (or the value of the workshop if the artist were the owner), the « *entratura* » (goodwill), « that is the right to exercise the trade apart from the value of the shop or its position », the equipment and materials and the finished work in stock, the assets and the liabilities and the location of the workshop itself. It will easily be understood what a precious and incomparable source of information these returns are for the historian, and no other city in the world has anything to compare with them. They are, moreover, proof of the high standard of economic administration in Florence, an exception in Renaissance times.

Most of the workshops in Florence were in the Corso degli Adimari, now the first section, starting at the Piazza del Duomo, of the Via dei Calzaioli. One of the biggest and best known was that of Pesello, a curious person, whose work as a painter is still unknown today because nothing has survived which can be positively identified as his. Yet he was continually being referred to in the chronicles of the time, and what we know of his life reads like a *novella*. We can follow in contemporary documents the history of this workshop, which soon became the centre of activity in the Corso degli Adimari, and the information we have is exceptionally detailed and vivid. It was opened in 1416 and saw a succession of *compagnie* (the *compagnie* had a limited life, three years at the most, after which contracts could be renewed, as generally happened, or they were dissolved). His associates came and went, but Pesello remained until his death in 1446, when he was succeeded by his young grandson Francesco, known as Pesellino, who also made his name in the history of art, but by his paintings as well as by frequent mention in contemporary records. Pesellino brought the workshop to the height of its prosperity, but after his early death on July 29th 1457 it declined rapidly. A note by the tax officials' lawyer in the margin of the return of March 21st 1461 shows that it had gone bankrupt.

By 1461, however, the whole complex of old workshops was changing rapidly under the influence of new knowledge, a new concept of art and developing social and political conditions in the city. The Medici family emerged as patrons of the arts, and the workshops of a few great personalities in the profession began to stand out far above the rest and to exercise a direct influence on prevailing culture. These famous artists were greatly sought after by princes and high church dignitaries, and were received at court with precedence over men of letters. The old Florentine workshops soon became forgotten with their many homely crafts and their popular humour.

When Lorenzo il Magnifico was a young man, Vasari spoke of the garden « which that most exalted citizen possessed opening on to the Piazza San Marco in Florence, full of fine and ancient sculptures; the loggia, the paths and the surrounding rooms had the finest ancient marble figures, paintings and other such things, all made by the hands of the greatest artists who ever lived in Italy or elsewhere. All these objects were as a school or academy to the young painters and sculptors, and to all who were interested in drawing, especially the young noblemen... » This passage of Vasari's gave rise to the myth of the « San Marco

garden school », a kind of *avant lettre* academy at which were supposed to have studied under Bertoldo, a former pupil of Donatello and now an old man, Michelangelo and a whole series of Florentine and foreign artists, of whom Vasari gives a list. Modern critics have shown that the « school and academy » was much more limited and of rather a different kind. Lorenzo had opened the collections of antiques, paintings and new and ancient sculptures which he, his brothers and their father Cosimo had assembled, not only in the San Marco garden, but also in the garden by San Lorenzo and in their palazzo in Via Larga, for the benefit of all, men of letters, teachers and young artists, who might care to see and to study them. Vasari projected backwards on to the San Marco garden and the atmosphere of the Florence of Lorenzo

Donatello entered Ghiberti's workshop as a very young man. His skill won him the friendship of Cosimo, but he preferred working in his shop to the brilliant society of the Medicis. His « Head of a Prophet » (Museo dell'Opera del Duomo).

Niche with the Four Saints by Nanni di Banco on Orsanmichele (1413), commissioned by the trade association of « builders, smiths and woodcarvers ».

the Magnificent his ideas of a school of art based on the Accademia del Disegno founded by the Grand Duke Cosimo in 1561.

Yet, however distorted, Vasari's view of artists practising their profession in Renaissance Florence shows how far they were moving away from the old workshops.

THE PAINTERS AND SCULPTORS

At the beginning of the fifteenth century the figure which all future developments in the artistic world will show to have been the most influential, not only in architecture but also in painting and sculpture, is Filippo Brunelleschi. He emerged as a sculptor in the famous competition for the second door of the Baptistery in 1401.

The competition was won by Ghiberti and the judges' decision was fully justified. The door was required to match the first one by Andrea Pisano (1330-1336) and had to be set in the same complicated gothic frame. Ghiberti's panels show a harmony of composition and a mastery of modelling and casting unequalled by any other competitor. But in its sharper, even excessive relief, and in some uncertainty in the balance of its composition, Brunelleschi's set of panels show a wealth and vitality of new technique which clearly point the way to the future.

Brunelleschi also worked as a painter, and here his work was even more revolutionary. He was the first (and the originality of his vision is now almost lost on us, until we realise how this extraordinary discovery of his has become a very part of our civilisation) to sweep away with virtually one stroke of his brush all the complicated ornamentation of the Gothic, its mannerisms of colour, its refined subtleties and its picturesque, fanciful flowing lines. This he achieved with his views of the Piazza San Giovanni and the Piazza della Signora with its palazzo and loggia, all based on the strictest perspective projections « with the plan and elevation constructed by means of intersection ».

This shook the very foundations of traditional workshop practice. Artists seized upon the revolutionary challenge of the Brunelleschi theories « which brought about a great awakening of the mind and caused artists to apply themselves greatly to study

The glazed terracottas of Luca della Robbia, with their marvellous blues and whites, offer a striking contrast to the decorative fantasies of Donatello with their balanced composition, their continuity of plane and their « classical » form.

them » (Vasari). Tradition has it that Brunelleschi taught Masaccio, who very soon abandoned the « old » method by which he had painted the delightful little triptych of 1421. In sculpture also Donatello immediately took up the teaching of Brunelleschi.

These three artists between them determined the course of Renaissance art in Florence. All three were called Filippo. Brunelleschi was the oldest, being born in 1377, Donatello was born in 1384 or 1386 (he himself having given the two dates on different tax returns) and Masaccio was much the younger, being born in 1401. Brunelleschi was unanimously recognised as the greatest, and his name became legendary; this is shown by, amongst others, the tribute paid to him by Alberti in dedicating to him his Treatise on Painting. To do this in 1435, when Brunelleschi was famous above all as an architect, was a significant recognition of the importance of his work in the field of painting as well.

ALBERTI'S TREATISE

Alberti's dedication is a great page of history: « I was wont to marvel, and at the same time to grieve, that such great divine arts and sciences as we see in the works of antiquity should be now missing and almost entirely lost ... But then when I returned from the long exile in which the Alberti family had grown old, and saw again my city, beloved above all others for its beauty, I came to understand by many, but firstof all by you, Filippo, by our dear friend Donato the sculptor and Nencio and Luca and Masaccio, that we should ever give praise that our great artists are worthy to be compared with those of any famous State of antiquity ».

In these few lines, and at so early a date as 1435, Leon Battista Alberti singles out with unerring judgment the greatest artists of his day in Florence: first Filippo Brunelleschi, then Donato, that is to say Donatello, Nencio, the shortened name of Lorenzo Ghiberti, and Luca della Robbia and Masaccio. These are the « great » ones of their time, and there only requires to be added to them a sixth, the writer of the Treatise, Alberti himself. He goes on to say, in moving terms, how amazed he was, after the lifting in 1428 of the ban under which his family had grown old (his grandparents, that is, not Leon Battista himself, who was young at the time, having been born in Genoa in 1404), to be able shortly afterwards to return to Florence where he saw for the first time Brunelleschi's dome, « a structure so large, that it stood higher than the hills and was wide enough to cover with its shadow all the people of Tuscany ».

The second of the artists recalled by Alberti is Donatello: « our dear friend Donato the sculptor ». The link between Brunelleschi and Donatello is shown

Donatello's « schiacciato » relief turns plastic art into painting: relief decreases to give an effect of depth until the classical buildings in the background are scarcely modelled at all: the groups of figures thus do not project forwards, but the whole composition has unity and a high dramatic effect, resulting from the play of light on the broken surfaces. The pulpit is in San Lorenzo church and was Donatello's last work, carved about 1460.

259

not only in documentary sources, but in their works, particularly in their spirit and style. They are as different as can be in temperament: the former all clarity and strict restraint, the latter dynamic and dramatic, his modelling, with its broken lines, full of movement and pictorial effects. Both, however, have great breadth of vision, their art is a synthesis and has great strength, both are moved by a spirit which is radically and consciously new, directed to the « imitation of nature ». There is a great difference between the Renaissance concept of nature, all-embracing, animist and convinced of the rationality of its laws, and the positivist concept of the nineteenth century. As for the much discussed principle of the « imitation of nature », the artists kept a clear distinction between « imitating », a moderately autonomous and creative act, and « copying ». « Our great artists, emulators of nature, were reluctant to bind themselves to the natural order ».

GHIBERTI AND DONATELLO

In this imitation of nature, the rendering of three-dimensional space and the plasticity of the figures were the two fundamental factors. The genius of Donatello achieved both together, grandly, even in sculpture, with effects in his bas-reliefs which rivalled those of painting. Donatello's famous « schiacciato » (flattening effect) was a clever stylistic invention. By foreshortening the planes, by gradually lowering the relief (an increased flattening of the figures until they were a mere outline in the background), and by softening the outlines to give an effect of distance (thus anticipating Leonardo's « perspective ») he achieved the integration of the figures with the space they inhabit and their attraction towards the background. Instead of projecting outwards in relief, the figures became a part of the whole and, fading into the distance, built up the perspective and the illusion of space.

Ghiberti too, like every Florentine artist of his day, was interested in the problems of perspective and wished to apply it to his bas-reliefs on the third door of the Baptistery, but his sensitivity was still attuned to the preciosity of the late gothic, and he was unable to relinquish the exquisite touches and the refined modelling and counterpoint in which

Detail from « The Adoration of the Magi » by Gentile da Fabriano (Uffizi), one of the masterpieces of the International Gothic style. It is more like a scene at court, a display of sumptuous clothes, heavy with gold and precious stones, and spectacular regalia, more dream-like than real.

he was a master. His shortening of forms and softening of outlines are quite different from Donatello's. Compared with the great revolution in art brought about by Brunelleschi, Donatello and Masaccio, Ghiberti's work shows that in the first half of the fifteenth century he was still deeply influenced by the past and was continuing into the new age features which could be traced back to the High Gothic.

Yet Alberti includes Ghiberti in the five artists he mentions in the dedication of his Treatise on Painting. In this he shows himself to be a wise and discerning critic, capable of seeing beyond dogmatic classification and of recognising the variety of styles which can coexist in one period, provided they are significant. It should be added that there is also a touch of formal classicism in Ghiberti's art. It is small-scale, and not monumental, almost purist (except that this word when applied to culture implies a certain rigid, bare formalism) in a word a purified, refined classicism: slender, elegant adolescent nudes, sharply-defined ornamentation of festoons and floral garlands such as

The art of Masolino marks a half-way point between the courtly, decorative style of International Gothic and the new human dimensions of Masaccio's Carmelite frescoes: the conventional gothic mannerism takes on a more refined and sensitive colouring, and there is the first attempt at perspective in the buildings.

In Masaccio's « Expulsion from Paradise » (Santa Maria del Carmine) the chiaroscuro distorts Eve's face into an expression of agony; the red of the angel's cloak, reflected on Adam's body, confirms the condemnation of the first two human beings, now expelled from their earthly paradise.

would appeal to the humanist of the second half of the century, and therefore to Alberti.

Alberti's inclusion of Luca della Robbia among the five is also important. For too long Luca della Robbia has been considered by modern critics to be merely the delicate artist in ceramics, the creator of those lovely blue and white glazed terra-cotta groups which so appealed to the tender sentiments of the age, with their youths, their pure madonnas, cherubs and « holy innocents » all grouped together and offered to the view in the circle of a simple, elegant cornice. Luca is much more than this. He certainly does not possess the fire or the transfiguring creative genius of Donatello, his inexhaustible wealth of invention, or his power to capture an idea in an outline, but he is a sculptor of great controlled strength, the creator of confidently modelled figures which could earn him the name of « classic », not in the literary sense, and even less in the sense in which the word was applied to Ghiberti, but in that his art has balance, his composition is clear, of harmonious proportions and his form full and serene.

The sixth name which might have been added, that of Alberti himself, is a separate case. Alberti was not trained in the Florentine workshops. He was brought up in a different cultural environment. After an early humanistic literary education in Padua and Bologna, he turned to art only on his return to Florence when he saw what was developing and when he made contact with the creators of the great new « Renaissance » of the arts. He always retained, however, a tendency of a different nature which inclined him towards the cultured and the theoretical, nurtured on examples from antiquity. In this respect he foreshadows the artistic climate of the last quarter of the fifteenth century and the beginning of the sixteenth.

This discrepancy in the most authentic native Florentine tradition is echoed a century later in Vasari's account of the way in which the written word can establish an artist's reputation. Some of his remarks are uncharitable, not to say downright unjust in their bitter observations: « having applied himself to the study of Latin and composed works on architecture, perspective and painting, he left behind him books written in such a manner that no artist of modern times has been able to surpass him in his style, although there have been very many more distinguished than himself in the practice of art, and it is generally be-

Detail from an altar-piece by Domenico Veneziano, the teacher of Piero della Francesca. He was interested in the effect of light on colour and his forms are softened in outline with a « new » liquid pink colouring. There is a delicate play of light and shade on the architectural background.

262

lieved ... that he was superior to all those who did, in fact, surpass him in their works ».

But when it comes to Alberti's works, Vasari shows himself to be a better and more impartial judge. Concerning the church which Alberti designed at Rimini for Sigismondo Malatesta, Vasari writes: « with triumphal arches and side walls pierced for sarcophagi for the illustrious dead ... he transformed the fabric of the old building into a massive construction and one of the most famous churches in Italy ». He picks up the boldness of design of the choir in the Annunziata in Florence, and recognises the important part played by Alberti in Rome under Pope Nicholas V, the Pope who « with his method of building had turned all Rome upside down », and who « in matters of architecture first consulted Bernardo Rossellino ... and from then on always took the advice of Leon Battista » ...

The case of Alberti, the son of a Florentine exile, who was quite at ease also outside Florence and spent long periods away from the city in Rome, Urbino, Rimini, Mantua and even abroad, is an exception in the first three quarters of the fifteenth century. Apart from the many gothic masters, still active in the workshops of the cathedral, minor figures who gradually became redundant and emigrated to the north, especially to Venice, the Florentine artists were deeply

The Blessed Angelico adapted Masaccio's style to a vision less epic, more direct and accessible to human understanding. Often considered purely mystic and religious, his style, with its apparent return to out-dated gothic mannerism, is nevertheless important in its new use of colour, in which he is a precursor of Domenico Veneziano. With Filippo Lippi he offers a contrast to Masaccio's humanistic art and plasticism. « The Descent from the Cross » (San Marco Museum).

Filippo Lippi: « Madonna and Child » (Uffizi). Lippi was a member of the Carmelite order, but had no sense of religious vocation. In his arabesque adornments and his elegiac naturalism he anticipated to some extent the pagan world of Sandro Botticelli.

rooted in the cultural climate of their city. Even when they did undertake commissions outside Florence (which happened often as their fame spread throughout Italy) they did not break with the city or change their style. They went away and returned, having left profound traces of their art in the places where they worked, and having absorbed nothing, or very little, themselves. The civilisation to which they belonged, and in which they played an active part, was so compact, homogeneous and in such a vital phase of development. Thus Paolo Uccello and Filippo Lippi went to Padua; Paolo Uccello again and Andrea del Castagno to Venice. Donatello especially worked in Padua for ten years and his activity there gave rise to the revolutionary school of Padua led by Andrea Mantegna, which had an immense influence on the whole art of Northern Italy. But Donatello himself, according to Vasari (and it does not matter if the fact is literally true or not, the sense is fundamentally

263

true): « having by a miracle come here, and being praised by all people of understanding, deliberated upon returning to Florence, saying that if he were to remain in Padua, he would soon forget all that he had learned, being so highly praised by one and all; that he would willingly return home, as there he was continually criticised, and such criticism gave him occasion for study and consequently led to greater glory ».

Throughout the first half of the fifteenth century and beyond, Florence was the centre of the most extraordinary artistic activity. Brunelleschi and Donatello dominated the scene, but had many famous contemporaries and disciples: Lorenzo Ghiberti, Luca della Robbia, Nanni di Banco, Michelozzo, Desiderio da Settignano, the two Rossellinos, Bernardo and Antonio, as well as many minor artists. Masaccio disappeared early, having died very young in Rome in 1428: « It is said that, hearing of his death, Filippo di Ser Brunelleschi remarked ' We have sustained a very great loss in Masaccio '» (Vasari). The activity

Drawing by Paolo Uccello. Once when his wife called him to bed, as he was still at his work-bench in the middle of the night, he begged her to leave him a little longer at his task: « this perspective is such a sweet thing ».

was centred on a few great workshops: first of all the Cathedral, not only on account of the building of the dome and the tribunes but also because of the many sculptures which were being commissioned for its embellishment. Nanni di Banco worked there, as also did Donatello, both sharing commissions for statues: the Prophets on the Porta della Mandorla; Saint John the Evangelist for one of the niches at the side of the main door, now in the Museo dell' Opera; the four Prophets on the bell-tower and finally the *Cantoria* (singing gallery 1433) to match the one by Luca della Robbia. Luca della Robbia also made the bronze doors of the Sacristy and some bas-reliefs for the bell-tower. Ghiberti worked on the Baptistery doors for fifty years from 1401. The other great sculpture workshop in these years was the Church of Orsanmichele, with its continuous series of external tabernacles, where Nanni di Banco, Ghiberti and Donatello also worked, the latter on a statue of Saint

Architectural drawing by Brunelleschi (Uffizi). He first codified the principles of linear perspective in his views of the Piazza della Signoria and the Baptistery. To demonstrate the accuracy of his theories he made a hole in the drawing-board corresponding to the vanishing-point. The spectator then stood behind the picture, looked through the hole and saw the scene reflected in a mirror. The suggestion of reality was almost perfect.

Perspective in a drawing by Leonardo (Uffizi). Leonardo discovered the rules of aerial perspective, which, together with his use of « luministic » colour, gave his paintings a striking spatial depth. In his « Treatise on Painting », which sets out the use of « sfumato », he says: « What is in the Universe in essence, the painter has first in his mind, then in his hands ».

George (1416), whom he made a young man, for the Cuirass-makers Guild. Later he made the statue of San Ludovico di Tolosa, now in the Santa Croce Museum, for the Parte Guelfa tabernacle, which was later to contain (and it is still there) Verrocchio's group of Saint Thomas's Disbelief. Donatello made sculptures also for other Brunelleschi buildings, such as the medallions on the vault and the bronze doors of the Old Sacristy of San Lorenzo. Other Brunelleschi buildings contain sculptures by Luca della Robbia, such as the cherubs in the medallions on the loggia of the Ospedale degli Innocenti.

PAINTING AFTER MASACCIO

After the death of Masaccio in 1428 there was no painter with a stature corresponding to that of Brunelleschi and Donatello in architecture and sculpture.

The greatest one, the Blessed Angelico, was working on his own in the seclusion of the Convent of San Marco. He was a Dominican Friar of the Order of Preachers, and his work is therefore devout and didactic, but of the highest artistic quality.

Paolo Uccello's reputation has suffered unjustly in the hands of modern critics. Andrea del Castagno, contrary to what was believed until recently, was not a contemporary of Paolo Uccello and Masaccio, but belonged to the following generation, having been born in 1423; he died young before the middle of the century. There remains Filippo Lippi, who, together with the Blessed Angelico, first learnt from Masaccio, and the exquisite Domenico Veneziano, one of whose *garzone* when he was working on the Sant'Egidio frescoes in 1439, was the future great Piero della Francesca. Alessio Baldovinetti appeared somewhat later, and his work extended over the whole of the second half of the fifteenth century.

The Florence of Lorenzo de' Medici has been called the Golden Age. In fact the great age in Florentine art falls in the first three quarters of the fifteenth century, and not in Lorenzo's lifetime, however rich that might have been in exquisite works of art. All the essential problems which made the Florentine school great were faced up to and solved in the first half of the century. This may seem a strange statement to make when the second half of the century saw the emergence of Pollaiuolo, Verrocchio, and especially Leonardo and Michelangelo. Yet the work of Pollaiuolo and Verrocchio cannot compare in originality and scope with that of Brunelleschi, Masaccio and Donatello, and neither Leonardo nor Michelangelo can be considered solely within the confines of the Florentine school: they dealt with other problems, in which the solutions arrived at by the Florentine school formed an essential, but not a unique, part.

Other artists came on to the scene, bringing great changes. It was now no longer the case, as it was with Donatello, that they felt the need to return to Florence to draw further inspiration from her local culture; on the contrary, they found greater opportunities for development outside the city.

Italian art was now in process of formation.

Until now the schools of different regions or individual cities had been strongly contrasted. From the last quarter of the fifteenth century we see the beginnings of an overall common culture, and Florence ceased to be the centre of the process. For twenty years it was Milan, then Rome and then Venice. The strong individuality of the Florentine school became local and conservative.

Antonio Pollaiuolo: « Hercules and the Hydra » (Uffizi). Pollaiolo expressed in painting the dynamism of Donatello. The figures unfold against an open, distant lanascape, in a perfect realisation of energy and movement.

THE SYSTEM OF PATRONAGE OF THE MEDICI

The largest workshops (the institution and the old name continues) in the second half of the fifteenth century were those of Pollaiuolo and Verrocchio, both of them primarily sculptors. The atmosphere changed and became civic-centred with the coming to power of the Medici, and the artists were gradually drawn into the service of the new *signori*, who went in for patronage on a large scale. Donatello himself, now an old man, worked for Cosimo, as also did Michelozzo, who became his architect. The type of work done by the artists also changed. Formerly they had been engaged on great collective commissions: the Cathedral, the Baptistery, the Guild and trade tabernacles in Orsanmichele, the great churches of San Lorenzo, Santo Spirito, and so on. Now they worked individually on private commissions for the great Florentine families: the Medici particularly, but also the Strozzi, the Gondi, the Sassetti, the Tornabuoni, the Scala.

Their paintings and sculptures also began to reflect the tastes of the humanists; the new *signori* and men of letters commissioned them and dictated the subjects. There was profuse secularised decoration, of a kind never seen before. The secular element was introduced also into the series of religious works done for the churches: in Ghirlandaio's frescoes in the Sassetti chapel of Santa Trinita and in the Tornabuoni chapel

Botticelli's recording on canvas of the neo-Platonic idealism embraced by the humanist movement in its maturity brought an original stylistic interpretation of Florentine linear composition. In the allegory of « Spring », perhaps suggested by Lorenzo de' Medici, the artist used arabesques and lines very different from the « functional » outlines of Pollaiolo. The suggestive colour and the gentle curves seem to evoke sweet harmonies (Uffizi).

of Santa Maria Novella. Groups of secular works became more frequent, particularly for the decoration of palazzi and villas. There was great building activity in the city: Benedetto Dei speaks of some thirty palazzi built between 1450 and 1480; Luca Landucci mentions many others in his diary in 1489; and the Medici palazzi! — at Cafaggiolo, Trebbio, Careggi, Fiesole and Poggio a Caiano, the last and the most grandiose, commissioned by Lorenzo de' Medici from Giuliano da Sangallo.

Many of the frescoes intended to decorate these villas and palazzi have been lost, destroyed or left incomplete, but what remains is still a precious heritage. To begin with, there was Andrea del Castagno's fresco of « Famous Men » in the Villa di Legnaia, painted just after the middle of the century, then the decorations of the chair-backs and the pictures in the ground-floor drawing-room of the Medici palace, including Paolo Uccello's three Battles, now divided between the Uffizi, the Louvre and the National Gallery in London. Then there were the frescoes of mythological subjects which Lorenzo il Magnifico commissioned for his villa at Spedaletti near Volterra from Botticelli, Ghirlandaio, Perugino and Filippino Lippi soon after 1483; Botticelli's frescoes in the Villa Lemmi, parts of which have been removed and are now in the Louvre; the series of frescoes in the villa at Poggio a Caiano, begun under Lorenzo and continued under Leo X, the Medici Pope.

Sculpture too began to draw its subjects from similar sources, testifying to the spread of humanistic culture among the *signori* and men of letters in Flo-

Leonardo replaced the analytical vision of the Renaissance with sixteenth-century synthesis. The master of the « sfumato » was a pupil of Verrocchio, who is said by Vasari to have laid down his brush for ever when he saw one of his precocious young apprentice's first attempts.

rence, and in this connection one of the outstanding artists was Giuliano da Sangallo. His workshop produced the bas-relief decorations of Bartolomeo Scala's little palazzo. Many of Botticelli's pictures originated in this way: Spring, and the Birth of Venus, for example, until his conversion to the *piagnone* cause, under the influence of Savonarola's preaching. This must not be regarded as reactionary on Botticelli's part, but was a serious and passionate protest against the often specious and sophisticated subtleties of the predominant neo-platonism.

Antonio Pollaiuolo also bowed to the current fashion in mythology with subjects such as Hercules and Antaeus, Hercules and the hydra, Apollo and Daphne, but he also carried forward into the second half of the century the naturalistic studies which were the basis of the Florentine school, especially anatomy. The latter part of his activities took place outside Florence, in Rome, where he died in 1498. Similarly Verrocchio, the other great master of this period, and only a few years younger than Antonio Pollaiuolo, ended his work in Venice where he had been summoned to execute the great equestrian statue of Colleoni, the condottiere. Forty years earlier, Donatello too had gone to Padua to work on the equestrian statue of Gattamelata.

In the later years of the century another young artist was working and studying in the workshop of Ghirlandaio and in the Medici Garden of San Marco — Michelangelo Buonarroti. Twenty years before the century ended Leonardo had left Verrocchio's workshop and was far away from Florence by 1482. It needs some mental effort to realise that Leonardo was an almost exact contemporary of Ghirlandaio. Only three years separate their births: Ghirlandaio's was in 1449, Leonardo's in 1452. There seems to be half a century between their work.

But with Leonardo a new age begins.

THE ARCHITECTS AND THE IMITATION OF THE CLASSICS

To us, who are now distant observers, Florence in the first quarter of the fifteenth century made a clear choice of spiritual direction in her attitude to nature and to knowledge. This was a result of long preparation throughout the fourteenth century, which can generally explain the new position, but in the field of architecture the background to the new developments has been glossed over as merely « imitation of the ancients ». How this imitation should have come about or why has not been explained. There is even disagreement about who the « ancients » were.

Who and where were they? If, for an immediate answer, we were to attribute the reasons for the choice of imitating the ancients to the work of Brunelleschi, as has often been done, there would be some truth in it, but such an answer would so distort the picture that any historical interpretation would be impossible and would put Brunelleschi himself out of his period. The fact that Brunelleschi had absorbed a culture which aimed at a generally classical ideal, and was particularly Florentine, having grown with the city in the preceding century, setting him problems to solve and at the same time giving him support and the necessary moral strength to turn certain pre-existing factors to his purpose, did not necessarily lead him to make the choice which he did make. He had to work out a pattern of life of his own, deriving from all that was best in Florentine art and culture and then express it in terms of architecture. For this he had first to win for himself complete autonomy and liberty of action in respect of the most deeply-engrained habits and attitudes of mind. Brunelleschi went to the greatest trouble to affirm this liberty and to explain and propagate his views to the Florentines. In doing this he was also clarifying his actions to himself. His intuition of the complexity of thought, not only humanistic but also mathematical and historical, required for the solution of his architectural problems, must have confirmed to him that his choice had been right. But this was after twenty years of hard work, from the almost symbolical result of the competition for the Baptistery door to the work on the Old Sacristy, by which time his views were accepted by most.

We may try to understand by reason what for him and for others was the result of a natural intuition of the events of the time. The life of Florence as a city of stone linked to the destiny of her architects was something recent. If the problem of the history of the Baptistery has always been a lively one for the Florentines, and the octagon is quoted as an example of Romanesque Florence (even so, there are others who date it back to the seventh or eighth century), there cannot be said to have been a distinguishable Florentine architecture until the twelfth century, for all that Florence had dependencies such as Lucca, Pisa and so on. The independence of Florentine thought is not, therefore, complete, and this is seen in the architecture of some churches and monasteries, where the powerful influence of the monastic orders propagated not so much the German gothic vision as the external trappings of gothic ornament on fundamentally classic designs.

THE RETURN TO ANTIQUITY

This conflict between the gothic and the classical is most evident in the thirteenth century, but seems to die down in the fourteenth with the prevalence of the gothic. At the same time, however, critical minds turn again to the ancient civilisations of the Mediterranean, and the classical begins to dominate in the last quarter of the century. Brunelleschi must have seen exactly how this antithesis between classical antiquity and gothic, or the Mediterranean and Central Europe, had been confirmed by recent historical events, and have realised what forces could bear in favour of one or the other on the historical or the theoretical plane. A new force had appeared in the Mediterranean, however: that of the Arabic world of mathematicians and scientists nurtured on the Greek and Byzantine classics. This had been brought to bear, for example, on the solution of mathematical problems connected with building since the Romanesque period, and these solutions were of the greatest interest to a builder such as Brunelleschi, who was henceforward to be involved in the mathematical problems of architecture.

Ancient Rome was an ever-present phenomenon, and Rome itself, together with the lands of Umbria and Tuscany, represented a part of the ancient world which seemed, to Florentines and Tuscans in general, still unspoilt. Arnolfo saw and worked in the classical manner even in his architecture, as well as in the fully-rounded figures which he developed independently of his great master Nicola Pisano. The classical vein, powerfully evident in Buscheto's architectural work for Pisa cathedral, lingered on here and there in Tuscany, especially in Siena and Florence, and influenced the proportions of Santa Maria Novella, the spaciousness of Santa Croce, the great dome of Santa Maria del Fiore and the church of the Santa Trinita, where the vaults with pointed arches are classical rather than gothic, where the proportions are clean and there is a serene sense of unity and inner spaciousness. Brunelleschi then realised intuitively that this classicism, transformed in the hands of architects, could become the life-blood of a new and vigorous young body. He gave the Florentines an architectural language which they could take for their own and use with confidence.

And so it was. In humanistic culture he had found a powerful ally and his first inspiration, for it opened his eyes on to the world of antiquity and gave him a criterion against which to judge the world of his day. The stimuli were the formal and structural unity, the harmony, the moderation, the clarity of thought and form of all works of antiquity. The other world of mysticism and gothic formalism offered neither problem, challenge nor risk. Our knowledge of the Florentine masters of mathematics before Brunelleschi is very limited, and we have little idea of what went on in that Paradiso of the Albertis which was a meeting-place between 1380 and 1400 for mathematicians such as Biagio Palancani, who knew the work of Roger Bacon and Alhazen, theoreticians of music and rhythm

The Baptistery is a key to the understanding of fifteenth-century Florentine architecture and the desire to « rediscover » the Romans' principles of building.

such as Francesco Landino, the blind organist who knew the works of Occam, and theologists such as Luigi Marsili.

But Florentine and Sienese painters since Giotto and Simone Martini had already abandoned the method of representing figures by frontal juxtaposition, and were gradually beginning to distribute them in depth in accordance with the subject of the painting. Current treatises on mathematical and geometric proportions in music were clearly related to studies of perspectives and distances in painting and constructional problems in architecture, and could well have led to the growth and development of Brunelleschi's theories. Leonardo Bruni penned many a pompous phrase in praise of Florence, but occasionally showed notable intuition and accuracy of judgment. Of the buildings and the appearance of the city he said that the Florentines generally were convinced that they belonged to an urban civilisation destined to pre-eminence and « sufficient and worthy to acquire dominion and power over the whole world ».

The knowledge of this superiority could not be an end in itself, and Bruni's praise would be misplaced if, out of this confused awareness that she was called to lead the way, Florence had not maintained a freedom of choice, independent, that is, of all outside influences. Bruni's words show clearly that when Florence chose to go her own way, this was a result of an irresistible natural force. It was an unhesitating choice made not to please others, but to follow her own impulse, and for this she was both ready and capable. The first obvious step was to turn her back on the gothic, which Vasari calls German, and to begin to assimilate those canons of architecture which, if not forgotten (Vitruvius was known throughout the Romanesque and Gothic periods in Italy) were at least misunderstood. In a period which demanded a rational organisation of the moral basis of society, Brunelleschi considered that the architect played a determining part, as the results of his work were seen by all and led, through the sense of formal beauty and stability, to the perception and evolution of the guiding principles of science.

The first twenty years of the fifteenth century in Florence were a period of deep reflection. After a long and difficult series of competitions and negotiations, after much thought and hesitation over whether to go in for something colossal, the Florentines had almost finished the first great cathedral in Italy which was not completely gothic, but which would have liked to be. The one who had put an insuperable barrier in the way of this aspiration, in the shape of the great dome to be built over the transept, was the cathedral's first designer, Arnolfo. In 1367, seventy years after building was begun, a commission of architects and painters were planning the erection of a dome on Arnolfo's design, but much larger. A few years later Giovanni di Lapo came forward with the

The Baptistery is considered by some to be a late Roman foundation of the sixth century, by others to date from the eleventh century. The octagonal structure nevertheless indicates the presence in Florence of a Latin spirit not yet extinguished or forgotten.

idea of supporting it on a large drum. This was the final blow to any overall gothic design, and imposed a predominantly classical form on the finished building.

THE CATHEDRAL DOME

Other domes were being built at this time: there was one of considerable size on Siena cathedral, and

Santa Croce (Arnolfo), an example of the partial acceptance in Florence of gothic themes which Vasari called German, but which never became widely used. Together with the gothic elements, there are paleo-Christian features such as the trussed roof, the octagonal pillars and the projecting balcony-type cornice. The result is a complex of vigorously articulated spaces.

a small, but very beautiful one by Orcagna, modelled on Arnolfo's or the one in Bonaiuti's fresco in Santa Maria Novella, on the top of his tabernacle in Orsanmichele. But the dome of Santa Maria del Fiore was a colossus of unimagined proportions. It gave rise to factions within the city and there were some who complained that the authorities had entered too lightly on the road to a megalomaniac quasi-Roman structure, a road which they considered a blind alley. Arnolfo died before the birth of the father of humanism, Petrarch, who was to be crowned in the Campidoglio dreaming of the grandeur of ancient Rome. He had therefore been able only to touch upon classical Rome, and that by himself. He revived the desire to give expression to the problems of great single spaces, not tackled in Tuscany since the first Cistercians came down into Latium with the pointed bows of their gothic naves and handed on their solution to their successors. Arnolfo, therefore, like the colossus of Rhodes, with one foot in Pisa and the other in Florence, seemed the only one capable of transferring the great mass of the ancient master-concept of Roman architecture to the place where it was most likely to bear fruit. He found that place in Florence. We shall not narrate the facts, but try to see behind the events as they occurred.

The whole of Brunelleschi's work was not to be found only in Florence, nor was he by any means the only artist working there: there were Donatello, Ghiberti, Paolo Uccello and Masaccio, Biagio Palancani, Paolo Toscanelli, Coluccio Salutati, Poggio Bracciolini and many others, each labouring unaided in his own field, but in a common endeavour, speculating and theorising about antiquity and the classics in this island of uncorrupt Latinity, the lands of Tuscany and Latium, and about their relationship with the contemporary world. The Romans and the Latins first, then the Greeks, now were understood directly in their language and seen in their monuments. Brunelleschi's work received general support and official approval. He had a commission from the *Signoria*, in the general fortification and restoration of the Castellina at Pisa in 1415, to repair the Ponte a Mare and adapt the Arsenal. From the Old Sacristy onwards, and in the competition for the cathedral dome he had the support of the craftsmen, the merchants and the painters. He then received a great number of commissions, including many from outside Florence at Mantua, Milan, Ferrara, Bologna and Rome. At Rome

The Old Sacristy of San Lorenzo (Brunelleschi, about 1419), a vigorous example of the new classical ideas. The building is a cube roofed with a twelve-ribbed dome. The sharpness of the volumes and the spatial geometry is underlined by the Corinthian pilasters, the rich entablature and the projecting bands of pietra serena.

The dome of Santa Maria del Fiore (Brunelleschi). The style is mainly gothic, and the height of the dome is twice its diameter. The drum is classical. This daring construction, carried out by new techniques, aroused great astonishment in the Florentines who saw it grow, as Vasari relates, without any external scaffolding. The lantern, the geometrical complement to the dome, was built after Brunelleschi's death from plans left by the great architect.

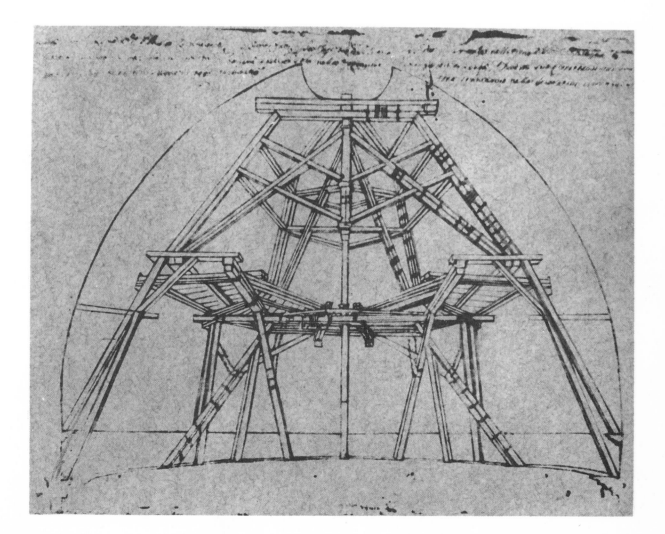

he made further studies of antiquity from those buildings whose ruinous condition Poggio had described in *De Ruinarum Urbis Romae*, predicting their destruction within a short time. There was little opposition to Brunelleschi's work within Florence itself. Ghiberti's real interests lay in the outgoing forms, and he clearly has close ties with his gothic predecessors, of whom he made himself the historian. Michelozzo approached the practical problem of a return to antiquity in a spirit of ambivalent expediency, and was an important channel for the transmission of Brunelleschi's influence to Venice, Milan and throughout Tuscany.

GHIBERTI AS AN ARCHITECT

There is possibly one single building which might be attributed to Ghiberti, and that is the Palla Strozzi chapel in the Santa Trinita, now the Sacristy, although Ghiberti never mentioned it in his *Commentari*, part of which contained his (incomplete) autobiography. There are certain resemblances between this building and those which figure in the second door of the Baptistery: the interior is supported on two square abutments and the outer wall has very long windows with embrasures in the gothic manner but a high tympanum clearly intended to give a classical effect; the door on the church side particularly has a classical style, is complicated in concept but timid in execution, thought out in bronze and realised in marble, the work of a sculptor, not a builder. This was Ghiberti's attempt to make his name as an architect independently of Brunelleschi, but it was in vain. His was also the only attempt, for his other great contemporary, Michelozzo,

although continuing the fourteenth-century styles of the rib vault, the pointed window and the compound tympanum, as in the Bosco ai Frati, San Gerolamo in Volterra and Montepulciano in Naples, nevertheless in his mature period used a style very much derived from Brunelleschi and his studies in perspective, as in the Palazzo Medici, the first tribune of the Annunziata, the Novitiate chapel in Santa Croce, and, if it is his, the Portinari chapel in Santo Eustorgio in Milan.

In addition to Brunelleschi and Ghiberti, Donatello also seems to have influenced Michelozzo, but Donatello's work as an architect is confused by his collaboration with Brunelleschi, except in the refuge doors of the Old Sacristy with their top-heavy overhanging tympanum. The new ideas began to be adopted almost immediately after Brunelleschi began work as an architect in 1418-1419 on the Old Sacristy and the Foundling Hospital. His rules on perspective had now been codified and illustrated by his views of the Piazza della Signoria and the Baptistery. The geometric theorem of the representation of objects in perspective on one plane was given a popular demonstration in the Trinita of Santa Maria Novella, where Brunelleschi designed the background for Masaccio's figures in 1424. Brunelleschi and his successors were also responsible for some town-planning, and this too was an outcome of his work on perspective. The Piazza dell'Annunziata, for example, was seen and planned perspectively, that is symmetrically around an axis, and regular and geometrical in shape like a closed space, whereas around the cathedral the need was not felt in the fourteenth century for a unified harmonious space in keeping with the grandeur of the building.

The Foundling Hospital in the Piazza SS. Annunziata (Brunelleschi, 1419-1426). The slender Corinthian columns, the pedimented windows from the Baptistery and the widely spaced arches from the SS. Apostoli show the formative process behind Brunelleschi's style. The terracotta plaques are by Luca della Robbia.

The villa of Lorenzo the Magnificent at Poggio a Caiano (Giuliano da Sangallo, 1480-1485). Against a sober façade Giuliano introduced a Greek temple, with a scenic effect less marked than in successive neo-classical experiments.

Brunelleschi's extension of perspective into town-planning clearly opened the way for other great artists to develop in an urban environment such as Michelangelo in the Piazza del Campidoglio, Bernini at Saint Peter's and Alberti himself and his successors in several places. The laws of linear perspective and the conquest of space, both real and imaginary, which Brunelleschi interpreted mathematically and which became his rules for all the arts, caused him frequently to evade the current attitude to antiquity, as in the Prophets at Pistoia, the wooden crucifix of Santa Maria Novella and the fragmented space in the Santo Spirito, suggesting to him that predominance of symmetry which is a characteristic of buildings with a vertical axis, such as Santa Maria degli Angeli and the lantern and blind tribunes of Santa Maria del Fiore. These buildings of Brunelleschi's maturity may have dominated the architectural scene, in spite, or rather because of the stimulus brought by Alberti, but they touch on the differences in attitude between the two men. If anyone had wished to criticise Brunelleschi after 1436 when he completed the skeleton of the dome, he could have pointed to the liberty Brunelleschi had taken in forcing the style of antiquity into a new mould.

Such criticism would never occur to us today, but the mistake of « imitating » the ancients, which could not apply to Brunelleschi nor, in a certain sense, to Donatello, could, however, be attributed to Ghiberti. It was quite clear that Ghiberti could never surpass Brunelleschi, as he lacked the necessary energy and vision, and he found it easier to content himself with the particular. When Brunelleschi had conceived the lantern of the cathedral dome or the rotunda of Santa Maria degli Angeli, there was no further development in this direction until Bramante's circular Tempietto of San Pietro in Montorio. In another ten years Brunelleschi would probably have astonished Alberti who, even a short time before his death, still found it difficult to accept what he considered defects in the tribune of the Annunziata, defects due, according to him, to an excessive reliance on the apparently natural process of inserting a domed cylinder on a rectangular cube. It has taken a long time to recognise that these two spatial forms can form a harmonious composition. The model of Santo Spirito, the chapel of the Santo Sepolcro, Alberti's late designs for Santo Andrea in Mantua, where Brunelleschi's proposals matured under a Roman sun, are all a last flowering of Brunelleschi's ideas. He died in 1445, and with him died the creative urge behind his greatest buildings. No one could take his place in the final execution of his ideas. When Brunelleschi was alive, Alberti seemed rarely to have looked beneath the surface of ancient and contemporary architecture, designing elegant compositions with arabesques and coloured ornamentation, but after Brunelleschi's death Alberti interpreted his doctrines to the letter. This seems to me the dominating factor, the risk run by Florentine architecture from 1418 to 1472.

THE NEW ARCHITECTS

Events after Brunelleschi's death show that Alberti's style gradually approximated to Brunelleschi's as he came to study and accept Brunelleschi's ideas. The important figures in Florentine architecture after Alberti are not Alberti's pupil Rossellino, although he was not unimportant, or Fancelli, but Giuliano da Sangallo and Cronaca. All of them, including later Michelangelo, wished to know at first hand the ancient world of Rome, to see the buildings, examine the material from which they were constructed, ponder over the many technological problems, and tap this world of forms and theories at its source. This was not the case with other men of the second half of the fifteenth century. Alberti was a man of letters who took the essence of Vitruvius and reshaped it into his own treatise, a modern treatise on architecture, adapted to its age and pruned of the Augustan's defects. Not that the Florentine found sufficient in Vitruvius to understand the organism of the Parthenon and to imitate it, but he did learn to appreciate from Attic Greece a refinement of carving, of symbolism, and a complete formal perfection which became part of his very being, guiding his theoretical researches to the very highest level. The façade of the Palazzo Rucellai, for example, was designed with the greatest care and deliberately introduced novelties to break up the rather severe geometry which might have resulted from regular rusticated stone, identical capitals and a rigid division into exactly equal parts. The stones are deliberately irregular, the capitals varied, the central section slightly wider than the others, and the treatment of the surface of the stones noticeably different here and there. All this betrays the sensitivity of the theoretical artist who had shown himself capable of assimilating forms from a world which had crumbled away, but which in its day had been glorious, yet accepting them eclectically, or, as we should say today, in the spirit of the archeologist.

If the theoretician could not afford to ignore the origins, no architect could now ignore the adaptation of the classical elements, orders, symmetry, symbolical ornamentation, to the decoration of buildings. Every would-be architect had to do his own researches, and thus Giuliano, the elder of the Sangallo brothers, virtually began his work with a book of designs of the monuments of Rome, a work of the greatest value to the student of architecture, but intended by its author merely as a guide to Rome's buildings.

In his life of Baccio d'Agnolo, Vasari says that he had the greatest artists in his workshop: Raphael, then very young, Andrea Sansovino, Filippino, Maiano, Cronaca, Antonio and Giuliano da Sangallo, Granaccio and occasionally, Michelangelo. Baccio had his workshop in 1490, or shortly before, and Raphael could only have been there around 1504-1505, whilst the Sangallo brothers only appeared in Florence at intervals, and when they did their presence often gave rise to important argument, not to mention occasional sprees and revelry. Only Bramante and Leonardo were missing to complete the picture. Cronaca might have been heard deriding the antiquated palazzo which the younger of the Maianos was erecting on the site of the old one for Filippo Strozzi, newly returned from Naples, loaded with money and wishing only to spend it in the city which had banished him for fifteen years. In this Cronaca would have had the support of Giuliano da Sangallo who, remaking the model of the palazzo, wished to replace the bipartite, arched, old-fashioned windows (Brunelleschi did not even use them fifty years previously) with windows with a tympanum. Cronaca did eventually finish it off with a courtyard and a large external cornice in an attempt to modernise it.

What things were debated in this workshop, and what did they mean for Florence? In simple terms, they were attempting to take up the theories of Brunelleschi, whilst at the same time giving due place to more recent studies in static and formal construction. The formula adopted for Santo Spirito is a good example for all those which will follow, as this seems to free the forces which will bring life to the plastic structures of Michelangelo, to Jacopo Sansovino's developments in ornamentation in Venice, whilst the Sacristy itself is the source of all that Raphael will do in Florence and Rome. Two men in particular took up at the end of the century the theme of plastically-organised volumes related to the structures of the buildings: Giuliano da Sangallo in the completion of the Piazza dell'Annunziata, in his study for the plan of the Crocetta, in the villa at Poggio a Caiano, Bartolommeo Scala's palazzo, the little Cocchi palazzo in Santa Croce, the Santo Spirito Sacristy and other works, and Cronaca in the Palazzo Strozzi courtyard, San Salvatore al Monte, the Santo Spirito Sacristy, the « baroque » church of San Giuseppe in the Via dei Malcontenti and a few others. Thus the fifteenth century closes, preparing the way for the new undertakings of the sixteenth, in which Florence will play but little part, but Rome and Venice a great one, both of them having had their beginnings in Florence. Leonardo returned to Florence right at the end of the century, and in a few most happy architectural designs took up again his impressions from Bramante, at once the son and grandson of the Florence of the great architects.

The designs to come are dynamically complex, yet they are still based on fifteenth-century volumes, symmetrical, enclosed and measurable.

DISTINGUISHED FOREIGNERS IN FLORENCE

In the Middle Ages and the Renaissance the Florentines, merchants or bankers, artists or adventurers, frequently appeared in many other parts of Europe. They were the genial ambassadors of an advanced, yet warm-hearted civilisation and the living witnesses of a breadth of mind and spirit hitherto unsuspected.

The name of Florence, the city of art and commerce, became a password to a new experience, a call to the ideal environment in which to spend a day, a season or perhaps one's whole life.

The presence of distinguished foreigners in Florence, beginning in the distant past, gradually became a fundamental part of city life through the sixteenth and seventeenth centuries, reaching its maximum in the nineteenth and continuing to the present day, in spite of two world wars. Hospitality to the foreigner is now part of the city's « vocation », and a duty of which it is most keenly aware.

Florence is therefore to be numbered among the great cities which have played a determining role in the growth of civilisation. Through the legacy of her distinguished past, men have been able to renew contact with ancient traditions, and foreigners from every country and every continent, especially the illustrious representatives of differing cultures and the world leaders of today, can move about, now as in the centuries past, among the unspoilt remains of the Florentine Renaissance, concrete evidence of the « rediscovery of man ».

The first year of the fifteenth century saw the death in London of England's greatest medieval poet, Geoffrey Chaucer, who had paid at least two visits to Italy on diplomatic and trade missions. He had thus had the opportunity to know and to appraise Florentine intellectual life, and was influenced by Dante and Petrarch, both of whose names occur in his works in confirmation of an effective and lasting interest.

This points to one of the fundamental attractions which Florence will exert over the world in the coming centuries: culture. Abroad, Florentine culture meant resplendent poetry, an ever-mounting patrimony of libraries, institutions, rich collections of Greek, Hebrew and Latin texts, coherent and scholarly research into the past, with the possibility of access to these sources of knowledge, allowing at one and the same time a synthesis and an analysis of human intelligence in its remotest and nearest point of time.

The fifteenth century saw the way open to Florence for foreigners, and the linking of various cultures had a profound effect throughout Europe. The cultural atmosphere of the city, now known widely abroad, attracted scholars who enjoyed, or were soon to enjoy, considerable fame in their own countries. One of the most notable was the German humanist Johann Reuchlin, who arrived in 1480 in the suite of Eberhard, Count of Württemberg, apparently as an interpreter. He stayed long enough to make contact with the most famous humanists of the time and to be presented to Lorenzo il Magnifico. He was to return twice: in 1490 to meet Pico della Mirandola, and in 1498 to acquire Hebrew texts and manuscripts for his library, as, in addition to Greek, he taught Hebrew first at Ingolstadt then at the University of Tübingen.

After 1453, the year of the fall of Constantinople, Florence had become a centre and a market of the first importance for Greek manuscripts. This attracted

Cosimo il Vecchio, founder of the first public library in Florence (Bronzino, Uffizi).

to the city many famous teachers of Greek, and the first printed edition of Homer was published in Florence by Demetrius Chalcondyles, whose presence in Florence attracted two famous English scholars. Thomas Linacre, an eminent doctor and student of the classics, came to Italy from Canterbury to improve his knowledge of medicine, Greek and Latin, which languages he studied in 1485 under Chalcondyles and Poliziano respectively. Linacre is justly famous as having been the physician of Henry VIII, thanks to his exceptional skill, and for having played a major part in the establishment of the Royal College of Physicians, which set up the medical profession in England. His humanistic training was even more noteworthy. He taught Greek to Sir Thomas More and Erasmus, Latin to the future Queen Mary, and published an elegant Latin translation of the treatises of Galen.

William Grocyn, one of England's greatest Greek scholars, came to Florence in 1488 to spend the next two years studying under Chalcondyles and Poliziano. After his studies in Florence, Grocyn established himself in Oxford in 1491, teaching Greek at Exeter College. He taught a new pronunciation, which caused heated arguments between his supporters and his opponents, but which earned him the esteem of Erasmus, as it helped him to a richer understanding of the language.

The desire to learn Greek, which was then little known in England, and an interest in humanism sent John Colet also to Florence in 1493. He studied with Pico della Mirandola, Poliziano and Marsilio Ficino and learned about Florentine teaching methods. The son of Sir Henry Colet and a man of considerable wealth, he gave part of his fortune to found Saint Paul's School in London, and was the author of noteworthy publications in Latin. For him too the experience of Florence was not lost after his stay, but it enriched and to a certain extent determined his future activity. Humanism, which was to give English culture a new and different conception of fundamental values for religion and the social conscience, was brought particularly from Florence towards the end of the fifteenth century by Linacre, Grocyn, Colet and others. The study of Greek and Latin and the assimilation of Florentine culture were an impulse to new thought and new learning in England, opening up a new and exciting world of poetry and philosophy.

In the second half of the sixteenth century visitors to Florence from France included, among others, the historian and bibliophile Jacques Auguste de Thou and the writer and philosopher Michel de Montaigne. The former came to Italy in 1573 in the suite of the ambassador de Foix and spent some months in Florence collecting material for his « Historia sui temporis » in which he was also assisted by Vasari. Michel de Montaigne undertook long journeys in Switzerland, Germany and Italy in 1580-1581 and elected to spend the summer in Florence, going on afterwards to Bagni di Lucca for hot bath treatment. He wrote critically of Florence at first, then more constructively, as if it had taken him some time to awaken to the great complex of activities and traditions which sometimes made it difficult for foreigners to understand her. It is possible that François Rabelais, who came to Rome in the suite of the Bishop of Paris, Jean du Bellay, in 1533 and

The library of the Convent of San Marco, founded by Cosimo, was open to all who sought to further their knowledge. Facilities were available, particularly to foreign scholars, for the consultation and study of the codices and manuscripts kept in the library.

1535, passed through Florence, as he speaks of the city with great admiration. There is, however, no documentary evidence to support the fact that he may have stayed in the city.

The city offered increasing facilities for students from all countries. Cosimo the Elder had already instituted in the San Marco Convent the first public library in Europe and the model for all those which followed it; he had expressly desired that it should be made freely available to all those who wished to deepen their knowledge. The Medicis' private library, after many vicissitudes due to the changes of fortune in the family's political life, was opened to the public for the first time on June 11th 1571. It took in the San Marco library and came to be called the Laurentine Library after Lorenzo the Magnificent who had enriched it with manuscripts from Italy and Europe. Flo-

rence was showing the way: the nucleus of the Vatican Library in Rome was constituted on the model of Florence, Pope Nicholas V (the humanist Tommaso Parentuccelli) having acted as adviser on the establishment of the Medici library.

The generous help she gave to scholars and her modern outlook in matters of culture and teaching made Florence a focal point of the widest intellectual interests and an important centre for the dissemination of knowledge.

The distinguished Europeans who stayed and worked in Florence for cultural purposes were in the main English, French and German, but there were others such as the Spaniard Mateo Alemán, the author of the picaresque novel *Guzmán de Alfarache*, although here again documentary evidence is lacking. The same is true also of the Dutch historian Pieter Corneliszoon van Hooft. Both these writers refer to the city in their works, the first virtually in the style of a modern reporter and the second in the vein of gentle lyricism. The Portuguese poet Francisco de Sa de Miranda, on the other hand, certainly stayed in Florence from 1521 to 1536, during which time he also visited Venice, Milan and Rome; he regarded the city of the Medici as the ideal place for the study of poetry and wished to introduce the Florentine style into the verse of his own country. There were also many Poles studying Latin poetry in Padua and Bologna who must have visited Florence to consult precious manuscripts, unique and indispensible sources for their work. Amongst these in the sixteenth century were several illustrious names, including that of Klemens Janicki, whose works show the influence of the Latin elegy.

The figurative arts also attracted to Renaissance Florence many well-known foreigners. Flemish, Spanish, German and French artists felt the need to develop their talents by a stay in the city which was constantly growing in beauty and becoming inseparable from the works of its architects, painters, sculptors and craftsmen.

Roger van der Weyden, one of the greatest Flemish painters with Jan van Eyck in the fifteenth century, came to Florence in 1449 for a long stay. He wished to acquire a thorough knowledge of the techniques of oil painting and at the same time to see what had been done in Florentine art. Cosimo commissioned from him a large Madonna for his collection. Whereas in literature the transmission of ideas was partly hindered by the language barrier, in art communication was immediate, and not only did the skill of the Florentines influence directly those who came to see it, but Florentine artists themselves felt the influence of Flemish painting, thanks to the personal contacts which were established.

The Spanish painter Alonso Berruguete came to Florence early in 1503 and was greatly attracted to Michelangelo whom he followed to Rome. He was favourably received by the great master and became his well-appreciated assistant on the statue of David; he was thus able to see a powerful statue created out of a huge block of stone, and learn technical devices and secrets by watching Michelangelo in action. Vasari refers to Berruguete several times in his *Lives*, calling him sometimes Alonso Berugetta, sometimes Alonso the Spaniard and also Barughetta, and, though not giving his biography, mentions him together with

artists of some distinction. Berruguete's return to Spain coincided with a vast activity in sculpture, painting and architecture, all connected with his experience of Florence.

The brothers Frans and Cornelis Floris were in Florence around 1545. The former, whom his fellow-countrymen called the « Flemish Raphael », stayed in both Florence and Rome to study the works of Raphael and Michelangelo. In the world of art, the sixteenth century brought a reversal of positions between Italy, and therefore Florence, on the one hand, and foreign painters on the other, as compared with the fifteenth century. In the fifteenth century Bruges had to a certain extent set the pattern, and Flemish painting was a source of inspiration to Florentine artists, as can be seen, for instance, in the success of Hugo van der Goes' triptych of the Nativity commissioned in Bruges by the Medici agent Tommaso Portinari and « imported » by him into Florence in 1470. In the sixteenth century, thanks to the three great names in art, Leonardo, Raphael and Michelangelo, the interest shifted from North to South and, consequent upon the visits of foreign artists to Florence, new influences were felt in Flemish painting, fresh commissions were given to Florentine artists and distinct classical schools arose in the Netherlands.

It should be noted that, although Florence played a major part in attracting foreign artists to Italy, she was not by any means the only city to do so. Under the prevailing political circumstances, it was not possible to concentrate the country's major interests in one city, as it was later with France and Paris, and there was a clear, though not harmful rivalry between Florence and Rome, the latter exerting exceptional attraction as the seat of the Papacy. Other centres such as Naples, Genoa, Milan, Ferrara and, within Tuscany also, Leghorn, Pisa and Siena, also had the benefit of contact with foreigners. Florence had the advantage of her geographical position, which made her an obligatory stage on the way to Rome, a most enviable political and economic situation and a pre-eminence, intelligently publicised by her diplomatic and commercial representatives abroad, due to the following reasons: Tuscany was the cradle of men of genius, who of necessity converged on Florence, the one city in the region which offered then the greatest opportunities, and a wise and sensitive public-spiritedness encouraged the right conditions of work for men of exceptional minds. The distinguished foreigners who chose to live and work in Florence showed great intelligence and understanding in appreciating the value of such a complex of complementary and contrasting activities, which led to artistic and cultural expression of the highest order.

Like his brother Frans, Cornelis Floris, architect and sculptor, also came to Florence to study art. He was particularly interested in great buildings, and on his return home he designed the Town Hall of Antwerp, giving it an articulated façade in which, in addition to his personal style, the influence of Renaissance forms is clearly evident.

For reasons previously mentioned, foreign artists came to Florence in the sixteenth century to study and then, in certain cases, stayed for a great part of their lives, having found a welcome, opportunities for work and a market for their products. Amongst these were the Dutchman Pieter de Witte and the Frenchman Pierre Franqueville, who lived in Florence for twenty and over thirty years respectively.

Pieter de Witte came to Florence about 1570, attracted like many others by the desire to study masterpieces of art on the spot and to learn as much as possible. He met Vasari, who was always willing to help foreign artists by finding them work to pay for their studies, and became a valued assistant on the frescoes on the cathedral dome. Pierre Franqueville (better known under his Italian name of Pietro Francavilla) came to Florence when he was quite young, probably in 1571, with a letter of introduction to Giambologna. He also worked in Pisa and Genoa, and when he left Florence for the French Court on the invitation of Henri IV, he had created in the city one of his most famous works, the statue of Spring on the Santa Trinita bridge. Better known, however, among the famous foreigners who became assimilated into Florentine life, was Giambologna, originally known as Jehan de Boulogne. He was a sculptor, born in Douai in 1529 and he died in Florence in 1608. He came to Italy together with Frans and Cornelis Floris to study antiquity and the works of Michelangelo in Rome. Francesco de' Medici summoned him to Florence in 1562 and he worked there not only as a sculptor but also as an adviser for the acquisition of works of art and for the planning of the Medici gardens.

Another artist who stayed in Florence for many years was Hans von Achen. He left Cologne in 1578

to study the great artists' use of colour. Specialising in portrait-painting, he received important commissions from the Grand Duke Francis I for his collection of paintings of Court personalities. He was to become one of the foremost practitioners of Mannerism in Germany and took back to his country a rich artistic experience gained in the main from Michelangelo and Correggio.

Some of the distinguished foreigners recorded in the annals of Florence were interested in music. One such was Heinrich Isaac, known in Italy as Arrigo il Tedesco (Harry the German), born, according to some,

« Spring » (Pierre Franqueville). This statue was made for the Santa Trinita bridge before the sculptor returned to his native country.

281

36

Many distinguished representatives of religion and culture came to Florence for the Ecumenical Council. The Patriarch Joseph of Constantinople was portrayed by Gozzoli in the « Procession of the Magi » in the Palazzo Medici.

in Flanders, according to others, in Prague, who came to Florence at the invitation of Lorenzo il Magnifico. He arrived in 1477 and stayed until 1492, then came again for a further period from 1514 to 1517, the year of his death. He was a composer of religious music, but was fascinated by popular songs, and set to music many of the choruses of the famous Florentine May songs.

Art, culture and the things of the spirit prevailed in Renaissance Florence over the material world, and this was clearly interpreted by, amongst others, Francisco de Sa de Miranda mentioned above. It is, however, necessary to add that these contacts with distinguished foreigners could not have been possible without a flourishing economy, the basis and prerequisite of the

city's artistic and cultural life and of its reputation abroad. It was their activities in the economic sphere which took Florentine merchants to various parts of Europe and of the then known world, enabling them to make contacts which did not stop short at the commercial level, but which awakened interest in their city and brought an ever-increasing number of visitors, understandably desirous of doing business. On their return these men related what they had seen and spread further the news of the wealth of masterpieces of art and literature in Florence, whose value they were sometimes quite unable to appreciate.

It was under Cosimo the Elder that Florence had begun to trade far and wide, and this expansion in commercial activity had also laid the foundations for intellectual development. The English historian Edward Gibbon went so far as to say that spices and Greek manuscripts were often imported into Florence on the same vessels. A network of bankers' agents, very extensive for those times, was set up in the major European centres and they performed functions which today would be those of a cultural attaché or even of a public relations officer. Tommaso Portinari, an agent first in Bruges, then in London and then ambassador in Spain, was one of those who exerted the greatest influence in presenting the city as an inviting centre for the élite of the times. Moreover the strong banking and commercial organisation in Italy in general, and particularly in her ports, made for easy contacts. In many respects, Leghorn was a very suitable gateway to Florence.

On the other hand, it is significant that the distinguished foreigners who came to Florence in the fifteenth and the sixteenth centuries were in the main, if not exclusively, artists, writers and scholars, that is from the world of culture. Commerce brought preeminence to Florentines, who as merchants were more active than those of other countries; banking techniques were jealously guarded and usually operations were entrusted only to famous bankers and their relatives. The visits of distinguished foreigners were never hindered by wars, except for the disastrous invasion of Charles VIII of France, who came to Florence not as a friend, but as an invader, in November 1494, only to leave almost immediately for the conquest of Naples. There were many embassies, of which the personnel changed much as they do in the diplomatic corps today. In the political and religious life of the Renaissance, Florence also played a part of unusual interest.

There was one great event which brought distinguished men of religion to Florence. This was the Ecumenical Council of 1439, intended by Pope Eugenius IV for Ferrara, but transferred to Florence for two very different reasons: plague in the city of the Marchese d'Este, and the political cunning of Cosimo. In February of that year its eminent members assembled to decide on the reunion of the Eastern and Western Churches. There were Joseph the Patriarch of Constantinople and Johannis VIII Palaeologus, the Byzantine Emperor, the former accompanied by a host of Eastern prelates and monks, and the latter by a large suite of knights and dignitaries. The visitors naturally included

Eleonora, daughter of Don Pedro Alvarez of Toledo, who married Cosimo I de' Medici in 1539 and lived in Florence for twenty-three years. She died in October 1562 of malaria which she contracted during a journey along the coast at La Maremma. She is shown with one of her eight children (Bronzino, Uffizi).

teachers and scholars such as Cardinal Bessarione, the Archbishop of Nicea, one of the most famous Greek scholars of the age who, after contact with the Florentine humanists, came to abandon his standpoint in the Greek church and pressed instead for unification.

Another distinguished personality who was to settle in Florence for several years at the invitation of Cosimo was the philosopher Gemisto Pletone. He had come to represent the Greek church at the Council and he fitted well into the cultural atmosphere of the city. The Patriarch Joseph died a month before the Council ended and was buried in Santa Maria Novella. The Council was also a success on other than religious grounds, and it brought to Florence what Cosimo had wanted: trade openings to the Eastern markets and an appreciation by the Greek scholars who had visited the city of Florence's cultural position. There was thus a possibility of creating a European centre for Greek studies, and these were to play a great part in the development of culture after the fall of Constantinople.

The history of Renaissance Florence is also a story of subtle diplomatic intrigue. Dynastic interests led to marriages for reasons of State between the House of the Medici and members of the royal and aristocratic families of Spain, France and Austria. Thus the Medici residences in Florence welcomed Marguerita, the natural daughter of the Emperor Charles V. In June 1536 she married Duke Alessandro, who was to be assassinated by Lorenzino barely six months after the wedding. Marguerita could leave no trace of her brief and unhappy stay in Florence. She was only fifteen, and destiny was keeping a more interesting role for her in other lands. On the other hand Eleonora, the daughter of Don Pedro Alvarez de Toledo, who in 1539 married Cosimo I de' Medici, Grand Duke of Tuscany, played a very notable part in the fortunes of the House of the Medici, bringing wealth and political influence through her father, the Governor of Southern Italy and Charles V's faithful lieutenant. Eleonora spent twenty-three years in Florence until, in October 1562, she went on a journey along the Tuscan coast with her husband and children and died there of malaria. She bore Cosimo eight children and was his best and most faithful adviser; as events subsequently showed, her influence was considerable. Francesco I, Cosimo's son, also married a foreign girl. His father arranged his union with the Archduchess Joanna of Austria, the daughter of the Emperor Ferdinand I and sister of Maximilian II. Francesco's successor, Ferdinando I, married Christine, the daughter of the Duke of Lorraine. The Medici fortunes were established and now the desire was growing for a royal alliance.

The city built by artists, enriched by poets and musicians, enlivened by commerce and by bold initiative in finance, was in the forefront of progress, and the landscape of her surrounding hills was an authentic framework to this unique picture of genius and power. But the life of the Renaissance was drawing to a close. The seventeenth century was on the horizon, yet the leaven in the arts and culture continued to work through succeeding ages, and intellectual activity continued undiminished, to the fascination of the whole world. Distinguished foreigners still came to Florence, which the fifteenth and sixteenth centuries had brought to the notice of everyone, for quiet meditation, to find a source of knowledge or a work of art to love. From Milton to Goethe, from Stendhal to Dumas, from Byron to Hawthorne, from Dostoievski to Andersen, to Dickens, Anatole France, Tchaikovsky, Debussy, Wagner, Oscar Wilde, Blasco Ibáñez, Rilke, Thomas Mann and many others. Thus, in our day as well, Florence, city of the Renaissance, whose paintings in the golden age are the subject of a work of rare value by Bernard Berenson, inspired Sidney Alexander, author of « Michelangelo the Florentine » to write: « When I go to Florence, I journey not only through space, but also through time; not only from America to Italy, but also from the twentieth to the sixteenth century. In Florence I can still walk round what was once the city's outer wall, though most of it no longer exists, and only a few of the ancient city gates are left. But when I am close to these places, to these nerve-centres of history, thousands of ideas crowd into my mind: in certain magical moments, the past ceases to be the past, paradoxically the sense of history liberates us from history, that is from Time ».

INDEX

37

Edited by Italo Salvan, Renato Caporali and Pier Paolo Donati.
Layout by Attilio Rossi and Gianfranco Bulletti.
Photographic consultants: Scala IFE, Florence.
Collaboration also with Alinari & Co., Florence.

Reproduction and printing: Offset Co., Zincotecnica
and Tipografia Bona, Turin, in collaboration.

Paper by Cartiere del Garda, Riva di Trento.
Binding by Legatoria. Degli Esposti, Bologna.

PRINTED IN ITALY
BY BEMPORAD MARZOCCO, FLORENCE